STUDIES IN WELSH HISTORY

Editors

RALPH A. GRIFFITHS CHRIS WILLIAMS
GLANMOR WILLIAMS

———

17

CIVILIZING THE URBAN

POPULAR CULTURE AND PUBLIC SPACE
IN MERTHYR, *c.*1870–1914

CIVILIZING THE URBAN

POPULAR CULTURE AND PUBLIC SPACE IN MERTHYR, *c.* 1870–1914

by

ANDY CROLL

*Published on behalf of the
History and Law Committee
of the Board of Celtic Studies*

UNIVERSITY OF WALES PRESS
CARDIFF
2000

British Library Cataloguing-in-Publication Data.
A catalogue record for this book is available from the British Library.

ISBN 0–7083–1637–9

Typeset by Aarontype Ltd., Easton, Bristol
Printed in Great Britain by Dinefwr Press, Llandybïe, Dyfed

EDITORS' FOREWORD

Since the Second World War, Welsh history has attracted considerable scholarly attention and enjoyed a vigorous popularity. Not only have the approaches, both traditional and new, to the study of history in general been successfully applied to Wales's past, but the number of scholars engaged in this enterprise has multiplied during these years. These advances have been especially marked in the University of Wales.

In order to make more widely available the conclusions of recent research, much of it of limited accessibility in postgraduate dissertations and theses, in 1977 the History and Law Committee of the Board of Celtic Studies inaugurated this series of monographs, *Studies in Welsh History*. It was anticipated that many of the volumes would originate in research conducted in the University of Wales or under the auspices of the Board of Celtic Studies. But the series does not exclude significant contributions made by researchers in other universities and elsewhere. Its primary aim is to serve historical scholarship and to encourage the study of Welsh history. Each volume so far published has fulfilled that aim in ample measure, and it is a pleasure to welcome the most recent addition to the list.

CONTENTS

ABBREVIATIONS

AT	*Aberdare Times*
CMG	*Cardiff and Merthyr Guardian*
CT	*Cardiff Times*
EE	*Evening Express*
GRO	Glamorgan Record Office
ILP	Independent Labour Party
MDT	*Merthyr and Dowlais Times*
ME	*Merthyr Express*
MP	*Merthyr Pioneer*
MS	*Merthyr Star*
MT	*Merthyr Times*
MTl	*Merthyr Telegraph*
PC	*Pontypridd Chronicle*
SC Report	*Royal Commission of Inquiry on the Operation of the Sunday Closing (Wales) Act, 1881,* 1890.
WM	*Western Mail*

ACKNOWLEDGEMENTS

This book is like the process it seeks to understand; it was a long time in the making and its completion was never a foregone conclusion. Moreover, along the way, numerous people played a part in shaping the final outcome. Work began on it when I enrolled as a Ph.D. student in the History Department at Cardiff University in 1990. However, in retrospect, I had spent much of the previous decade unconsciously preparing myself for the task. Two schoolteachers, Sandra Davies and Gloria Newlove, knew – better than I – that history had a future, and I am grateful to them both. At Cardiff, a Philosophy course on Aristotle persuaded me of the sense in converting to Welsh history. After hearing Professor Dai Smith's first lecture, I needed no further convincing. Throughout my studies, he was an inspirational teacher who always managed to convey the excitement that could be had from studying past societies. As a supervisor, he was invaluable as a source of support, encouragement and guidance. I'm not sure that this is the book he thought he was supervising, but without him, none of it would have been written. Similarly, Dr Chris Williams has played an important part at every stage of this project. He saw the Ph.D. through to the end, and then, as one of the series editors, had to go through it all again. While I could have done without the endless thrashings on the squash court, I could not have done without his friendship.

A number of people have helped during the transition from Ph.D. to book. I have benefited enormously from the comments of my examiners, Professor John Belchem and Dr Bill Jones. The series editors, Emeritus Professor Sir Glanmor Williams, Professor Ralph Griffiths and Dr Chris Williams have improved the manuscript in multifarious ways, as have the staff of the University of Wales Press, and especially Ceinwen Jones. My colleagues in the History section at the University of Glamorgan have made being at work an enjoyable and stimulating experience; I would particularly like to thank Neil Wynn and Peter Mercer for their support. Numerous students at

Cardiff and Glamorgan have shared with me their ideas on Victorian social, cultural and urban history, and made me rethink my own. I have discussed many aspects of the book with Kevin Passmore and Garthine Walker who have always proved themselves to be perceptive critics and generous friends. Another friend, Angela Gaffney, set an example in terms of productivity that I have failed to live up to. Denna Jones and Simon Brilliant gave me a place to stay while researching parts of the book. For that, and much else besides, I am extremely grateful. Some of chapter I was written on Rob Eva's computer, just before it broke. Any offer of recompense would only offend, and could not, in any case, make up for the huge debt that I already owe him, Paula, Alice and Jenny; they have been the very best of friends. In a like fashion, the friendship of Bill and Val Jones, and Sara Spalding, has proved crucial in more ways than I thought possible.

Thanks are due to the British Academy for providing me with funds to carry out the research, while the staffs of the following libraries and archives have provided much help: the Arts and Social Studies Library at Cardiff University, the British Library, the British Newspaper Library, Cardiff Central Library, the Hugh Owen Library at Aberystwyth, the Learning Resources Centre at the University of Glamorgan, the National Library of Wales and Swansea University Library. The bulk of the newspaper research was carried out at the Glamorgan Record Office where the staff were always full of encouragement. Carolyn Jacob, at Merthyr Tydfil Public Library, also deserves a special mention. Her endless supply of cups of tea was greatly appreciated. The late Victorian boosters would surely have approved of her enthusiasm for all things Merthyrian. Bill Aird, Andy and Rhian Cornish, Philippa Davies, Spencer Hawkridge, Rob Humphries, Mike Jones, Martin Johnes, Steve Jones and Emma Fillmore, Phil Macdonald, Ian and Clare Morris, Mike Reader and Victoria Coy, Gareth and Anya Seymour, Paolo Sidoli, Keith Strange, Jeremy Thomas, Elaine Williams and Ian O'Connor, and Mari Williams have all, in various ways and at different times, provided help and encouragement.

My greatest thanks go to my family. I would like to thank George Croll and Margaret Croll for their support, and Anne

Croll for not doubting that it would get finished one day. My Gran – Lillian Sang – has shared with me stories of my rugby-playing, brass-band-loving, great grandfather from Penryn, Cornwall, Richard Francis Penver. Unfortunately I never met him, but I hope that he would have recognized at least some of what follows. I am grateful to her for those memories and for giving me many happy ones of my own. Finally, special thanks go to my Mum, Mary Croll. Without her help and support this study would not have been possible, which is why it is dedicated both to her and to the memory of my Dad, Harry Croll.

I

INTRODUCTION

Here humanity attains its most complete development and its most brutish; here civilization works its miracles, and civilized man is turned back almost into a savage.

Alexis de Tocqueville[1]

Nothing is fundamental. That is what is interesting in the analysis of society. That is why nothing irritates me as much as these inquiries – which are by definition metaphysical – on the foundations of power in a society or the self-institution of a society, etc. These are not fundamental phenomena. There are only reciprocal relations, and the perpetual gaps between intentions in relation to one another.

Michel Foucault[2]

The nineteenth-century city 'mocked every boast of material success that the "Century of Progress" uttered'; it was a place in which 'the taste for ugliness became ingrained'.[3] Few urban settlements appear to fit the Mumfordian vision more completely than Merthyr Tydfil. The quintessential 'frontier town', industrial Merthyr managed to shock, horrify and depress generations of Victorians. Conjured into existence by the efforts of a band of ironmasters in the late eighteenth century, the town's rapid and unplanned development was determined by the exigencies of the iron industry. Such a situation allowed little room for civic niceties. At a time when many other towns and cities were investing in sewers, public lamps and parks, Merthyr remained a place in which blast furnaces, foundries and rolling mills counted for more. The consequences of this neglect in terms of human misery were appalling. Death rates soared, social unrest reached unprecedented levels, and areas of the town fell outside the pale of civilization altogether. Little wonder that by the mid-Victorian period, the name of Merthyr

[1] Commenting upon the early industrial 'shock cities' of the north of England. Alexis de Tocqueville, *Journeys to England and Ireland*, tr. G. Lawrence and K. P. Mayer, ed. J. P. Mayer (New Jersey, 1988 edn), p. 108.
[2] 'Space, knowledge and power', in Sylvère Lotringer (ed.), *Foucault Live* (New York, 1989), p. 341.
[3] Lewis Mumford, *The City in History* (London, 1961), pp. 466-7.

was synonymous, in the minds of many, with the darker side of
the British urban experience.

Much is familiar about Merthyr's history. We have fine
studies of the late eighteenth- and early nineteenth-century iron
industry that so dominated the district, and of the cataclysm
that was 1831, the year of the famous rising.[4] The terrible 1830s
and 1840s, decades which saw the town secure for itself an
unenviable reputation as one of the most unhealthy settlements
in Britain, have not gone unnoticed, while the subsequent (and
often unsuccessful) attempts to initiate sanitary reforms have
also been extensively written about.[5] Meanwhile, historians of
crime have carried out their investigations into activities of the
'criminal class' that resided in the 'China' district during the
middle years of the century.[6] Yet no sooner have the new police
chased the last pimp out of the rookeries than something of an
historiographical silence descends upon the town. We catch
occasional glimpses of Merthyr, usually in the company of
political historians, who have found more than enough to keep
them occupied.[7] But it takes the misery, dislocation and deprivation of the interwar period to begin to break the silence.[8]

This silence is unfortunate because those late Victorian and
Edwardian years were vital ones in Merthyr's urban history.
At the point when social historians have taken their leave of
the settlement – the 1860s – it still occupied the predominant
position in the urban hierarchy of Wales, albeit retaining more

---

[4] Chris Evans, 'The Labyrinth of Flames': Work and Social Conflict in Early Industrial
Merthyr Tydfil (Cardiff, 1993); Gwyn A. Williams, The Merthyr Rising (Cardiff, 1988).
[5] Keith Strange, 'The condition of the working classes in Merthyr Tydfil, c. 1840–
1850', Ph.D. thesis, University of Wales (Swansea), 1982; Raymond K. J. Grant,
'Merthyr Tydfil in the mid-nineteenth century: the struggle for public health', Welsh
History Review, 14, no. 4 (1989), 574–94; Ieuan Gwynedd Jones, 'Merthyr Tydfil: the
politics of survival', Llafur, 2, no. 1 (1976), 18–31; Christopher Hamlin, 'Muddling in
Bumbledom: on the enormity of large sanitary improvements in four British towns',
Victorian Studies, 32, no.1 (1988), 55–83.
[6] David Jones and Alan Bainbridge, 'The "Conquering of China": crime in an industrial community, 1842–64', Llafur, 2, no. 3 (1978), 7–37; Keith Strange, 'In search of
the Celestial Empire: crime in Merthyr, 1830–1860', Llafur, 3, no. 1 (1980), 44–86.
[7] See, for example, Ieuan Gwynedd Jones, 'The election of 1868 in Merthyr Tydfil: a
study in the politics of an industrial borough', in his Explorations and Explanations: Essays
in the Social History of Victorian Wales (Llandysul, 1981), pp. 193–214; Kenneth O.
Morgan, 'D. A. Thomas: the industrialist as politician', in Stewart Williams (ed.),
Glamorgan Historian, Vol. 3 (Cowbridge, 1966); Kenneth O. Morgan, 'The Merthyr of
Keir Hardie', in Glanmor Williams (ed.), Merthyr Politics: The Making of a Working-Class
Tradition (Cardiff, 1966).
[8] J. W. England, 'The Merthyr of the twentieth century', in Williams (ed.), Merthyr
Politics.

than a hint of its 'frontier' qualities in the process; by the time they return to it, it is a profoundly different place. No longer the premier urban centre in south Wales, it had, by way of compensation, achieved county borough status. Replete with all the institutions and amenities that one might expect to find in any truly civic settlement – including free libraries, parks and a town hall – Merthyr had matured; the 'Samaria of Wales' had apparently been civilized. Yet, notwithstanding this reversal of fortunes, the making of 'civic Merthyr' has gone unnoticed by urban historians. It is suggested in this book that one of the most compelling reasons for studying this dramatic refashioning of the town's identity is the opportunity it provides to generate fresh understandings of the workings of the nineteenth-century British 'civic project'.

I. REFRAMING THE CIVIC PROJECT: 'CLASS', IDEOLOGY AND CIVILIZATION

The multifarious schemes to civilize the nineteenth-century British town and city constitute one of the most compelling of narratives. Many scholars have been keen to retell it.[9] What follows is a consideration of some of the ways in which they have approached their object of study. Such an endeavour is necessarily selective for if one defines the civic project broadly as that which attempted to order, civilize and rationalize the urban experience, a whole raft of initiatives, schemes and programmes comes within our purview. These include philanthropic ventures, the introduction of the new police, slum clearance programmes, the erection of civic buildings and the rational recreation movement, to name but a few. To add to the problem, historians have often written about such topics without making explicit the connection with the 'civic' dimension. In the face of such diversity, it is difficult to point to a coherent historiography of the civic project. Nevertheless, it is possible to identify certain shared assumptions that have united many of these narratives.

[9] See, for instance, Asa Briggs, *Victorian Cities* (Harmondsworth, 1990, paperback edn); Helen Meller, *Leisure and the Changing City, 1870–1914* (London, 1976); Martin Hewitt, *The Emergence of Stability in the Industrial City: Manchester, 1832–67* (Aldershot, 1996).

Perhaps most striking is the extent to which 'class' has occupied a privileged place in these histories. With good reason, both
Marxists and non-Marxists alike have often identified the project to civilize urban life with a particular social class, the middle
class. This was the group that provided many of the most
prominent supporters of the project, and this was the group best
placed to install the architectural features – the town halls, the
public parks, the statuary, and such like – that together comprised a civic landscape. Indeed, middle-class urbanites displayed such levels of commitment to the promotion of all things
'civilized' that it has been possible to suggest that the civic gospel
should be seen as an expression of middle-class 'consciousness',
'values', 'morality' or 'interests'. Martin Hewitt, in explaining
'the emergence of stability' in mid-nineteenth-century Manchester, has identified a middle-class 'moral imperialism' at
work in the city, an imperialism rooted in bourgeois culture, and
propagated through a range of bourgeois-dominated (or -run),
institutions including churches, chapels, Mechanics' Institutes
and temperance societies.[10] Similarly, R. J. Morris has discerned
a bourgeois 'sense of moral responsibility for the development of
urban society'.[11] Once possessed of such a responsibility, the
middle class set about remaking that society in its own image.
Thus, Alan Kidd has contended that the social problems
encountered in Victorian Manchester fired 'the middle-class
impetus to social and cultural intervention in the lives and habits
of the lower social classes and groups'. This impetus included a
'desire to reform morals and "civilize" the senses of the working
class'.[12] Likewise, Simon Gunn has described how the middle
class was able to 'project its impress over a considerable part of
urban existence from the spheres of work, leisure and education
to the physical layout of the town, civic architecture and sanitary
improvement'.[13] And Neil Evans, in his investigation of the

[10] Hewitt, *Emergence of Stability*, ch. 3, especially pp. 87–91.
[11] R. J. Morris, 'The middle class and British towns and cities of the industrial
revolution, 1780–1870', in D. Fraser and A. Sutcliffe (eds), *The Pursuit of Urban History*
(London, 1983), p. 303.
[12] A. J. Kidd, 'Introduction: the middle class in nineteenth-century Manchester', in
A. J. Kidd and K. W. Roberts (eds), *City, Class and Culture: Studies of Cultural Production
and Social Policy in Victorian Manchester* (Manchester, 1985), p. 15.
[13] Simon Gunn, 'The "failure" of the Victorian middle class: a critique', in J. Wolff
and J. Seed (eds), *The Culture of Capital: Art, Power and the Nineteenth-Century Middle Class*
(Manchester, 1988), p. 32.

development of a civic consciousness in Cardiff, has suggested that the civic spirit could *only* reside in the minds of the bourgeoisie: 'It was vital for the growth of civic responsibility that the emergent middle class should assert itself against the estate.'[14] Had it been left in the hands of the land-owning Bute family, Cardiff's civic consciousness would have remained a stunted and sickly plant indeed.

As descriptions of middle-class involvement in the project to civilize and govern the urban, these accounts are perfectly acceptable. Citizens drawn from the ranks of the social élite did involve themselves in various activities designed to fashion civic identities (and will be shown to have done so in late Victorian Merthyr), and they did initiate schemes that had the explicit brief of 'reforming' or 'civilizing' the working class. Moreover, that there was an ideological dimension to the civic project is undeniable: that the working class was often targeted by the middle-class 'missionaries' and their agents is clear; and that the 'civilizing mission' helped to buttress a sense of class unity amongst 'well-to-dos' is also apparent.[15] This study does not attempt to overturn such an understanding. But it does ponder further the implications of an argument which – in certain renderings – perceives the civic movement as somehow imma-nent within the culture of the British middle class, soaked in that class's values and shaped by its interests. Furthermore, it quizzes the notion that there was a sole object against which the civilizing power was to be unleashed, namely the working class. Both these suppositions have surfaced repeatedly in many studies dealing with different aspects of the civilizing pro-ject. Historians of leisure have often examined the Victorian 'rational recreation' movement in ways that fit neatly into the ideological paradigm.[16] Similarly, nineteenth-century philan-thropy has been interpreted by many as an attempt to remake the urban poor in the image of the ideal bourgeois: morally

---

[14] Neil Evans, 'The Welsh Victorian city: the middle class and civic and national consciousness in Cardiff, 1850–1914', *Welsh History Review*, 12, no. 3 (1985), 350–87, 351.

[15] This point has been made by Simon Gunn. See his article, 'The ministry, the middle class and the "civilizing mission" in Manchester, 1850–1880', *Social History*, 21, no. 1 (1996), 22–36. Also see the suggestive comments in Patrick Joyce, *Democratic Subjects: The Self and the Social in Nineteenth-Century England* (Cambridge, 1994), pp. 161–76.

[16] An example of this approach is Peter Bailey's, *Leisure and Class in Victorian England: Rational Recreation and the Contest for Control, 1830–1885* (London, 1978).

upright, independent and eminently respectable. In this analysis the oft-made distinction between 'deserving' and 'undeserving' becomes a means of 'socially controlling' the working class.[17] And, if techniques of moral suasion failed, the middle-class reformers could always rely on the 'new police' to spread the civic gospel.[18]

Such understandings capture significant truths about the civic project. However, it is suggested here that other truths can be obscured by an assumption that the civilizing project was a class project in any straightforward or singular sense, truths that this book seeks to uncover. To this extent it is a product of its time, for recent years have seen the interrogation of many of the assumptions that governed the writing of the 'new' social history. In particular, postmodernists and post-structuralists have expressed their dissatisfaction with 'hard' 'master' concepts such as 'class' and Marxian (and other) 'meta-narratives'. The ensuing debates may have been conducted in a bad-tempered and sometimes churlish key, but they have at least enabled old certainties to be questioned. 'Class' has come under some of the heaviest fire. For so long the basic building block of social history, its power as a category of analysis now has to be argued for, rather than assumed. And as an identity, it is now seen as just one amongst many: at certain times and in certain contexts privileged above others, but at other times and in other places occupying a less exalted position. This, it should be emphasized, does not entail its wholesale rejection. As Patrick Joyce has put it, class has a place in our histories, 'though it does from time to time need to be put in it'.[19] This book is written in that spirit, and is shaped by the belief that the 'linguistic turn' has much to offer the cultural and social historian. Nevertheless, we need to exercise caution at this point for – as many

[17] David Fraser, *The Evolution of the Welfare British State* (2nd edn, Basingstoke, 1984), p. 128.
[18] Allan Silver, 'The demand for order in civil society: a review of some themes in the history of urban crime, police, and riot', in D. J. Bordua (ed.), *The Police: Six Sociological Essays* (New York, 1967); Robert D. Storch, 'The plague of the blue locusts: police reform and popular resistance in Northern England, 1840–57', *International Review of Social History*, 20, no. 1 (1975), 61–90; Robert D. Storch, 'The policeman as domestic missionary: urban discipline and popular culture in Northern England, 1850–80', *Journal of Social History*, 9, no. 4 (1976), 481–509.
[19] Patrick Joyce, *Visions of the People: Industrial England and the Question of Class, 1848–1914* (Cambridge, 1991), p. 1.

others have pointed out – as a theory postmodernism contains more than a few ahistorical (indeed, even anti-historical) tendencies.[20] Bearing this in mind, this work attempts to integrate some of its more useful insights (such as the insistence upon the importance of language in the creation of identities) in a work that does not hold that we have witnessed 'the end of social history', nor which lapses into linguistic determinism. Along the way, other identities and other dynamics can be introduced into the historical equation in an effort to broaden our understanding of the drive to civilize the urban.

Such a theoretical positioning admits the argument that while ideology may have been an attribute of the civic project, it should not be seen as its essence. Linked to this is the suggestion that it is unsatisfactory to conceive of power as a relationship simply structured along class lines. The assumption that, in the final analysis, the middle class was the subject of the power relations enacted by the civilizing initiatives, while the working class was constituted as the object of that power, is too crude to do justice to the complexities of the project. One of the reasons why the civic project could never have merely been a class project lies in the fractured and de-centred nature of power. Here the insights of Michel Foucault are particularly apposite.[21] Foucault conceptualized power as being dispersed throughout a range of complex social networks; it is not something that is unproblematically possessed by a dominant agent, or set of agents. This is useful as it allows the development of a more sophisticated analysis of the workings of the civic project. For in this account, all urbanites were implicated in the civilizing project; all were – to varying degrees and at various times – constituted as both subjects *and* objects of the civilizing power. Moreover, we are alerted to the fashion in which a range

[20] Contributions to the debate include Patrick Joyce, 'The end of social history?', *Social History*, 20, no. 1 (1995), 73–91; Patrick Joyce, 'The return of history: postmodernism and the politics of academic history in Britain', *Past and Present*, 158 (1998), 207–35; Geoff Eley and Keith Nield, 'Starting over: the present, the post-modern and the moment of social history', *Social History*, 20, no. 3 (1995), 355–64; Joyce Appleby, Lynn Hunt and Margaret Jacob, *Telling the Truth about History* (London, 1994); James Epstein, 'Spatial practices/democratic vistas', *Social History*, 24, no. 3 (1999), 294–310.
[21] Many of Foucault's works were concerned with the analysis of power. See, for example, his *Madness and Civilization: A History of Insanity in the Age of Reason* (London, 1967), and *Discipline and Punish: The Birth of the Prison* (London, 1977). See also Colin Gordon (ed.), *Power/Knowledge: Selected Interviews and Other Writings, 1972–1977, by Michel Foucault* (Brighton, 1980), and Lotringer, *Foucault Live*.

of identities (including those of religion, class, gender and ethnicity) could be inscribed within the civic project, often in antagonistic ways. It should be noted that this approach neither precludes the idea of class power, nor shuts down the possibility of resistance, although Foucault himself had relatively little to say on this important theme.[22]

Building upon this conceptualization of power, a potentially fruitful way of understanding the civic project (which again looks to Foucault for inspiration) is to conceive of it as a particular mode of 'governmentality' – nineteenth-century liberalism. Liberalism in this rendering denotes not a set of philosophical observations upon the problem of rule, but rather a formula of government, a political rationality.[23] This approach has the virtue of freeing us from an over-reliance upon the ideological paradigm. Barry and others make the point: 'for Foucault, political rationalities are more than just ideologies; they constitute a part of the fabric of our ways of thinking about and acting upon one another and ourselves.'[24] This is important. Liberalism, as understood in this account, is not reducible to an ideology that emanates from an anterior class (or other) structure. Rather it is a set of ruminations on 'the conduct of conduct' which themselves have a part to play in the constitution of collective identities such as 'class', the 'public' and the 'citizenry'. Liberalism is marked out from other modes of governmentality (such as sovereignty, for instance) in its concern with freedom, as various spheres are defined as being outside the influence of the state. As Nikolas Rose explains it:

> the achievement of liberalism as an art of government was to begin to govern through making people free. Liberalism 'freed' persons in the realms of the market, civil society, the family – it placed them outside the legitimate scope of the political authorities, subject only to the limits of the law. Yet the 'freeing' of these zones was accompanied by the

[22] For more on 'class' power, see Joseph Rouse, 'Power/knowledge', in Garry Gutting (ed.), *The Cambridge Companion to Foucault* (Cambridge, 1994), pp. 104–7. Foucault asserted that resistance was possible without effectively allowing a theoretical space for it. See Lotringer, *Foucault Live*, pp. 239–40.

[23] See Nikolas Rose, 'Governing "advanced" liberal democracies', in Andrew Barry, Thomas Osborne and Nikolas Rose (eds), *Foucault and Political Reason: Liberalism, Neo-Liberalism and the Rationalities of Government* (London, 1996), p. 39.

[24] Andrew Barry, Thomas Osborne and Nikolas Rose, 'Introduction', in A. Barry et al. (eds), *Foucault and Political Reason*, p. 7.

intervention of a whole series of attempts to shape and manage conduct
within them in desirable ways. On the one hand, the 'public' activities
of free citizens were to be regulated by codes of civility, reason and
orderliness. On the other, the private conduct of free citizens was to be
civilized by equipping them with the languages and techniques of self-
understanding and self-mastery. Freedom thus becomes inextricably
linked to the norm of civility; from this moment on, even when freedom
is practised as calculated resistance to civility, its exercise entails
extrapolating, parodying or inverting its valuations.[25]

Thus, instead of merely being interpreted as a particular
manifestation of a class ideology, the civic programme becomes
a vital feature of a particular mode of governmentality which
itself entails the construction of social identities and the
enactment of power relations. Moreover, 'civilization' can be
seen not simply as a synonym for 'middle-class' values but
rather as a key concept in framing and shaping social relations.
Of course, middle-class urbanites still feature prominently in
the effort to create civic identities. As promoters of schemes to
open public parks, museums, libraries and the like, they were
important actors in the civic drama; but others have to be
brought into the frame. For while civic landscapes may have
been fashioned by a social élite, they were overwhelmingly
populated by a non-élite citizenry. This is significant because
urban meaning was largely dependent upon the uses to which
public urban spaces were put. When urbanites entered the
streets – spaces shot through with notions of 'freedom' – they
(unwittingly perhaps) contributed to the identity of their own
town. 'Civilized' behaviour added lustre to a town image;
'uncivilized' practices in these most sensitive of public spaces
called into question a settlement's civic credentials. In some
cases there was broad agreement when it came to deciding
whether various types of public behaviour were barbaric or
civilized. Public drunkenness was a clear example of the former.
One did not have to be a teetotaller to take offence at the
disorderly inebriates as they staggered through the streets on
their way from one pub to the next. Contrariwise, contemporaries from all social classes could welcome crowds gathered

[25] Nikolas Rose, *Towards a Critical Sociology of Freedom* (Inaugural Lecture,
Goldsmith's College, University of London, 3 May 1992), reprinted in Patrick Joyce
(ed.), *Class* (Oxford, 1995), p. 215.

together to hear performances of choral music, a cultural practice that was generally believed to be morally uplifting. In other
cases, it was more difficult to categorize behaviour. For instance, depending upon one's point of view, sporting urbanites
could be dismissed as 'roughs' or lauded as 'respectables'. Thus,
as citizens 'read their streets' they could reach different conclusions about how 'civilized' their town was. Hence, a town
image was always in flux, always contested.

As the above examples indicate, popular cultural practices
frequently made demands upon the urban landscape. It is for
this reason that they are singled out for particular attention
here. And it is at this point that we are reminded of the
advantages of picking Merthyr as a case study. For as a late
developer in civic matters, the settlement found itself caught up
in the civic project at a time when the popular cultural life of
Britons was being profoundly transformed. The commercialization of leisure, while not new in itself, was massively
intensified during the late Victorian and Edwardian periods.
One consequence of these changes was the formation of the so-
called ' "traditional" working-class culture', a culture based on
new forms of collective leisure experiences which were conducted on an ever bigger scale, and along ever more formal and
organized lines.[26] With the rise of the new model sports, the
music hall, the cinema and other forms of mass entertainment,
new spatial practices, and new recreational crowds, were called
into existence. That so many of these changes can be understood in 'class' terms makes Merthyr an ideal location in which
to test new understandings of the civic project. We should
expect to be able to find an ideological dimension to that project in a town with Merthyr's striking social structure. Similarly,
with the rise of so many new forms of popular leisure involving
large numbers of working-class urbanites, it would be easy to
construct a history of 'middle-class' efforts to 'tame' the worst
excesses of that 'working-class' culture that simply mobilized
notions of 'social control'. However, if it is possible to discern
other identities and other dynamics at work in a town in which

---

[26] The classic accounts of this cultural formation are Gareth Stedman Jones,
'Working-class culture and working-class politics in London, 1870–1900: notes on the
remaking of a working class', *Journal of Social History*, 7, no. 4 (1983), 460–508; Eric
Hobsbawm, *Worlds of Labour: Further Studies in the History of Labour* (London, 1984),
chs. 10 and 11.

'class', in key respects, was the very touchstone of its historical experience (Merthyr, after all, has been identified by one author as the birthplace of the Welsh working class[27]), some idea of the complexities underpinning the nineteenth-century British civic project can be grasped. Before we set about that task, it is necessary to ponder certain features of the district's historical legacy that weighed heavily upon the civic projectors of the late Victorian years.

II. MERTHYR: THE PARADIGMATIC INDUSTRIAL SETTLEMENT

Some places have a lot of … [local] culture: songs that memorialize their great streets or side streets, homes once occupied by the famous or infamous, a distinctive dialect or vocabulary, routine festivals and parades that selectively dramatize the past, novels, dirty lyrics, pejorative nicknames, special holidays, dead heroes, evangelical moralists, celebrated wastrels, and so on. Other cities seem only the product of recent mass manufacture. Generally, the accumulation of local culture is a matter of age; the process of selective memorialization takes time. But it must also be said that some cities emerge quickly with a strong image of themselves often repeated in their appearential order and in the statements of outsiders. Others seem to remain practically nonentities no matter what their age.

Gerald D. Suttles[28]

No one could ever accuse Merthyr of being a nonentity. Perhaps life would have been more agreeable for its civic 'boosters' if it had been, for by the latter decades of the nineteenth century they were living in a town with a surfeit of 'local culture', much of it charged with extremely negative meanings.[29] This is not the place to construct in full the urban biography of Merthyr. However, it is important to identify some of the particularities of its urban history, particularities that had to be confronted by the late Victorian civic projectors.

---

[27] Williams, *Merthyr Rising*, especially pp. 224–30.

[28] 'The cumulative texture of local urban culture', *American Journal of Sociology*, 90, no. 2 (1984), 283–304, 284.

[29] The term 'booster' is used at various points throughout this study as a convenient means of describing those who engaged in the process of fashioning positive images of their town. The label had its origins in a discrete period in American urban history (the so-called 'Booster Era' (*c.* 1885–*c.* 1925)), during which individuals promoted their home towns in the hope of attracting settlers and businesses.

The brute fact that determined so much of Merthyr's development was the extent to which the settlement's growth was dependent above all else upon industrialization. While scholars rightly caution against understanding urbanization as a simple function of industrial growth, in the case of Merthyr such caution is wholly misplaced;[30] in the late eighteenth century the ironmasters magicked a settlement out of thin air. Certainly, traces of an earlier history did survive into the nineteenth century. For instance, the boundaries of the sprawling Merthyr parish – which stretched for some fifteen miles from the Brecon Beacons down to the confluence of the Rivers Taff and Cynon – had been drawn sometime in the thirteenth century.[31] And, importantly, the very existence of the 'old village' had an influence on Merthyr's subsequent development.[32] Yet, for all that, the urban history of Merthyr effectively dated from the arrival of the would-be ironmasters. The result of their activities was a complex of settlements in the upper reaches of the Taff Valley that secured for itself the top spot in the urban hierarchy of south Wales, a position it was to retain until the late 1860s. At the time of the first census (in 1801), Merthyr had already emerged as the largest 'town' in the region with a population of just over 7,700. Over the course of the next half-century, and in step with the continued expansion of the iron industry, the district continued to experience dramatic rates of urban growth. The 1810s and 1830s were particularly dislocating decades: between 1811 and 1821 Merthyr's population increased by 56 per cent, whilst between 1831 and 1841 the figure was 58 per cent. By 1851 there were some 46,378 souls living in the district.[33]

Such was the importance of the ironworks that distinct urban communities grew up in their shadows.[34] The 'big four' works

[30] F. M. L. Thompson, 'Town and city', in F. M. L. Thompson (ed.), *The Cambridge Social History of Britain, 1750–1950*, 3 vols. (Cambridge, 1990), Vol. 1, 'Regions and Communities', p. 9.
[31] Charles Wilkins, *The History of Merthyr Tydfil* (2nd edn, Merthyr Tydfil, 1908), p. 64.
[32] Harold Carter and Sandra Wheatley, *Merthyr Tydfil in 1851: A Study of the Spatial Structure of a Welsh Industrial Town* (Cardiff, 1982), p. 9.
[33] 1801 Census Report; 1811 Census Report; 1821 Census Report; 1831 Census Report; 1841 Census Report; 1851 Census Report.
[34] Carter and Wheatley, *Merthyr Tydfil in 1851*, pp. 9–13; Harold Carter, 'The structure of Glamorgan towns in the nineteenth century', in Prys Morgan (ed.), *Glamorgan County History, VI: Glamorgan Society, 1780–1980* (Cardiff, 1988), pp. 159–64.

spawned their own satellite settlements populated by workforces that defined themselves, often riotously, in terms of Cyfarthfa, Dowlais, Penydarren and Plymouth. By the end of the nine-teenth century, Dowlais emerged as the most developed of these settlements. It looked like a separate town situated, as it was, approximately two miles to the north-east of Merthyr, and some 500 feet above the 'old village'. As the century progressed, so did Dowlais's integrity as a distinct urban unit. It developed its own commercial centre with its own High Street. In 1834, it was constituted an ecclesiastical parish.[35] With its own railway stations, public halls (the Oddfellows' Hall was built in 1878), a separate Burial Board, its own gas works and a branch bank, Dowlaisians could think of themselves as living within the Merthyr district, yet residing in a discrete urban settlement that had its own interests, demands and identity.[36]

The same came to be true of those living in the villages and townships that appeared in the south of Merthyr parish during the second half of the nineteenth century. However, in their cases a sense of a different history also fed into the construction of independent, yet interconnected, identities. For, unlike the older iron townships, it was the imperatives of the coal trade that led to the creation of settlements such as Troedyrhiw, Bedlinog, Treharris and Merthyr Vale. Although the iron com-panies had mined coal on a large scale, it was not until the 1860s that the sale-coal trade took off in the Taff Valley.[37] By the early 1880s about 10 per cent of all Glamorgan steam coal came from the Merthyr district, and in particular from those townships located to the south of Merthyr town.[38] On the back of the burgeoning coal trade, within three decades Treharris and Merthyr Vale were transformed from sites in which 'one or two farms' could be found, into urban centres boasting several thousand inhabitants each.[39] In the early 1880s, Merthyr Vale was home to some 3,600, whilst Treharris hardly registered as a

[35] *Kelly's Directory of Monmouthshire and the Principal Towns and Places in South Wales* (London, 1884), p. 391.
[36] John G. E. Astle, *Illustrated Report of the Merthyr Tydfil Incorporation Inquiries, 1897 and 1903* (Merthyr, 1903), p. 58.
[37] J. H. Morris and L. J. Williams, *The South Wales Coal Industry, 1841–1875* (Cardiff, 1958), pp. 9–10; R. H. Walters, *The Economic and Business History of the South Wales Steam Coal Industry, 1840–1914* (New York, 1977), p. 11.
[38] Walters, *Economic and Business History*, p. 9.
[39] Charles Wilkins, *Merthyr and Aberdare Illustrated* (Merthyr Tydfil, 1902), p. 62.

centre of population at all. Thirty years later over 8,500 dwelt in the former, while Treharris had over 8,800 inhabitants living within its limits.[40] Meanwhile, Troedyrhiw and Abercannaid, small settlements that had been established before the coal boom, benefited enormously from an increase in the output of the Plymouth Collieries during the early 1890s. Over the course of two decades, Troedyrhiw's population had increased by a factor of five-and-a-half.[41]

This rise of the southern mining townships took place against a backdrop of stagnating iron settlements in the north of the parish. Iron, and increasingly steel, still had a part to play in the economic life of Merthyr and Dowlais. In the early 1880s, the Dowlais Iron Company employed approximately 60 per cent of Dowlaisians.[42] Nevertheless, the decline of the iron trade was all too clear. Penydarren Works closed in 1859; those at Plymouth ceased operation in 1880. Cyfarthfa struggled on until 1910 after a successful takeover bid by the Dowlais Company in 1902. The consequences of the demise of iron were twofold. On the one hand, it led to many inhabitants of the 'outlying districts' resenting the influence (expressed in terms of local government, administration and justice) that Merthyr Tydfil continued to exercise throughout the late Victorian and Edwardian periods. Certainly, all manner of civic schemes were scuppered by individuals who feared that inhabitants of Merthyr town would benefit at the expense of those living in Merthyr Vale and Treharris. This distrust of all things Merthyrian was in place from an early stage, as is witnessed by the actions of eighty-eight ratepayers from Merthyr Vale in 1869. Already wary of the old iron town, and armed with a precocious sense of their own historical destiny, they petitioned the General Board of Health in the hope that the settlement be removed from the jurisdiction of the Merthyr Tydfil Local Board of Health.[43] Although their request was refused, it was an ominous portent of the prickly relationship that was to

[40] *Kelly's Directory* (1884), p. 391; *Kelly's Directory* (1920), p. 621.
[41] John G. E. Astle, *The Progress of Merthyr* (Merthyr Tydfil, 1894), p. 26; *Royal Commission on the Church of England and Other Religious Bodies in Wales and Monmouthshire*, 1911, Cd. 5435, Vol. 4, Minutes of Evidence, Book 3, Q. 45346 (hereafter *Report on Religious Bodies*). Troedyrhiw's population in 1880 was 2,360. In 1906 it was 12,951.
[42] *Kelly's Directory* (1884), p. 391.
[43] Ieuan Gwynedd Jones, *Communities: Essays in the Social History of Victorian Wales* (Llandysul, 1987), p. 142.

develop between Merthyr and 'the outlying districts' in the course of the next half-century, a relationship that did much to frame the efforts of Merthyr's civic boosters.

Just as the particularities of the district's industrial development shaped the built form, and determined many of the fault-lines along which urban identities were to begin and end, so they were also responsible for moulding a distinctive social structure, something of no small consequence when it came to civic matters. Most striking of all was the fact that Merthyr was packed with working-class urbanites. This was a result of the dominance of industries that relied primarily on muscle-power.[44] In the early 1830s, one in every three Merthyrians was directly engaged in the production of iron.[45] By the late 1840s, one commentator suggested that the inhabitants of the district were employed 'almost entirely' in the four great iron works.[46] And, despite the decidedly shaky position of the industry at the start of the late Victorian period, in 1871 one quarter of all males over twenty years of age worked in iron manufacture. Thereafter, 'King Coal' took over where the ironmasters had left off. Some 27 per cent of Merthyr's adult male population were employed in mining in the early 1870s, while in 1911 a massive 55 per cent were working in the district's collieries.[47] So, although in that year only 5 per cent of Merthyr's males over ten years of age were involved in the iron and steel trade, the overall picture remained the same; in demographic terms at least, Edwardian Merthyr was still an overwhelmingly 'working-class' town.

The corollary of this was that the middle class was noticeable by its absence. Such was bourgeois dislike for the harsh conditions in the 'Samaria of Wales' that it was possible for one observer to report in 1850 that 'there are no men of middle station, none of the ordinary class of "residents" who are to be found, more or less in number, in every other town in England'.[48] This was an overstatement of the case, but it did point

---

[44] Jones, 'The politics of survival', p. 23.
[45] Williams, *Merthyr Rising*, p. 34.
[46] *Royal Commission of Inquiry into the State of Education in Wales*, Report, 1847, XXVII (870), Part 1, p. 304. Hereafter *1847 Report.*
[47] 1871 Census Report; 1911 Census Report.
[48] T. W. Rammell, *Report to the General Board of Health into the Sewerage, Drainage, and Supply of Water, and the Sanitary Condition of Merthyr Tydfil* (London, 1850), p. 6.

to a striking social fact.[49] Taking the number of retailing outlets
as one, albeit imprecise, indicator of a bourgeois presence, the
contrast between Merthyr and other towns was indeed great.
Notwithstanding a rapid growth in the number of shops set up
in the period stretching from the early 1820s through to the late
1840s, by the century's mid-point Merthyr was still a long way
behind other settlements of comparable size. In 1822 there was
one shop for every 400 Merthyrians, while by the late 1840s this
ratio had fallen to 145 inhabitants per shop. Yet urbanites in
York were much better served with one shop per sixty inhabitants.[50] The census returns expressed in another way what the
built form of Merthyr displayed for all to see. In York in 1851
22 per cent of the population were in socio-economic groups
1 and 2, whilst in Merthyr the equivalent figure was a mere
6.2 per cent.[51]

Historians have cited this absence of a strong middle class as
the key to understanding many aspects of Merthyr's turbulent
early history. In common with many contemporaries, they
have identified a 'lack of governance' that stemmed from a
skewed social structure composed of the omnipotent ironmasters on the one hand, and the working class on the other.[52]
For example, when pondering the rising of 1831, R. J. Morris
has suggested that 'Merthyr demonstrated what happened
when an industry grew without a traditional work relationship
to pattern its conflicts, and when a town grew without being a
town and without a strong and secure middle class'.[53] Similarly,
the 'ecological disaster' which beset Merthyr in the 1830s and
1840s has also been explained in terms of the weakness of the
bourgeoisie, the group that in other towns was populating
the organs of local government and effecting the necessary
sanitary reforms.[54] Their inability to do the same for Merthyr
meant that by the middle years of the century diseases such as
typhoid, smallpox and scarlet fever stalked the numerous slum

---

[49] *1847 Report* Part 1, p. 304. In 1853 Dr William Kay estimated that some 4,000 out
of a population of over 46,300 belonged to the middle and upper classes, although this
was something of an exaggeration. William Kay, *Report on the Sanitary Condition of
Merthyr Tydfil* ... (Merthyr, 1854), cited in Jones, 'The politics of survival', p. 26.
[50] Carter and Wheatley, *Merthyr Tydfil in 1851*, pp. 17–18.
[51] Ibid., p. 18.
[52] Jones, *Communities*, p. 337.
[53] Morris, 'The middle class and British towns', p. 292.
[54] Williams, *The Merthyr Rising*, p. 51; Jones, *Communities*, pp. 338–9.

areas, picking off inhabitants at will; when cholera visited the town in 1849, one in twelve of the population was attacked, while one in twenty-eight actually succumbed.[55] Stratospheric mortality rates, and particularly high infant mortality rates, were chilling testaments to the extent of the problems facing Merthyrians in their battle through life. And, although such problems were encountered by all urban settlements during this period, the district stood out as suffering more than most; in 1845, Merthyr was rated the second most unhealthy town in Britain.[56]

Late Victorian civic boosters had to wrestle with this legacy. The establishment of sewerage systems and pure water supplies, the clearance of slum housing and the improvement of streets, all dominated the local political agenda for years to come.[57] Furthermore, given the persistence of these problems, it was extremely difficult to shake off the stigma that had attached itself to Merthyr's name. Not only had all manner of government inspectors, social explorers and the like found Merthyr an excellent object of study in the 1840s and 1850s (and been careful to publicize their findings in the process), but their successors returned and did the same thing throughout the latter decades of the century. Indeed, as will be shown later, special sanitary commissioners were still descending upon the town and describing the 'hell' that they found well into the twentieth century. Unfortunately for the civic projectors (and the rest of the inhabitants), Merthyr's official status as a place 'prejudicial to human life' was constantly reaffirmed.[58] As late as 1915, for instance, it was revealed that the town had one of the highest maternal death rates in Britain.[59]

Yet, notwithstanding some terrible similarities, the Merthyr of the later nineteenth century was, in important respects, a world away from the frontier settlement that had been so traumatically hurled into history. During the early phases of its

---

[55] J. Ginswick (ed.), *Labour and the Poor in England and Wales, 1849–51*, Vol. 3 (London, 1983), p. 11.

[56] See Chris Evans, *'Labyrinth of Flames'*, p. 56. Liverpool occupied the premier position.

[57] Grant, 'The struggle for public health'; Hamlin, 'Muddling in Bumbledom'.

[58] Ginswick (ed.), *Labour and the Poor*, p. 11.

[59] Anthony S. Wohl, *Endangered Lives: Public Health in Victorian Britain* (London, 1984, paperback edn), p. 30.

development, it was the transitory nature of the population that marked it out from older urban centres. Days of prosperity and high wages saw a stream of human labour head into the Taff Valley in search of work; hard times and wage cuts had the effect of reversing the flow. The presence of this floating population gave the town many of its 'frontier' qualities. As long as Merthyr remained a place to make – and take – money from, rather than a town in which to live, there was little reason to develop a machinery of local government that could temper the worst excesses of urban growth. By the late Victorian and Edwardian periods, the situation had altered decisively. On Census Night 1871, just under 60 per cent of Merthyr's inhabitants were recorded as having been born in Glamorgan, although how many of these had actually been born in the town is difficult to assess. By 1911 the census abstracts are more forthcoming; six out of every ten Merthyrians were living in their place of birth.[60]

They found themselves in a community that had shed many vestiges of its frontier past. For not only was the population becoming more settled, but an infrastructure of local government was also slowly developing. The process had begun as long before as 1836, when a Board of Guardians replaced the Select Vestry. Fourteen years later a Local Board of Health was set up, and it remained the main focus of power until 1894, when an urban district council was established.[61] And as the iron trade entered a period of decline, so the grip of the ironmasters on the levers of political power weakened. The election of Henry Richard as Liberal MP in 1868 marked a significant break with the past, ushering in, as it did, a new era of increased middle-class and even working-class participation in the formal structures of politics. This is not to say that industrial might was no longer a force to be reckoned with. In Merthyr, as in the rest of south Wales, coal magnates and colliery companies were not averse to involving themselves in the political process. Nevertheless, there had been a fundamental shift away from the almost feudal situation that had obtained in the earlier phases

[60] 1871 Census Report; 1911 Census Report; P. N. Jones, 'Population migration into Glamorgan 1861–1911: a reassessment', in Morgan (ed.), *Glamorgan County History*, VI.
[61] R. S. Evans, 'The development of local government', in Merthyr Teachers' Centre Group, *Merthyr Tydfil: A Valley Community* (Cowbridge, 1981).

of the iron town's history. Then power – be it defined politically, economically, socially or culturally – seemed to reside in
the hands of a few iron kings; now it was dispersed more widely
throughout 'the town'.

Hand in hand with this broadening of the political sphere
went a proliferation of all manner of institutions that one might
expect to find in a maturing civil society. For instance, the
number of voluntary organizations increased during these
years. Many of them were concerned, to a greater or lesser
extent, with effecting reforms at the local level. Ratepayers'
societies, chambers of trade, licensed victuallers' associations,
debating groups, branches of the Young Men's Christian
Organization, temperance societies and improvement societies
all competed for the support of interested inhabitants. The
chapel towered above them all. Nonconformists had long been
to the fore when it came to promoting the cause of 'civilization'
in Merthyr. As early as the 1790s and 1800s Baptists, Inde-
pendents, Wesleyan Methodists, Calvinistic Methodists and
Unitarians had registered their presence in the district.[62] They
continued to thrive throughout the century. During the later
Victorian period, when the most significant nodes of urban
growth were located in the south of the parish, the Free
Churches put down roots swiftly. Over £33,000 was invested in
Troedyrhiw as part of a chapel-building frenzy. As a result, 80
per cent of the township's 13,000 inhabitants could find a seat in
a place of worship if they so desired.[63] Meanwhile, a sharp eye
was also kept on developments in the older settlements. Any
house-building project was likely to be accompanied by the
appearance of a chapel. For example, amongst the 460 new
houses that were constructed in Penydarren, two chapels were
placed 'in the midst of them'.[64] By the early years of the
twentieth century, Merthyr was blessed with eighty-two Nonconformist chapels. Between them they could accommodate
44,330 (or 77 per cent) of the population deemed to be 'available for Protestant places of worship'.[65] From these chapels
emerged some of the most enthusiastic of all the civic projectors.

[62] Anthony Jones, *A Thesis and Survey of the Nonconformist Chapel Architecture in
Merthyr Tydfil* (Merthyr, 1962).
[63] *Report on Religious Bodies*, Q. 45346.
[64] Ibid., QQ. 45346, 45349.
[65] Ibid., Q. 45338.

They took their place alongside a citizenry that was increasingly used to debating a variety of *local* issues in an ever more robust public sphere. The chapels themselves were a significant part of the infrastructure of that sphere. Utterances from the pulpit about the 'condition' of Merthyr, the spiritual health of the town and the morality of the townsfolk carried weight throughout the late Victorian years. The institutions of local government were also prime sites in which debates could rage over the nature of Merthyr society. Meanwhile, a flourishing print culture immeasurably strengthened the public sphere. Antiquarians such as Charles Wilkins invented an urban history for Merthyr that stretched back to the very dawn of time itself. His *magnum opus* took its place amongst a host of local guides, directories and almanacs celebrating all things Merthyrian. However, the most significant space within which a 'public opinion' could be formed and re-formed, was that described by the local newspapers. The *Merthyr Express* stands out as particularly important, appearing, as it did, weekly from 1864 and running throughout the entire period. Its proprietor and editor, Harry Southey, proved himself one of the most committed of all the civic boosters. Yet the *Cardiff and Merthyr Guardian* (1845–74), the *Merthyr Telegraph* (1858–81), the *Merthyr Star* (1859–72), the *Fellten* (1868–76) and the *Merthyr and Dowlais Times* (1891–9), amongst others, all had their part to play in augmenting the public sphere.[66] With their 'local intelligence' and gossip columns, their editorials and correspondence columns, they provided members of the district's reading public with an opportunity to discourse upon the kind of town they thought Merthyr had been, was now and could be in the future. At the same time, all promulgated some of the key assumptions which underpinned the civic project, including notions of public duty and civility. Incidentally, they provide us with the richest source we have of the multifarious efforts to civilize the urban settlement that was Merthyr.

The very existence of such a vibrant public sphere is itself evidence of a profound move away from the frontier days, and provided interested Merthyrians with a solid base from which to promote the civic project. This book considers aspects of that

---

[66] Wilkins, *History of Merthyr*, p. 499.

project by concentrating upon the often complex relationship
that obtained between popular culture, public space and urban
meaning. It is argued throughout the following chapters that
the public spaces of the town were heavily implicated in the
mission to civilize the urban; certainly when contemporaries
wandered Merthyr's streets they frequently drew conclusions
about the morality of the inhabitants that populated them.
Various popular cultural practices made demands upon those
public spaces and brought townspeople (both as individuals
and as members of recreational crowds) into the heart of the
town. The civic projectors had to deal with these spatial
practices. Some were deemed inimical to the cause of urban
civilization and had to be discouraged. Others could be
accommodated more easily into civic images of the district.
In almost all cases there was room for disagreement and
negotiation. (This should not surprise; 'civilized' behaviour was
never an uncontested virtue.) The ensuing debates and the
numerous initiatives to protect the civility of the streets fed into
the very identity of Merthyr itself.

As noted in Chapter II, by the 1870s that identity was in
desperate need of improvement. At a time when Merthyr was
falling behind the likes of Cardiff, Newport and Swansea in
terms of both size and civic accomplishment, the old iron town's
decline was frequently prophesied. To the fore in agitating for
reform were representatives from the middle class. Thanks
largely to their untiring efforts, and with help from influential
'friends', progress was made; in July 1905, the town was
granted a charter of incorporation, and something approaching
a civic landscape was eventually fashioned for Merthyr. Running through the heart of this landscape were the streets and
thoroughfares. These spaces – charged with notions of 'freedom' and intimately connected to the idea of 'the public' – are
examined in Chapter III, where consideration is given to some
of the ways in which 'civilized' norms of street behaviour were
both assembled and challenged. Public drunks are singled out
as especially troublesome individuals who possessed an unner-
ving ability to disrupt a civilized street etiquette. Some of the
strategies developed to regulate these inebriates, and to encourage 'self'-control, are considered with particular emphasis
placed upon the role of the local newspaper as a 'technology of

rule'. In Chapter IV the first recreational crowd marches across
the pages of the book. The musical crowd was a gathering
generally welcomed by respectable inhabitants. The reasons for
this acceptance lie in the socially inclusive characteristics of late
Victorian musical culture. These characteristics are examined
in some detail, and it is suggested in the process that in music the
civic projectors' vision of a harmonious and civilized 'town'
came closest to being fully realized. Representations of the
musical crowd were frequently constructed in ways that emphasized the unity and coherence of Merthyr society; yet for all
that, it is noted that 'musical Merthyr' remained an inherently
unstable compound. An equally noisy, though often more
boisterous, collection of urbanites, the sporting crowd, heaves
into view in Chapter V. This was a far more difficult gathering
to accommodate within the civic vision of Merthyr. In explaining why this was the case, the inadequacies of an analysis that
stresses the project as a simple manifestation of middle-class
'interests' are brought into sharp focus. Local tradesmen played
a pivotal role in encouraging various sports in the central spaces
of the town, sports whose moralizing qualities were disputed
by many Merthyrians (including Nonconformists) wedded to
notions of urban civilization. Thus, the pursuit of profit (surely
a middle-class interest if ever there was one?) can be seen in this
instance to have severely problematized certain conceptions
of a civic identity. If nothing else, we are reminded of the
plural nature of the civic project. Taking this theme further, the
final chapter concentrates upon the complex relationship that
obtained between Merthyr's Nonconformists and popular
leisure. Given that the project, and notions of civility, were
often articulated in a religious key, such a study is a useful
means of underlining the problems that the spiritual civic
projectors had to encounter. It is argued that during the late
nineteenth and early twentieth centuries the Nonconformists
were less able to dominate Merthyr's public sphere, partly as a
consequence of the rise of commercialized sports and entertainments which facilitated the generation of more secular town
images. The use of an outdated condemnatory discourse to
make sense of entertainments that were eminently respectable
(and marketed as such) did little to strengthen the hand of the
more extreme Nonconformists. All the chapters, in different

ways, emphasize a major theme throughout the book, namely, that for all its obvious successes, the civic project was a fractured, incomplete, often contradictory, and always contested, process. It is to that process, as it unfolded in Merthyr, the 'old metropolis of Wales', that attention is now turned.

II
THE 'OLD METROPOLIS OF WALES':
AN URBAN SETTLEMENT
WITH CIVIC PRETENSIONS

> Years ago, when Merthyr was but a village, it was called the Metropolis
> of Wales, but since Aberdare had risen up their estimation had been put
> down. A year or two ago, an Aberdare gentleman, at a dinner in
> Merthyr, had the impudence to say that Merthyr was going to the dogs,
> and they would be glad to go to Aberdare as rag-tag and bob-tails and
> gather rags and bones (laughter). But Merthyr would be the new
> Jerusalem when Aberdare would be Babylon (laughter and applause).
>
> A speech delivered by John Jones to the Merthyr Friends
> in Distress Society, 1901.[1]

I. MERTHYR: THE 'OLD METROPOLIS OF WALES'
AND THE NARRATIVE OF DECLINE

In 1882 the periodical *The Red Dragon* opened its pages to a
number of contributors who had been invited to explain why
their home towns should be chosen as the site of the new Welsh
university college. Three towns were singled out as possible
venues, the ports of Cardiff and Swansea, and the industrial
community of Merthyr Tydfil. The ensuing debate constitutes
an interesting expression of late nineteenth-century civic pride,
as well as illuminating the competitive edge which characterized the relationship between the three towns. It also hints at
the dynamic and shifting nature of that relationship.

The first town to have its case considered was Merthyr Tydfil.
Its advocate was Nestor R. Williams, a Unitarian minister
who had been a resident of the town for over twenty-one years.[2]
The contrast between his argument and that put forward by
his two opponents on behalf of Swansea and Cardiff is instructive. Whereas the latter concerned themselves with detailed

---

[1] *Merthyr Express (ME)*, 23 November 1901.
[2] *Kelly's Directory of Monmouthshire and the Principal Towns and Places in South Wales*
(London, 1884), p. 394.

explanations of the importance of their respective towns, drawing upon such statistics as population figures, growth rates, the
number of new houses built, trading figures and even the number of letters delivered weekly by carriers, Williams was hard
pressed to construct anything but the most general of pleas.
Merthyr was 'a cheap place to live in', had good rail links and,
somewhat improbably, was a town without 'many temptations
to dissipated habits'.[3] Moreover, he suggested that it would be
unjust if Merthyr were not granted the honour:

> It might be urged with considerable force that, as Merthyr is known far
> and near to be the *Metropolis* of Wales, it would be unfair to ignore the
> claims of a town for scholastic purposes which has so largely
> contributed, by its commercial industries, to make Wales famous
> among the civilized countries of the world.[4]

Williams's italicization of the term 'Metropolis' can be
interpreted as more than just an adherence to stylistic niceties,
for by 1882 the idea that Merthyr was the premier urban settlement of Wales was one that had to be forcefully emphasized
rather than simply assumed. Ten years later, it seems that few
Merthyrians would even attempt such an exercise. Take, for
example, the scenes that accompanied the opening ceremony
held in the old iron town to celebrate the long-awaited completion of the new Cantref reservoir in 1892. This was financed by
Cardiff Town Council during a period of high expenditure
on civic schemes and a number of notables from the port –
including the mayor and a cohort of the borough's aldermen –
arrived in Merthyr eager to mark the occasion.[5] During the
course of the celebrations, one of the Cardiffians – Alderman
Lewis – proposed a toast to Merthyr's high constable.

> [T]he humorous alderman referred to 'salubrious Merthyr'. The Car-
> diff people thereupon indulged in ironical laughter, and this was just
> one of those little sarcastic references that naturally made the gorge of
> the Merthyr men rise. The word was repeated again and again, and as
> often as it was repeated the Cardiff men laughed. Now this laughter

[3] For more on Merthyr's reputation as a centre of drunkenness, see ch. 3.
[4] Nestor R. Williams et al., 'Where ought the Welsh university to be located?', *The
Red Dragon*, 1 (February–July 1882), 186–90, 188.
[5] M. J. Daunton, *Coal Metropolis: Cardiff, 1870–1914* (Leicester, 1977), pp. 160–1.

threw doubt upon the salubrity of Merthyr, and one Merthyr man was so indignant at the affront that he was about to indulge in a flood of medical statistics showing the superiority of Merthyr over Cardiff.

Such behaviour did not go unnoticed by the reporter from the *Merthyr Express*. But despite his anger, the defence he offered was weakened somewhat by a grudging acknowledgement that all the sarcasm and ironical laughter did have some justification:

> Towns which have sprung up in a comparatively short space of time to important positions have a good many of the faults of the parvenu who has made his money quickly and likes to bounce about it, and Cardiff is not altogether free from those faults . . . [I]t was impossible to help detecting the patronising air in which the old metropolis of Wales was referred to; and while wincing under the treatment (as every patriotic Merthyrian ought), I could not help feeling that the patronage was not altogether undeserved.[6]

On one level, this incident simply reflected the feisty nature of the inter-town rivalries that were so characteristic not only of Victorian south Wales, but of a number of other regions in Britain during this period. Yet at the heart of the newspaper's attempt to deflect Alderman Lewis's criticism lay a recognition of the shift that had occurred in the urban hierarchy of south Wales. For the honour of Merthyr Tydfil was now being defended by deployment of that key descriptive phrase, 'the old metropolis of Wales'. It was the adjective and not the noun which signified to many observers the reality of Merthyr's late nineteenth-century position. While one Merthyrian might still have been tempted to maintain that his home town was superior to the sea-port in matters of public health, many more, the reporter included, were forced to admit that in all other respects Cardiff was indeed the region's premier urban centre.[7] Such a conclusion would have been unthinkable a mere thirty years earlier. Indeed, the rapidity of Merthyr's fall from grace was in some respects remarkable, especially given its

---

[6] *ME*, 17 September 1892.
[7] Martin Daunton remarks upon the confidence with which Cardiffians were describing their home town as the 'metropolis of Wales' at the turn of the century. See his 'Coal to capital: Cardiff since 1839', in Prys Morgan (ed.), *Glamorgan County History, Vol. VI: Glamorgan Society, 1780–1980* (Cardiff, 1988), p. 203.

breathtaking rise to a position of importance in the early years of the nineteenth century. As has been noted, rapid urban growth was the key theme of the history of early industrial Merthyr. At the start of the century the iron town stood out as the largest urban settlement in Wales. Four times bigger than Cardiff and six times the size of Newport, only the old borough of Swansea with its population of 6,100 posed any serious threat. By the early 1830s Merthyr's population had mushroomed to an impressive 22,000 as compared with the mere 6,200 living in Cardiff. Newport had yet to reach Merthyr's 1801 figure, whilst even Swansea with its 13,700 inhabitants had been left behind. And at the mid-point of the century the town's domination of the urban hierarchy of the region seemed unassailable. Its almost 46,400 inhabitants could look back over fifty years which had seen their town's population increase by a massive 38,700. Yet twenty years later the census returns revealed a dramatic turn-about in fortunes. Cardiff had usurped Merthyr's crown. At a little under 57,400, the port boasted some 5,000 more inhabitants than Merthyr, whose new position as Wales's second urban community was now threatened by a Swansea that was only two hundred inhabitants smaller.[8]

Cardiff's meteoric rise was based firmly upon its transformation into a coal-exporting port. The exploitation of the region's coal reserves that was proceeding apace in such valleys as the Cynon and especially the Rhondda, marked the second phase of Wales's industrial revolution. As the output of coal from south Wales increased from 4.5 million tons in 1840 to 8.5 million tons in 1854, rising again to just under 18 million tons by the end of the 1870s, so Cardiff reaped the benefits.[9] In the first half of the century, any growth it had experienced stemmed largely from the enterprise and industry of the iron-producing Merthyrians. It was perfectly placed to act as an outlet for the ironmasters' products, and by 1767 a road had been constructed along the floor of the Taff Valley enabling small quantities of iron to reach Cardiff.[10] With the opening of the Glamorganshire Canal in 1798, the relationship between Merthyr and the

[8] John Williams, *Digest of Welsh Historical Statistics*, 2 vols. (London, 1985), Vol. 1, pp. 63–4.

[9] See Daunton, *Coal Metropolis*, p. 4; Williams, *Digest*, Vol. 1, p. 300.

[10] Dennis Morgan, *The Cardiff Story* (Cowbridge, 1991), p. 123.

port was firmly established, and by the late 1830s some 130,000 tons of iron were being transported south along the canal. In 1841 a rail link was opened, further strengthening the ties between the two settlements.[11] Nevertheless, as a satellite of Merthyr, Cardiff's expansion was limited. In the first four decades of the nineteenth century the population of the port increased from 1,870 to 10,077, significant enough perhaps, but a pale reflection of what was to occur in the later years of the century. For as the coal industry developed, so Cardiff broke out of Merthyr's orbit in spectacular fashion. The 1840s and 1850s witnessed population growth rates in Cardiff of 82.1 per cent and 79.6 per cent respectively, and whilst such figures were never to be reached again, the late Victorian period was still one of impressive urban growth.[12] The decade between 1881 and 1891 saw Cardiff's population lurch from 82,761 to 128,915, and by 1911 there were 182,000 inhabitants living in a city known variously as the 'Queen of the South' and the Chicago of 'American Wales'.[13]

Just as Cardiffians were busy turning their town into a major world port, their counterparts in Merthyr were undergoing a particularly dislocating and worrying time. The iron industry that had breathed life into the settlement was entering a period of prolonged, and ultimately terminal, decline. Perennial concerns about the state of the international market for iron were exacerbated by more local factors, most notably the unease regarding the fortunes of the ironworks that had made the upper Taff Valley their home. Periodically throughout the mid-Victorian years, the iron settlements in Merthyr were seized by paroxysms of fear as news broke that one ironmaster or another was experiencing difficulties in renewing the all-important leases that enabled them to continue operations. Notwithstanding the angst that such intelligence could produce, Merthyr's industrial demise was in fact a protracted affair. The works at Penydarren and Plymouth had both closed by the 1880s (Penydarren in 1859 and Plymouth in 1880), although those at Cyfarthfa and Dowlais were left to struggle on. Meanwhile,

[11] Daunton, *Coal Metropolis*, p. 2.
[12] Ibid., p. 10.
[13] See Williams, *Digest*, Vol. 1, p. 63; Neil Evans, 'The Welsh Victorian city: the middle class and civic and national consciousness in Cardiff, 1850–1914', *Welsh History Review*, 12, no. 3 (1985), 350–87, 367, 368.

Merthyr was not untouched by the forces that were so radically affecting the rest of south Wales, and the district enjoyed at least some of the fruits of the sale-coal trade in the latter years of the century. Yet many contemporaries found it difficult to place an optimistic gloss on the district's economic situation.[14] The dismantling of the iron trade was a profound blow to a town which had liked to think of itself as the 'metropolis of iron-masters'.[15] Moreover, the habit of prophesying Merthyr's doom was firmly ingrained, and proved difficult to break.

Inhabitants began worrying about the district's future almost from the moment that urban Merthyr had been created. In 1850 the *Cardiff and Merthyr Guardian* recalled the various events which had led 'prophecy mongers' to proclaim that the town had 'seen its best days'. The cutting of the Glamorgan-shire Canal, the opening of the railway, the expiry of the Dowlais lease, had all prompted the pessimists to forecast Merthyr's terminal decline.[16] In 1860, Charles Wilkins, local antiquarian and civic booster, wrote about the gloomy prospects for the iron industry and, by extension, his home town.[17] These concerns were amplified by the closing of the Penydarren Works the previous year. By 1870 no less a figure than William Menelaus, the general manager of the Dowlais Works, felt moved to speak publicly about the precarious nature of Merthyr's position.[18] At the quarterly meeting of the South Wales Institute of Engineers held in Merthyr, Menelaus responded to a toast to the 'Success of the Coal and Iron trade of this district'. He 'hoped the generous terms of the toast would be realised, for the iron trade of the district was in a desperate condition'.[19] Others were already thinking about the implications of this situation. In 1869 members of the Rate-payers' Protection Society pointed to the need for new industries to be attracted to the town. A Mr Rosser 'drew attention to the gradually lowering condition of the town of Merthyr. There was

[14] See, for example, the pessimistic editorial in the *Pontypridd Chronicle* (*PC*), 14 May 1881.

[15] B. H. Malkin, *The Scenery, Antiquities, and Biography of South Wales* (Wakefield, 1970 edn), p. 169.

[16] *Cardiff and Merthyr Guardian* (*CMG*), 27 July 1850.

[17] Charles Wilkins, *The History of the Iron, Steel, Tinplate and Other Trades of Wales* (Merthyr Tydfil, 1903), pp. 96–7.

[18] For more on Menelaus, see ibid., pp. 290–2.

[19] *Merthyr Star* (*MS*), 31 December 1870.

an increasing number of vacant houses, and every day in
consequence of the emigration going on was increasing that
number. What could be done to improve the place?' One of the
participants in the ensuing debate suggested the establishment
of a tin works and a screw and nail plant. The idea of sending
'two or three of the shrewdest practical men in this district' on a
fact-finding tour to Newcastle, Sheffield and Birmingham was
floated although seemingly not acted upon.[20]

The direct consequence of, first, the stagnation and, then, the
demise of the iron industry was that by the 1880s Merthyr
Tydfil could appear to be a town out of step with the rest of the
region. It was an iron town of the 'hills district' that had
suddenly awoken and found itself in a buoyant coalfield. Whilst
geographically it was in close proximity to Cardiff and the
Rhondda, economically – and in terms of civic accomplishment – it seemed light years behind them. This idea of backwardness was one that was commonly expressed during these
years. In April 1889 one vociferous supporter of all things
Merthyrian, the solicitor E. P. Biddle, remarked sadly that
'there could not be the slightest doubt that Merthyr was not
moving with the times'.[21] He returned to this notion some six
months later in a speech about the town in which he informed
his audience that 'he was sorry to say its present condition was
not up to the nineteenth-century mark'.[22] So pervasive was this
way of thinking about Merthyr by the late 1880s that in June
1889 a correspondent to the *Express* could refer to 'the oft-
repeated question "Why is Merthyr so lamentably behind the
times?"'[23] He decided that it was so 'oft-repeated' that there
was little point in asking it any more.

This was the context in which the debates concerning the
epithet 'the Metropolis of Wales' were played out. That by the
1890s Merthyrians were increasingly forced to argue for their
town's historical as opposed to contemporary importance is
worthy of note, as is the gloomy nature of many of their assessments of the town's position. Perhaps the fact that Cardiff's
population on Census Day 1891 was 128,915 as compared with
Merthyr's 58,080 hardly allowed any other.

[20] Ibid., 12 April 1869.
[21] *ME*, 6 April 1889.
[22] Ibid., 26 October 1889.
[23] Ibid., 29 June 1889.

II. A 'VILE AND WRETCHED PLACE': REPRESENTING MERTHYR'S BUILT ENVIRONMENT

Merthyrians' concerns regarding the town's diminished position in the urban hierarchy of Wales were worsened by the condition of the built environment. The 'salubrity' of Merthyr – or, more correctly, the lack of it – which had provided the visiting notables from Cardiff with a convenient hook upon which to hang their amusing observations in 1892, had in fact for long been remarked upon by both inhabitants and non-inhabitants alike. Travel books, public health reports and newspaper articles were media through which certain representations of the town were constructed. And, as befitted Merthyr's status as a frontier town, perhaps it should not surprise that the settlement evoked some particularly strong images.[24] The fashion in which the unattractive quality of the town itself was frequently singled out by commentators is a particularly striking feature of these literary evocations of 'Merthyr Tydfil'.

As early as 1813 readers of the *Cambrian Traveller's Guide* were informed of Merthyr's grim appearance. Comparing Swansea with the iron town, the *Guide* noted that 'the external appearance of the former is far superior. The splendours of this town [i.e. Merthyr] begin and end with the house of mr.[*sic*] Humphrey, at Penydarren, which is large and elegant, with fine gardens, green-houses, hot-houses, &c.' As for the rest of the built form, 'Merthyr Tydfil is composed chiefly of irregular streets and small buildings'.[25] Such was the appalling condition of the environment that fifteen years later one scribe likened Merthyr to Hades itself (and not for the last time) via the medium of verse:

> O Merthyr, thou the vile, the wretched place,
> Peopled by the scum of the human race:
> Thy air is tainted with the breath of hell,
> And in thee none but rogues and rascals dwell.[26]

[24] Gerald D. Suttles has argued that American shock cities generated the most powerful images because they challenged the moral, political and social orders. Industrial Merthyr fits this model on all three counts. See his 'The cumulative texture of local urban culture', *American Journal of Sociology*, 90, no. 2 (1984), 283–304, 285.

[25] George Nicholson, *The Cambrian Traveller's Guide* (2nd edn, London, 1813), p. 893.

[26] *Greal y Bedyddwyr*, June 1828. Cited in the *Western Mail* (*WM*), 29 June 1907.

By the mid-nineteenth century there was evidence that the urban landscape was somewhat more varied in its appearance. In 1850, the *Cardiff and Merthyr Guardian* congratulated High Street tradesmen on the improvements they had made to their shop fronts; they marked 'a progress in civilization'.[27] Likewise, in 1868, *Black's Picturesque Guide Through Wales* could note that in recent years the town's built form had 'undergone much improvement'.[28] Yet, despite this upbeat assessment, older ways of describing the urban landscape persisted well into the late nineteenth and early twentieth centuries. Most damning of all the works produced during these years were those penned by that highly specialized band of authorial figures, the 'social explorers'.[29] Drawing upon the long-established conventions of their genre, a number of these observers descended upon the locality from the 1890s, all intent upon laying bare the social inequalities that still plagued the 'Samaria of Wales'. Before they could begin to describe the inhabitants of the district, such writers felt obliged to introduce their readers to the full horrors of the built environment. In 1898, for example, readers of the *Western Mail* were treated to a journey through the slums of 'Dismal Dowlais – A Dilapidated Town'. A few key trigger-words punctuate the writing. Dowlaisians were daily confronted with 'the squalid surroundings' in which they lived 'a dull, cheerless life'. Meanwhile, 'the houses occupied by the better class artisans are ugly, mean, squalid, in narrow streets, cheek by jowl with here a "disused slaughter-house", there a pigsty'. For those who belonged to the lower classes of workmen their lot was even worse. 'They work hard day after day for a crust of bread and fester and die in fetid sties, huddled in horrid slums, in vile, unhealthy streets, where decency is well-nigh impossible.'[30] This was hardly an environment in which one was likely to live the good civic life.

[27] *CMG*, 23 March 1850.
[28] Adam Black and Charles Black, *Black's Picturesque Guide Through Wales* (Chester, 1868), p. 328.
[29] There is a growing literature on the work of the nineteenth-century social explorers. See, for example, Peter Keating, 'Fact and fiction in the East End', in H. J. Dyos and M. Wolff (eds), *The Victorian City*, 2 vols. (London, 1973), Vol. 2.; Peter Keating, *Into Darkest England, 1866–1913: Selections from the Social Explorers* (Glasgow, 1976); Alan Mayne, 'Representing the slum', *Urban History Yearbook*, 17 (1990), 66–84, and his *The Imagined Slum* (Leicester, 1993).
[30] *WM*, 8 December 1898.

In 1907 the *Mail* published the observations of no less a figure than George R. Sims, a journalist who had sparked a renewed interest in the social problems of the East End of London in the early 1880s.[31] His visit to Merthyr and Dowlais resulted in a series of articles which took as their focus one particular aspect of the all-too-blighted landscape, the slums. His descriptions of the lower class of the residential areas were bleak indeed. Merthyr was a settlement comprised of 'hovels' which were 'dirty, dilapidated and evil-smelling'. The inhabitants of this wretched place were characterized as poor imitations of human beings. The women were 'pale, emaciated and spiritless', the children 'ill-clad and dirty', and the populace as a whole 'as desolate, as colourless and as gloomy as the towering grassless summits of the coal tips that look down upon them night and day'. Sims went on to remark:

> hundreds of human lives are being sacrificed year after year in Dowlais and the other bad districts by the failure of the capitalists employing labour to rescue that labour from the foul and filthy dwellings which are death traps and murder holes.
> ... Merthyr does not destroy its refuse, but it destroys its children.[32]

In order to press the message home, the following edition of the newspaper included a graphic cartoon, drawn by J. M. Staniforth, featuring a grieving young woman – who symbolized Merthyr – weeping in a graveyard full of her departed offspring.[33]

In forging the link between Merthyr and 'Death', Sims pre-empted the author of a series of articles published in the medical journal *The Lancet* in 1911. A 'Special Sanitary Commissioner' was appointed by the editors to visit urban south Wales and report back his findings. The world that he described to his well-to-do readers was as strange and terrifying

---

[31] George R. Sims (1847–1922) was most famous for his work, *How the Poor Live*. See Peter Keating, *Into Darkest England*, p. 65.

[32] *WM*, 28 June 1907.

[33] Ibid., 29 June 1907. Merthyr and other settlements in the coalfield were invariably represented in such cartoons as virtuous females, notwithstanding the masculine associations with iron- and steel-making and coal-mining which also featured in the town image of Merthyr; the town was something to be cherished and protected by the public men of the day. For more on Staniforth, see Peter Lord, *The Visual Culture of Wales: Industrial Society* (Cardiff, 1998), pp. 164–7.

as any imaginable.[34] This was a region in which it was implied
that the Devil himself held court and where Death was the
leitmotif that ran throughout the town's history. The naming of
the settlement after the Christian princess, Tydfil, who was
martyred in the sixth century, provided the commissioner with
the perfect opportunity to establish his sombre theme early on,
and the journey from the Dark Ages to the twentieth century
was one that was made effortlessly:

> The church subsequently raised to commemorate this martyrdom has
> become the centre of a great manufacturing district where many
> thousands have been brought prematurely to the grave – martyrs to the
> Moloch of modern industrialism. Indeed, the Merthyr Valley, or the
> Valley of Martyrdom, is no misnomer, and its sinister appearance does
> not belie its reputation.[35]

This 'sinister appearance' could only be conveyed to his readers
through the deployment of the most diabolical imagery:

> It is black, its people are dirty, many have but miserable rags to wear,
> there is smoke and coal-dust and soot suspended as a pall over the whole
> scene, while from the centre terrible volcanic eruptions constantly occur
> that suggest an invasion from the lower regions.
>   . . . It is no unusual thing for a person to say he has come from hell
> when he has been to Dowlais. The ironworks for which Dowlais is
> renowned are situated in a valley, and the hill overlooking them is
> covered by some of the worst slum dwellings. It was while visiting after
> dark these hovels where the wealth producers of Dowlais dwell that I
> was able to contemplate what has so often been compared with the
> infernal regions.[36]

This was a landscape dominated by the ironworks, increasingly
automated, and in which 'red-hot iron railway lines glide along
like great incandescent serpents'. After being shaped and cut,
'the fiery serpent makes a horrible hissing noise and squirts out
in all directions, as if it was its life blood, a shower of red-hot
iron drops'. Once again, where humans appear at all in this

---

[34] His observations were given an added *frisson* as a consequence of the Tonypandy
riots which had occurred only two months before the articles were published.
[35] Special Sanitary Commissioner, 'The housing problem in south Wales', *The
Lancet*, 21 January 1911, 193–4, 193.
[36] Ibid., p. 193.

nightmare-scape they are something rather less than human. There are the unemployed who 'clamour at the gates or shiver and starve in the hovels on the hill close by', and the blast furnace workers who 'grope about, stoop, lift and run like so many pigmies in the caves of Vulcan'.

The importance of this treatment of Merthyr in the newspapers, learned journals and the like was clear to contemporaries. As literary representations of the district, they had the power to fix meanings and add to an already negative image. Moreover, given their wide circulation – at least within south Wales – they could affect the perceptions of a large number. Even *The Lancet*'s potential in this respect was increased courtesy of the *Merthyr Express*'s decision to reprint it. The willingness of inhabitants of the district to rush to the defence of Merthyr is an indication of the seriousness with which these assaults upon the reputation of the 'old metropolis' were taken.[37] The slums of the district, so the counter-argument ran, were no longer representative of the whole, and attempts were made by local figures to redress the balance and offer descriptions of the built environment which stressed the positive.[38]

One such example was the survey produced by John G. E. Astle in 1897. A significant booster of the town's image, Astle was alive to the importance of the printed word in the battle to construct urban meaning, and he displayed this sensitivity by stepping out of the narrative of decline altogether. In his *The Progress of Merthyr* the plot structure was centred on the classic themes of the Enlightenment project – improvement, rationality and modernity.[39] In a section subtitled 'The Contrast 1848–1897', great emphasis was placed upon the improvement of the sanitary condition of the town. If still not perfect by any means, great leaps forward had been made in recent years which allowed Astle to invoke the notion of modernity in describing Merthyr. An ignoble past was something that was literally being destroyed as he wrote. Indeed, the traces of that past which yet remained on the urban landscape only served to make the contrast between 'the old state of affairs' – which

---

[37] See for instance a letter in the *WM*, 29 June 1907.
[38] For more on housing in the district, see Kate Sullivan, ' "The biggest room in Merthyr": working-class housing in Dowlais, 1850–1914', *Welsh History Review*, 17, no. 2 (1994), 155–85.
[39] John G. E. Astle, *The Progress of Merthyr* (Merthyr Tydfil, 1897).

'must have been horrible' – and the present all the clearer.[40] The notorious slum area of China 'is still visible . . . but it is a modified "China" which, it may devoutly be hoped, will go on improving'. Slums were 'doomed'.[41] '[M]odern colliery practices' were being introduced into the valley, as well as a 'modern system of water supply' which was playing 'an important part in the improvement' of the town. Merthyrians could congratulate themselves upon the development of 'an efficient network of educational establishments' whilst noting that progress was being made 'residentially' with the construction of attractive housing.[42]

Astle's attempt to provide an alternative reading of Merthyr's urban landscape is interesting because of its emphasis on progress. However, his effort also highlighted the need for yet more improvements; there were still features that by their absence were cause for complaint. For example, the dearth of public parks in the district was lamentable, as was the lack of a Free Library and a town hall. These omissions from the inventory of Merthyr's buildings and amenities were offset somewhat by the recent erection of the New Public Offices in the High Street, an event which was to be celebrated.[43] Astle was not alone in voicing his concern on such matters. On the contrary, there was a sizeable phalanx of observers who found the lack of public and other buildings disturbing. Their criticism was born out of a highly specific conception of what a late nineteenth-century town should look like, a conception framed in terms of the 'civic' that once again threw into sharp relief the backwardness of Merthyr.

III. 'A VILLAGE AS FAR AS PUBLIC INSTITUTIONS WENT': CONSTRUCTING A CIVIC MERTHYR

The main features of nineteenth-century civic consciousness are familiar enough and need only the briefest of introductions here. A strong attachment to one's home town or city, a commitment to effecting improvements at the local level and, as

40 Ibid., p. 22.
41 Ibid., pp. 30–1.
42 Ibid., p. 48.
43 Ibid.

already clear, a strong rivalry with neighbouring settlements were some of the general manifestations of this civic pride.[44] More specifically, the Victorian period saw 'the creation of the concept of the town as a discrete, self-aware integrated social and constitutional unity'.[45] By the later years of the century there was in place a highly developed idea of what an ideal town or city should look like, the sort of facilities that it should possess, and the kind of governmental and administrative structures that should oversee its affairs. Such a notion turned upon a particular conception of the social order, and has come to be equated by historians as being immanent in the developing culture of the British middle class. In this analysis, the urban was not simply a neutral site in which the bourgeoisie came to power. On the contrary, the 'town' was instrumental in facilitating such a process.[46] Thus, the struggle to obtain parks and free libraries, swimming baths and publicly owned brass bands can be viewed as part of the same impulse which led to efforts to obtain charters of incorporation and town halls. All had come to be markers of civic status and useful indicators of how urbane the urban had become. All could also be viewed as evidence of the level of activity of the local social élites and their ability to develop networks of influence.

Not surprisingly, the Merthyr Tydfil of the 1880s and 1890s fell short of the required criteria. It was not simply that the presence of slums, pollution and ugliness conspired to frustrate the hopes of the town's social élite. Even obviously civic communities such as Cardiff, Leeds and Manchester had their fair share of squalor and slum-scapes. Rather it was the absence of key features of the urban landscape and key institutions in the political and social spheres which called into question Merthyr's very status as a town.[47] This was a point which even Astle – in his enthusiastic attempts to weave Merthyr into the

---

[44] See, for example, Asa Briggs, *Victorian Cities* (Harmondsworth, 1990, paperback edn), ch. 4.

[45] R. J. Morris, 'The middle class and British towns and cities of the Industrial Revolution, 1780–1870', in D. Fraser and A. Sutcliffe (eds), The *Pursuit of Urban History* (London, 1983), p. 299.

[46] Mike Savage, 'Urban history and social class: two paradigms', *Urban History*, 20, pt. 1 (1993), 61–77.

[47] Christopher Hamlin, 'Muddling in Bumbledon'; Raymond K. J. Grant, 'Merthyr Tydfil in the mid-nineteenth century: the struggle for public health', *Welsh History Review*, 14, no. 4 (1989), 574–94.

narrative of 'Progress' and 'Improvement' – could not side-step. Not only was there no public park and no free library, but Merthyr had to endure the indignity of remaining a lowly urban district council as opposed to an elevated borough. As for these deficiencies, the best that he could do was to note rather wistfully that they ' "must come" we are told "some day" '.[48] Others shared his concern. In a speech delivered to the Hearts of Oak Society in 1891, the prominent local figure, Colonel D. Rees Lewis, touched upon the nub of the problem as he saw it.[49]

> In speaking of the town he was prompted to ask, Is there a town? Has there ever been a town? Will there ever be a town? He regretted to have to acknowledge that Merthyr was nothing more than a village as far as public institutions went, and it had lost thousands of pounds owing to the fact that it was a village. If there had been any public spirit in the inhabitants twenty years ago the aspect of that village would be vastly different, and they would not be so far behind in the race with Cardiff and Swansea (loud applause).[50]

W. L. Daniel echoed these sentiments in 1903 when he argued that 'I ... feel that Merthyr ... deserves to be incorporated, and not regarded to the end of time as an overgrown village'.[51]

The distress of Merthyrians interested in such matters was compounded by the way in which the town fared badly when compared with neighbouring settlements. It could be accepted perhaps that Cardiff, by virtue of size alone, would be well equipped with public buildings, parks and the like. However, the manner in which smaller towns, considered to be less significant presences in the social, economic and political life of the region than Merthyr, still managed to outdo the 'old metropolis' in civic matters rankled greatly. Aberdare was a case in

[48] Astle, *Progress of Merthyr*, p. 48.
[49] Lewis was a lawyer by training who returned to Merthyr and carved out a successful career in the Volunteers. See Charles Wilkins, *The History of Merthyr* (2nd edn, Merthyr, 1908), p. 494.
[50] *ME*, 31 January 1891.
[51] John G. E. Astle, *Illustrated Report of the Merthyr Tydfil Incorporation Inquiries, 1897 and 1903* (Merthyr, 1903), p. 177. W. L. Daniel – a resident of Merthyr for over forty years – had held positions on the Local Board of Guardians, was chairman of the School Board, official Receiver in Bankruptcy, and chairman of the South Wales and Monmouthshire Joint Truant School Committee. He was Merthyr's high constable in 1896 and also president of the Chamber of Trade. The idea that Merthyr was little more than a village was one that enjoyed much currency. See, for example, the editorial in the *Merthyr Telegraph* (*MTl*), 4 July 1873.

point. As a centre of population, it can scarcely be said to have challenged the old iron town.[52] Yet, notwithstanding the settlement's diminutive stature, when it came to the built environment Aberdare towered over its older, larger neighbour. Known variously as 'Athen Cymru' (or 'The Athens of Wales'), the 'Queen of the Hills' and 'Sweet Berdâr',[53] the town had won for itself a reputation as something of a flourishing cultural centre. Martin Barclay, commenting upon this image of the town, has drawn attention to the divergence between the extravagance of the claims and the meagreness of the reality. 'What is surprising, given the nature of the reforms [achieved by the 1870s] and the crabbing opposition to "unnecessary expenditure", is the strength of the "Queen of the Hills" legend.'[54] But if legends grow in stature simply through the retelling, then the part played by Merthyrians in the construction of this particular urban myth should not be underestimated.

That Aberdare was apparently so far ahead of Merthyr in civic matters was a constant source of complaint. That it was possible in the mid-1880s to read almanacs which narrated the *history* of Aberdare town hall grated with townsfolk on the other side of the mountain, as did the announcement that a Free Library was to be built in Athen Cymru.[55] However, it was Aberdare's seeming surfeit of public parks which invited the most unfavourable and frequent comparisons with the 'old metropolis of Wales'. When, in 1881, the Merthyr Chamber of Trade declared that it was to embark upon an – ultimately unsuccessful – attempt to secure for the town its first recreation ground, Harry Southey, the editor of the *Merthyr Express*, congratulated them, pointing out that whilst inhabitants had access to 'delightful sylvan scenes ... there is nothing akin to the great boon which our Aberdare friends possess in their public park'.[56] The park to which the paper referred was a 49-acre piece of common land at Trecynon which had been secured for

[52] The 1871 population figure of 36,112 actually dropped by over 2,000 by 1881, only to climb back to some 38,400 ten years later. Yet it was still almost 20,000 short of Merthyr's population.
[53] Martin Barclay, 'Aberdare, 1880–1914: class and community', MA thesis, University of Wales (Cardiff), 1985, p. 6.
[54] Ibid., p. 15.
[55] Anon., *Aberdare: A Descriptive and Historical Sketch* (Aberdare, 1885), reprinted in Cynon Valley History Society, *Old Aberdare*, Vol. 1 (Newport, 1976), p. 59.
[56] *ME*, 18 June 1881.

the public during the late 1850s. The local authority spent
approximately £10,000 on draining, clearing and laying-out, a
sum that was paid for by the levying of a penny rate over a
period of thirty years so that by the 1890s it had become a truly
'free' park.[57] With its two ornamental lakes and accommoda-
tion 'for cricket, football and tennis playing', it was a perfect
manifestation of civic consciousness.[58]

Some fifteen years later, in August 1896, Councillor David
Davies drew the attention of his colleagues to the lack of
suitable open spaces in the 'old metropolis'. In so doing he was
able to deploy an all-too-familiar rhetoric. 'The more he saw of
other towns, and the way they looked after the wants of the
people, the more he was able to see that Merthyr was a long
way behind the spirit of the age', and he urged the council to
take seriously 'the urgent necessity of having open spaces' in the
town.[59] That Aberdare was one of the 'other towns' Davies had
in mind is highly likely. Some five months later, it would have
been almost impossible for him not to think of Athen Cymru,
for by January 1897 Merthyrians were presented with the
rather unpalatable news that Aberdare was to be endowed with
a second park. Whilst offering its congratulations, Southey's
Express could not help simultaneously 'lament[ing] the ill-
fortune which denies a similar boon to Merthyr'.[60]

IV. 'PUBLIC SPIRIT', 'LEADING INHABITANTS' AND
THE CIVIC PROJECT

The absence of a town hall, a public park and all manner of
other civic ornaments in Merthyr during these years can
perhaps be explained most satisfactorily by considering the role
of the district's social élite. As already mentioned, historians
have been keen to identify the middle classes with the civic
gospel. One does not have to accept the crude notions of
'social control' put forward by some to acknowledge fully the
importance of their role in securing these symbols of civic

---

[57] Ibid., 16 January 1897.
[58] Anon., *Aberdare: A Descriptive and Historical Sketch*, p. 59. For a general discussion of
the development of parks, see Mark Girouard, *The English Town* (London, 1990),
pp. 270–8.
[59] *ME*, 8 August 1896.
[60] Ibid., 16 January 1897.

accomplishment for towns and cities up and down the country.[61] They had the financial and political resources to embark upon the often expensive civic schemes. It is thus significant that the latter decades of the nineteenth century witnessed both the development of a more settled bourgeois population and the establishment of a more effective system of local government in Merthyr.

It was always the case, of course, that Merthyr's middle classes were swamped in absolute terms by the labouring classes. Nevertheless, even as a frontier town it evidently had its attractions. Tradesmen of all descriptions were drawn to the district, although it appears that many were loath to put down roots. As one elderly townsman of the 1880s recalled of the booming days after the 'Riots' (that is, the 1830s and 1840s), many looked upon the settlement as a temporary resting place only. 'The shops were crowded with customers, and the shop-keepers strove hard to make *their pile* as rapidly as possible, with a view to leaving the town as soon as it was made – as most of them did – Merthyr not being then a choice abiding place.'[62] However, by the time that such an observation was being made, it was the contrast with the present that was most striking. By the 1870s there were signs of an élite residential area developing in the town, focused primarily upon Thomas Street and Courtland Terrace, a clear indication of the presence of a more permanent middle class.[63] This social group was also beginning to organize itself. The existence in the 1860s and early 1870s of a Ratepayers' Protection Society open to any ratepayer 'interested in the local government of Merthyr Tydfil' is emblematic of a shift in perceptions. By 1878 the commercial population of the town was settled enough to form a Chamber of Trade with the primary object of 'safeguarding the interests of commerce'.[64] That the Chamber's second avowed aim was that 'of suggesting *local* reforms' is indicative of

[61] See Barclay, 'Aberdare, 1880–1914', for an analysis which holds that civic pride was essentially part of the class struggle in Aberdare.
[62] J.H., 'Reminiscences of Merthyr Tydvil', *The Red Dragon*, 2 (August–December 1882), 337.
[63] Of the 141 private addresses recorded in Charles Wilkins's trade directory of 1873, one-third were in these two streets. Cited in Harold Carter and Sandra Wheatley, *Merthyr Tydfil in 1851: A Study of the Spatial Structure of a Welsh Industrial Town* (Cardiff, 1982), p. 34.
[64] Wilkins, *History of Merthyr*, p. 533.

the way in which the commercial sector increasingly identified
its interests with those of the town itself.[65] Dowlais tradesmen
had organized themselves along similar lines by the winter
of 1893–4.[66] And when one supporter of the incorporation
movement looked back from the vantage point of 1897 to the
last inquiry into the matter, he concluded that a primary reason
for failure in 1876 was the unsuitable 'character of the
population'. He went on to suggest that 'after the last twenty
years, he thought they were not likely to hear an argument of
that sort advanced at the present day'. After all, the rateable
value of the town was now above £220,000, a sure sign that the
'right sort' of people were living and working in the district.[67]

Although the number of tradesmen and professionals in
the town was relatively small during the late Victorian and
Edwardian years, this group occupied a powerful position in
local society. From the middle years of the century their
influence had grown at about the same rate as that of the
ironmasters had declined. The Second Reform Act of 1867 did
much to break the dominance of the latter in terms of parliamentary politics, as did the (long-overdue) development of
structures of local government in Merthyr.[68] The town's middle
classes were the direct beneficiaries of these changes, with the
result that they were well placed to introduce civic initiatives.
The property qualifications that had to be met before one could
stand in elections for town councils kept lower social groups
beyond the pale of local government until 1888 at the earliest.[69]
And, after that date, factors such as the time at which the
meetings were held, the difficulty in actually travelling to the
meetings, and the continued potency of the idea that a certain
type of individual was 'naturally' suited to positions of responsibility could all combine to maintain the older ways.

The bourgeoisie's political power was buttressed by its ability to influence other aspects of the public sphere. The local

[65] Ibid. (emphasis added).
[66] Ibid.
[67] Astle, *Illustrated Report*, p. 4.
[68] See Ieuan Gwynedd Jones, 'The Merthyr of Henry Richard', in Glanmor
Williams (ed.), *Merthyr Politics: The Making of a Working-Class Tradition* (Cardiff, 1966),
especially pp. 32–40.
[69] Pat Thane, 'Government and society in England and Wales, 1750–1914', in
F. M. L. Thompson (ed.), *The Cambridge Social History of Britain, 1750–1950*, 3 vols.
(Cambridge, 1990), Vol. 3, 'Social Agencies and Institutions', p. 45.

newspapers played a vital role in this. Both the *Merthyr Express* and the *Merthyr and Dowlais Times* carried detailed reports of the meetings of a whole host of bodies, including those of the town council, the Chamber of Trade and the Board of Guardians. As a consequence, the district's middle-class public men (much less the women) could set agendas and influence debates, including those centred on civic issues. The *Express*, with circulation figures of some 11,000 copies in the mid-1890s, was particularly important in this respect, courtesy of the fact that Harry Southey, the editor and proprietor, was one of the most enthusiastic of all the town's boosters.[70] A member of the Merthyr Chamber of Trade, a justice of the peace for the county of Hereford, and, by the late 1890s, an inhabitant of the town for over forty years, Southey was in many ways representative of the sort of figure who subscribed to the basic tenets of the civic gospel.[71] As someone who played an active part in the public life of the district, contributing to a number of worthy causes, his whole outlook was shaped by a commitment to the town. He adopted an aggressively pro-booster stance in his editorials and opened the correspondence columns to those wishing to join the debate. Through organs such as the *Express*, the main arguments in support of the civic project were regularly articulated during the late Victorian and Edwardian eras.[72]

The newspapers were also central in the construction and dissemination of one of the major concepts associated with the attempts to civilize Merthyr, namely the notion of 'public spirit'. The 'public-spirited' inhabitant stood at the heart of the whole venture, and featured prominently in many contemporary analyses of Merthyr's lack of civic progress. As far as many commentators were concerned it was the dearth of public spirit that acted as a brake on civic progress, rather than a straightforward lack of a middle class in the town. Colonel Lewis's contention that Merthyr remained a village as a consequence of

[70] The *Merthyr Express* started in 1864. Southey became manager in 1865 and proprietor in 1874. The paper's circulation spread to include large areas of the Aberdare Valley and Monmouthshire. See Wilkins, *History of Merthyr*, p. 449.

[71] Astle, *Illustrated Report*, p. 50.

[72] The *Merthyr and Dowlais Times* played a similar role. See, for example, the *Merthyr and Dowlais Times* (14 October 1892) for a report bemoaning the lack of civic feeling in Merthyr. For more on the editor of this Liberal paper, see David Pretty, 'John Owen Jones ('Ap Ffarmwr') and the labour movement in Merthyr Tydfil, 1894–96', *Morgannwg*, 38 (1994), 101–14.

its deficit of public spirit has already been noted.[73] In July 1887 a correspondent to the *Express* explicitly referred to the concept when discussing the differences that separated progressive Aberdare from slovenly Merthyr:

> Our Aberdare neighbours set us a good example in the matter of public spirit. In Merthyr it would be impossible to form a debating society or social institution which would last more than a few months. At Aberdare there are several well instituted clubs and debating societies, which continue to flourish with youthful vigour. Then they have a park which I am afraid Merthyrians will never be able to boast of. Their board meetings are held in a public building, and their overseers' offices are convenient ... Bravo Aberdare! There's nothing like public spirit and public enterprise.[74]

This was one of many observations made during the 1880s and 1890s about the death-wish that seemed to befall a number of movements of a public nature started in the town. Whether a Merthyr House of Commons, a debating society or a branch of the Young Men's Christian Association, such schemes were constantly in danger of collapsing due to the lack of right-minded supporters. Even initiatives by the local licensed victuallers – those masters of sociability – were threatened by the apathy which was taken to be endemic in Merthyr. The *Merthyr Express Almanack* commented upon the history of the Licensed Victuallers' Banquet which 'like all well-intentioned meetings promoted in the district, in time waned and died a natural death'.[75] This problem was picked up by C. A. Cripps, QC, MP, advocate for the promoters of the incorporation scheme during the inquiry held in the town in 1897. According to Cripps, Merthyr's past failings could be blamed upon the scarcity of public-spirited individuals. If the charter was granted it would have the effect of increasing such sentiments amongst the population. The reciprocal nature of the relationship between the formation of the social élite and the idea of the 'town' was thus emphasized.

> They knew it would be argued that there was not much difference between the powers of the present Urban District Council . . . and the

[73] See above, p. 38.
[74] *ME*, 28 July 1887.
[75] *Merthyr Express Almanack 1894*, p. 64.

powers of a municipal body. But if they took a wider view, it made all the difference. They would get the spirit of municipal life, which had always been found to lead to an important expansion of public life and the establishment of public institutions such as free libraries, parks; whereas in the case of the Urban District Council, where they had nominally the same power, they had not the same spirit (applause); and if he might take Merthyr Tydfil, it was a good illustration – they did not get the same public spirit shown in their institutions which it was necessary now-a-days to have, in order that the interests of a town should be enabled to attain their due expansion. It seemed incredible, but he was told that with all the wealth really made in the town of Merthyr Tydfil, there was not a single institution which had been given to the town as a public gift. Of course, people did not make gifts to an Urban District Council, but would do so to municipal societies (applause).[76]

In his analysis, 'public spirit' would be encouraged if one of the most important of civic institutions, a borough council, was established. Past inactivity on the part of the leading inhabitants of the district would be replaced by industrious altruism.

These assessments should not be taken as evidence that a lack of 'public spirit' had only recently been identified by Merthyrians as a cause of their undoing. On the contrary, the concept had been placed right at the top of the agenda by the proponents of civic improvement. Through various media the notion of the 'leading inhabitant' and the responsibilities that went with such a title were created, articulated and naturalized. The almanacs, with their endless lists of local 'notables', rein-forced the idea that holders of public office were literally noteworthy. Celebratory town guides like Astle's fulfilled a similar function. Trades directories also privileged such 'useful' information, while town histories (and here Charles Wilkins's mammoth work occupies pride of place) were peppered with the actions and thoughts of these individuals, while the lower orders were almost completely absent.[77] Taken as a whole they provided anyone intent upon entering the pantheon of local notables with a series of role models and a blueprint for success.

[76] Astle, *Illustrated Report*, p. 5. A similar argument was also put forward by the high constable, Cornelius Biddle, in 1903. See ibid., p. 154.

[77] Charles Wilkins, *The History of Merthyr Tydfil* (Merthyr Tydfil, 2 edns, 1868 and 1908). Patrick Joyce considers the importance of these town histories, almanacs and guides in his *Visions of the People: Industrial England and the Question of Class, 1848-1914* (Cambridge, 1991), pp. 180–1.

To be a worthy son or daughter of one's home town, one had to cultivate a public persona.[78] A brief case-study of Charles Herbert James is doubly instructive at this point. First, a consideration of his career throws light on the broad range of public commitments that such figures were expected to undertake courtesy of their social position. Secondly, the very fact that such activities were so widely reported in the local newspapers and elsewhere highlights the importance of such organs in the encouragement of popular expectations.

Born in Merthyr in June 1817 into a family of Unitarians, in the late 1830s Charles Herbert James left for London to study law. Upon qualifying, he returned to his home town and practised as a solicitor with his partner (and cousin) Frank James. Already financially secure, the young professional's personal wealth grew sizeably when he inherited mineral rights in the parish of Gelligaer and then went on to purchase others in both Glamorgan and Monmouthshire. Yet, notwithstanding his business and professional interests, James was also extremely active in the social and political life of the town. On his death in 1890 an obituary in the *Merthyr Express* traced his public career. The extent of his activity is impressive. He interested himself greatly in educational matters, supporting the Merthyr Library and occupying the position of president of the library committee for several years.[79] He offered £100 towards the building fund of a British school in the mid-1860s, was a keen advocate of the movement for public education following the Act of 1870, and became one of the first members of the School Board. He went on to secure the post of chairman of the General Purposes Committee. He subscribed to the University Colleges of Aberystwyth and Cardiff, was chairman of the local Science and Art Committee, and taught in the Unitarian Sunday school as well as delivering numerous lectures to various bodies. Despite these already significant outside interests, the author of his obituary noted that James's retirement from the legal business in 1876 meant that he was 'now at liberty to devote himself to public life'. This he did by becoming a justice of the peace for the

---

[78] For a stimulating discussion of the changing relationship between the private and the public during the eighteenth and nineteenth centuries, see Richard Sennett, *The Fall of Public Man* (London, 1993, paperback edn).

[79] This was not a Free Library. It was founded in 1846 'by a few thoughtful men of the town' (Wilkins, *History of Merthyr*, pp. 404–5).

county of Glamorgan and by securing for himself one of Merthyr's two parliamentary seats. He held the position of member of Parliament until 1888 when he was forced to stand down due to ill health.[80]

As represented in his obituary, James appears to have been the embodiment of the notion of the 'public man'. Moreover, there can be little doubt that he was conscious of the social role that he was playing, as evidenced by a remark he made at the start of a lecture delivered to the Merthyr Temperance Society in March 1850. After expressing his sympathy with the tee-totallers' cause, he explained why he had agreed to talk to them. 'Conscience, duty – that still small voice within, which is as audible to the listening soul as the thunder-peal – tell me to help you with any petty offering I can make; and you have it.'[81] Although remarkable in terms of his ultimate achievement of being returned to Westminster, in many ways he was simply one amongst a sizeable number of Merthyrians who heard similar 'thunder-peals'. Members of his own family were moved by the same impulses. His nephew, Charles Henry James, an engineer, was appointed to the Merthyr Police Court in 1893 as a justice of the peace. He also sat on the Merthyr School Board for three years.[82] Likewise, Frank Treharne James, son of Charles Herbert James's cousin and business partner Frank, was of the same stamp as his illustrious relative.[83] During the late 1890s he was clerk to the Penderyn School Board, the Gelligaer School Board and the Gelligaer Rural District Council. Moreover, like his father before him, he was clerk to the Merthyr Board of Guardians.[84] He was a member of the Vaynor and Penderyn Rural District Council, treasurer of the Merthyr Chamber of Trade, and became a vice-president of the Merthyr General Hospital as well as occupying a position on the hospital's executive board. The hospital, with its 'Ladies' Committee', also provided his wife with an opportunity to contribute to the life of the community. In addition to his already heavy workload, F. T. James was a captain in the Merthyr detachment of the Volunteers. However, it was in the field of local government

---

[80] *ME*, 11 October 1890.
[81] C. H. James, *Lectures* (Merthyr Tydfil, 1892), p. 21.
[82] Astle, *Progress of Merthyr*, p. 53.
[83] Wilkins, *History of Merthyr*, pp. 451–2.
[84] Ibid., p. 452.

that his career as a public man reached its zenith. In 1896 he was elected to the office of high constable of Caerphilly Higher, a position to which he was returned in 1897.[85] A devoted supporter of incorporation, he became mayor of Merthyr in 1907.[86]

The literary construction of the 'public man' was neatly illustrated in Charles Herbert James's own obituary. It both detailed his various interests and explained his motivations for such heavy commitments. 'He recognized his duty as a man and a citizen in a populous community.'[87] Thus, whilst highly commendable, James's almost pathological desire to get himself elected onto public bodies and his fervent interest in securing his home town's social advancement was not presented as being an extraordinary phenomenon requiring further analysis. On the contrary, it was his ordinariness that was emphasized. This was the sort of life that all (male) members of the town's élite should live if only they 'recognized' their duty.[88]

If the idea of the 'public man' could be used to praise individuals such as James, it could also be mobilized to discipline those who had failed to live up to expectations. In the case of E. P. Martin – James's son-in-law, and manager of the Dowlais Iron and Steel Works from 1882[89] – this discipline was administered after his death in the form of an obituary published in the *Merthyr Express* in October 1910.

> It was always a matter of public regret that Mr. Martin did not, like his father George Martin, take a leading part in the public life of the community of Merthyr and Dowlais. He had his own reasons for keeping out of this sphere, and without doubt, cogent ones, too. Nevertheless, after the long experience of his predecessors at the head of the Dowlais Works, and their active participation in the local government of the town and district, it would have brought Mr. Martin much nearer to

[85] Astle, *Progress of Merthyr*, p. 54.
[86] For F. T. James's obituary, see *ME*, 21 February 1942. I am grateful to Angela Gaffney for this reference.
[87] Ibid., 11 October 1890.
[88] The local papers are scattered with such obituaries. See, for example, the editorial which appeared in the *Merthyr Times* (8 August 1873) detailing the career of Evan Williams: a teacher at Tydfil School, an active member of the Liberal Party, secretary of Merthyr Nonconformist Association, member of the Merthyr School Board, a deacon and secretary of the Market Square Congregational Church. '[H]is manhood-life, brief as it was, afforded an example of industry, devotion to duty, and conscientiousness which will not be lost upon society . . . The late Mr. Williams was in many respects a public man.'
[89] *ME*, 11 October 1890.

the hearts of the people if he could have seen his way to have shared the
duties of public administration and entered more into the Social Life of
the Community.[90]

While too late for Martin, the obituary served as a warning to
any readers who had themselves shied away from the public life.
The 'long experience' of Martin's predecessors at Dowlais,
mentioned in the obituary, is a reminder that the public men
and women were never drawn solely from the ranks of the
commercial and professional bourgeoisie. On the contrary, as a
category of social analysis, the 'public citizen' was elastic
enough to include the great landowners and industrialists of the
district. Dowlaisians were well aware of this fact. For notwithstanding the appalling conditions endured by many of those
employed in the Dowlais works during the reign of ironmaster
Sir John Josiah Guest and his wife, Lady Charlotte, the couple
had at least attempted to demonstrate a concern for the inhabitants of the town.[91] John Guest supported all manner of educational, recreational and religious causes in Dowlais. As Charles
Wilkins noted, 'Sir John was unremitting in good works' and 'in
every movement that had for its object the welfare of the district
he took a lively interest'. 'Uninterruptedly the kingdom of
Dowlais prospered under the judicious rule of Sir John.'[92] Lady
Charlotte was similarly remembered. On her death in January 1895 obituary writers concentrated on her willingness to
concern herself with the lot of the common people. The *Cardiff
Times* made a point of proclaiming her beneficence towards the
community in which she lived, reminding readers that 'Lady
Charlotte evinced great interest in the improvement of the
social condition of the workmen and their families connected
with the Dowlais Works'. Only then did it proceed to proclaim
her status as a 'literary genius'.[93] Meanwhile, in an editorial,

[90] Ibid., 1 October 1910.
[91] Revel Guest and Angela V. John, *Lady Charlotte: A Biography of the Nineteenth
Century* (London, 1989), pp. 71–3. For differing assessments of industrial paternalism,
see Patrick Joyce, *Work, Society and Politics: The Culture of the Factory in Later Victorian
England* (London, 1980), p. 154; David Roberts, *Paternalism in Early Victorian England*
(London, 1979), pp. 180–1; Geoffrey Finlayson, *Citizen, State, and Social Welfare in
Britain, 1830–1990* (Oxford, 1994), pp. 56-8.
[92] Wilkins, *History of Iron*, pp. 108–9, 111.
[93] *Cardiff Times*, 19 January 1895. Her reputation as a cultured individual was well
founded; she produced a translation of the *Mabinogion* (published 1838–49).

the *Western Mail* noted the warm relationship that had existed
between Charlotte and the nation. 'Ever since she made Dowlais her home Welshmen of all classes have taken an interest
in Lady Charlotte, and, though she had for some years dis-
appeared on the horizon, many a kind inquiry about her lady-
ship's health and welfare came from Wales, where her decease
is now sincerely mourned.'[94]

Subsequent events were to make the death of Charlotte Guest
appear all the more lamentable given the failure of her son, Sir
Ifor Bertie Guest (later Lord Wimborne), to live up to the ideal
of the benevolent public man. He was largely absent from
Dowlais, took little interest in either the social life of the town or
the welfare of those working in the ironworks that had provided
him with his wealth. Absence, in this case at least, did not make
Dowlaisian hearts grow fonder. The local newspaper, once
again, served as a forum in which Wimborne's numerous shortcomings were paraded before the reading public. If Dowlais,
and indeed the Merthyr district more generally, was to become
a civic settlement, Wimborne – and others like him – needed
to be constantly chivvied and cajoled into action.[95] All public
men, bourgeois and landowner alike, had their part to play in
effecting the necessary reforms. Thus, in 1897, 'Polonius' urged
that 'some of our rich landowners or works proprietors' should
act to mark the Queen's jubilee. He suggested the provision of a
public park. Similarly, in an understated although charged
observation, Sir W. T. Lewis remarked that 'he thought it was a
pity that Merthyr, considering the number of men who had
made fortunes there, had no park'.[96] Lewis was well qualified to
discourse upon the subject.[97] He was one of the 'great philan-
thropists' to whom one commentator referred when noting that

[94]   *WM*, 17 January 1895.
[95]   For more on Wimborne's chilly relationship with Dowlais, see Andrew J. Croll,
'Civilizing the urban: popular culture, public space and urban meaning, Merthyr
c. 1870–1914', Ph.D. thesis, University of Wales (Cardiff), 1997, pp. 72–5.
[96]   *ME*, 16 January 1897. 'Polonius' was the author of the weekly 'gossip' column in
the *Merthyr Express*. His columns appeared in the paper throughout the period under
investigation. The extent to which his views mirrored those of the editor, Harry
Southey, is noteworthy. However, Polonius's true identity remains a mystery: he could
have been another journalist, or, indeed, several other journalists.
[97]   W. T. Lewis was a coal magnate and leading figure in the South Wales and
Monmouthshire Coalowners' Association. He was knighted in 1885 and became Baron
Merthyr of Senghenydd in 1896 (*The Dictionary of Welsh Biography* (London, 1959),
p. 564).

'Merthyr has done better than Dowlais in the matter of friends'.[98] This was, of course, meant as a commentary upon the state of affairs in Dowlais; as we have seen, unfortunately for Merthyrians, 'better' was still barely adequate.

V.   UNITING 'A TORTUOUS CONCOURSE OF ATOMS'

In the light of the inactivity of such figures as Wimborne and E. P. Martin, it is perhaps surprising to note the success that attended the supporters of the civic project in the Merthyr district. The 1900s in particular witnessed great strides on a whole host of matters that had for so long appeared intractable. It seemed that public spirit had begun to work its magic with the result that by the first decade of the twentieth century Merthyr at last was beginning to approach the civic ideal.

A raft of public institutions and amenities made their long-awaited appearance in the district. After decades of discussion, frustration and inactivity, May 1896 saw the completion of a town hall.[99] In January 1897 there was the formal opening of the Merthyr County School, while in 1899 news broke that the Thomastown Tips were to be refashioned into a recreation ground. By 1902 the Park Recreation Ground was laid, with seats given 'by the townspeople and public bodies and companies', and a fountain provided by D. A. Thomas MP, all under the control of the Urban District Council. Three years later the amenities had been increased to include a drinking fountain. Even the district's canine population benefited from the explosion of public spirit with the inclusion of a 'necessary trough' to satisfy their needs.[100] In 1905 the district was finally awarded borough status, while three years later the distinction of County Borough was conferred upon Merthyr.[101] In the years after 1908 the public park became a favourite venue for the 'Cyfarthfa and Merthyr Municipal Band', itself a symbol of the burgeoning of civic sentiments.[102] In February 1899 another drawn-out battle

[98]   Merthyr Tydfil Public Library, Henry Allgood, Notes on Dowlais (1910).
[99]   See *ME*, 23 May 1896; *WM*, 22 May 1896. The frustration stretched back at least to the 1870s. See *MS*, 3 December 1870, 7 May 1870.
[100]   Wilkins, *History of Merthyr*, p. 570.
[101]   Margaret S. Taylor, *The County Borough of Merthyr Tydfil: Fifty Years a Borough, 1905–1955* (Merthyr Tydfil, 1955), pp. 12, 21.
[102]   For more on the municipal band, see below, ch. 4.

entered its last stages with the announcement that the District
Council had adopted the Free Libraries Act. The Public
Reading Room was opened in the Town Hall in 1900, one
of six that was eventually to be scattered throughout the district. The District Council was aided in its efforts by an initial
gift of £6,000 from the Scottish-born American steel magnate
and philanthropist Andrew Carnegie in 1902.[103] By September
of that year D. A. Thomas and County Alderman Thomas
Williams JP opened the Penydarren Reading Room, with
further branches established at Abercannaid, Troedyrhiw and
Merthyr Vale, all within the next six months.[104] Dowlais got its
own free library in 1907.[105]

Notwithstanding the fact that Merthyr's history appeared to
follow the trajectory of progress delineated by Astle in the late
1890s, it would be a mistake to assume that the movement
towards the civic was either inevitable or ever completely
accomplished. The very process of constructing an urban identity necessarily precluded such outcomes. 'Civic Merthyr' was a
town image that had constantly to be maintained and defended.
The arrival of the totems of a civilized town was a great step
forward, but the nature of urban meaning was (and is) such as
to deny closure. Competing understandings of Merthyr always
challenged the image projected by the civic boosters. As we shall
see in later chapters, the district's popular culture generated all
manner of alternative visions of the urban; public spaces could
be used in a variety of ways by urbanites, not all of them
respectable. However, for the moment it is important to note
another major threat to the concept of urbane, incorporated
Merthyr, namely the problem of the 'outlying districts'.[106]

As contemporaries were all too aware, there were a number
of powerful centrifugal forces at work in the Merthyr district,
forces that threatened to explode the idea of a 'Merthyr district' altogether. This concept was vital to the boosters, for one
of the strongest arguments that could be deployed in support of
the incorporation bid was that which referred to the sheer
size of Merthyr's population. Time and again, the injustice

[103]   *WM*, 11 July 1905; *ME*, 12 January 1907.
[104]   Astle, *Illustrated Report*, p. 123.
[105]   *ME*, 12 January 1907.
[106]   A point made by Ieuan Gwynedd Jones. See his 'Politics of Merthyr Tydfil', in
Stewart Williams (ed.), *Glamorgan Historian*, Vol. 10 (Barry, 1974), p. 50.

of a settlement of its magnitude suffering the indignity of not possessing a charter was cited as a compelling argument for action.[107] Such claims rested upon population figures for the whole of the upper Taff Valley rather than just the 'old village'. This strategy, whilst sensible enough, had the drawback of assuming something that in fact had to be argued. For so entrenched was the notion of 'the town' as a discrete social unit, with its own economic, political and social interests, that attempts to override this and create a district-wide conscious-ness were consistently opposed. Thus, Merthyr's civic identity contained within it elements that promoted instability. Put another way, the 'Other' – in the shape of a competing town identity, be it 'Dowlais', 'Merthyr Vale' or 'Treharris' – was ever present within the larger identity of 'Merthyr' itself.

A variety of individuals from these outlying settlements employed the very arguments that supporters of incorporation advanced. Take, for example, the testimony of Mr Balfour Browne QC who, when summing up the case for the opposition during the inquiry of 1897, highlighted the power of the idea of the town as a natural focus for interests. After arguing that 'public opinion' was decidedly against incorporation, Browne told the Commissioner that he thought it

> one of the most extraordinary propositions that this little community of Merthyr town should force those people [the inhabitants of Merthyr Vale] into extra expense, merely in order to give some honour to some professional men or shopkeepers. Honour can be bought too dear, and I think it would be bought too dearly by bringing this old district together for all time.[108]

He did not doubt that the inhabitants of Merthyr town were decidedly in favour of the scheme. However, it was wrong to force the outlying settlements down the same road. In part, the venture was flawed because of the inequalities that would result:

---

[107] See, for example, the observations of W. L. Daniel, who argued: 'Merthyr is the most populous town in Wales without a Charter, and yet it has considerable public spirit, and has shown indomitable pluck in its repeated applications for a Charter, and it deserves to be placed in the same position as other surrounding towns by being Incorporated' (Astle, *Illustrated Report*, pp. 177–8).

[108] Ibid., p. 97.

> Where we find all the people could profit by the institutions of the place,
> they are one. Where on the other hand, we find a group of people
> separated by nine, ten, or eleven miles ... who could not profit by baths
> and wash-houses, this hall, and so on, they are not one, there is no
> community of interest, and we shall be doing the worst thing in legis-
> lation if we allow people here to take large sums of money from people
> at a distance for the benefit of people here.[109]

This idea of there existing no 'community of interest' in the
Merthyr district was one that enjoyed much currency amongst
the opponents of incorporation.[110] As Browne himself contended, 'You have not one town; you have half a dozen towns.
You have not one body of people, but a tortuous concourse of
atoms, Merthyr Vale, Treharris, Dowlais, Merthyr, Cyfarthfa,
Plymouth, Troedyrhiw.'[111] He suggested that these atoms were
separated by 'almost impenetrable' physical barriers such as
hills and bleak pasture lands.[112] But far more significant were
the imagined boundaries that divided a district of a mere ten-
and-a-half miles in length. Merthyr Vale and Treharris,
according to a number of witnesses, were far removed from
Merthyr and Dowlais. Treharris, in the words of H. E. Gray,
had 'nothing' in common with Merthyr; moreover, it had its
own mining population, its own commercial population, its
own public hall and library and possessed 'fairly good shops'.[113]
Undoubtedly Gray's opposition to incorporation sprang largely
from his position as mining engineer and manager of the
Nixon's Navigation Colliery, a company that stood to pay
higher rates if the district was turned into a municipality. Yet
the significant point is the extent to which he, and others,
appealed to the notion of their own town's interests over those
of a district that could appear to outsiders as a homogeneous
area apparently united by common economic interests, occupa-
tions and social lives. That some seriously suggested otherwise
may appear disingenuous. Nevertheless, the frequency with
which this card was played is suggestive of its potency, a potency

---

[109] Ibid., p. 98.
[110] For another example, see the testimony of R. H. Rhys (ibid., pp. 57–8).
[111] Ibid., p. 98.
[112] These boundaries were breached to some extent by the railway links. By 1901
Merthyrians enjoyed all the benefits of an electric tramway (*ME*, 6 April 1901).
[113] Astle, *Illustrated Report*, p. 65.

which allowed some witnesses to make outlandish claims. At the 1897 hearing one witness declared that some 5,000 inhabitants of Treharris had never even seen the town of Merthyr.[114]

If attempts to incorporate Merthyr could provoke unpleasant outbursts, the same was true of other civic initiatives. As Charles Herbert James once remarked, the 'disconnected nature of the parish' militated against any projects in which ratepayers were asked to contribute and yet, potentially, gain very little in return. Take, for example, the struggle to obtain a free library for Merthyr. Widely accepted as a public 'good', the library movement attracted many supporters during the barren years of the 1880s and 1890s. As a correspondent to the *Merthyr Express* put it in October 1890,

> I am of the opinion that it reflects discredit on our leading men that we have not had a Free Library these years. A parish like Merthyr Tydfil, where such trade and commerce have been carried on, and where all the thousands of poor working toilers have been living and dying in the last 50 or 60 years, why, it is a disgrace to our so-called civilization.[115]

Nevertheless, although all good citizens doubtless agreed with these observations, this did not prevent a feisty local patriotism from surfacing. One library scheme had already come to grief as a result of opposition from Dowlais in 1887. Consequently, during the resurrection of the plan, advocates were careful to acknowledge the feelings of Dowlaisians. When the Merthyr Chamber of Trade approached their colleagues in Dowlais, they were pointedly informed that 'there would be no objection offered on the part of Dowlais people, provided that Dowlais had the proper share of the advantages'.[116] Yet this was the nub of the issue, for many inhabitants of Merthyr town were loath to accept a plan that involved building a number of small branches as opposed to one large central library. The benefits in terms of civilization and urbanity may have been unaffected by such a scheme but civic reputation was severely diminished. This position was articulated by David Evans, a member of the Chamber of Trade. He informed his fellow

---

[114] Taylor, *County Borough of Merthyr Tydfil*, p. 13.
[115] *ME*, 18 October 1890.
[116] Ibid., 12 February 1887.

tradesmen that he 'should like to see an institution equal to those of the more important towns in England'. Obviously aware of the library's potential as a civic status symbol, he played on the established rivalry with the new metropolis of Wales in order to make his point. Here was an opportunity for them to equal the efforts of their counterparts in the port:

> Cardiff, notwithstanding the extent to which it was expanding, and had expanded, had a large library in the centre of the surrounding districts. To subdivide the district would considerably lessen its importance, and they should endeavour to educate the people up to this point. Small reading-rooms in by-places would be unworthy of the parish; and if they were going to consider the exigencies of Dowlais, the exigencies of Troedyrhiw and Merthyr Vale, that would be the result.[117]

Rather than see such a proposal passed, he would vote against the whole scheme.

It was just this sort of unbending commitment to principle which was to hamper so many of the initiatives to improve Merthyr's built form. Boosters were relentless in their efforts to break through the impasse. Harry Southey pursued an aggressive pro-library editorial policy in the *Merthyr Express*. He included letters on the subject in the correspondence columns, faithfully reported the latest efforts of the Chamber of Trade, and carried extensive reviews of books such as Thomas Greenwood's *Free Public Libraries*. The paper's readership was assaulted with numerous arguments detailing why an institution of this sort would prove to be an unalloyed blessing. Meanwhile, disgruntled ratepayers were singled out for special treatment, their complaints addressed in a forthright manner.[118] If appeals to the public good were unsuccessful, Southey was quite prepared to appeal to baser instincts. A large extract of Greenwood's book was printed as a means of conjuring an image of Merthyr's future with a library. Not only would there be an increase in the rates of a mere one penny in the pound, a decrease in the number of youths loitering on the streets, and a facility of which 'all classes, rich and poor' could avail themselves, but tradesmen would actually find that their business would increase as

---

[117] Ibid., 12 February 1887.
[118] See, for example, ibid., 19 February 1887; 26 February 1887; 30 April 1887.

they could advertise their establishments in terms of being located at so many minutes' walk away from the library.[119]

Despite these valiant efforts, the barriers constructed out of a combination of local interests and financial considerations proved insurmountable (on this occasion at least). By July, the Merthyr Chamber of Trade had all but abandoned the scheme, deciding to postpone any further efforts until the autumn when public meetings could be arranged.[120] The venture sank without trace, marked only by a lone letter to the *Merthyr Express* from 'Progress' in December in which all the tired debates were rehearsed for a final time: a fitting requiem to yet another failed attempt to recast urban Merthyr in the civic mould.[121] That the seemingly intractable problems presented by the 'outlying districts' were eventually overcome with the help of a philanthropist from America and not one from Merthyr was apt. Certainly it did not pass unnoticed. Sydney Simons, the chair of the Free Library Committee, wrote first to Lord Wimborne and W. T. Crawshay (whose family owned the Cyfarthfa Iron Works) in the hope of receiving financial support. Such efforts were 'to no avail'. Only then was it decided to make overtures to Andrew Carnegie. This was done with the help of the industrialist and local member of Parliament, D. A. Thomas, with the result that Carnegie agreed to give £6,000 towards the scheme in 1902.[122] Although grateful to the American ironmaster, Simons could not help but use the incident to berate local industrialists. Once again, the notion of a neglected public duty was invoked. Carnegie's 'was an example that might well be followed by local ironmasters – people who had made their millions in the district, but who had done nothing for the place in return'.[123]

The problem of the Free Library stood as a symbol of the shortcomings of many of Merthyr's social élite as well as serving as a reminder of the difficulties faced by those engaged in the civic project. Little wonder that its eventual appearance was so warmly welcomed. That only three years later the charter of

[119] Ibid., 9 July 1887.
[120] Ibid., 16 July 1887.
[121] Ibid., 3 December 1887.
[122] *ME*, 6 June 1903; *WM*, 11 July 1905; *ME*, 12 January 1907.
[123] *ME*, 28 June 1902.

incorporation was finally granted led many to believe that a truly civic Merthyr had finally been born. 'Charter Day' was certainly understood by many contemporaries as a defining moment, a realization of both their own and their town's true destiny. As one observer at the celebrations put it,

> Monday was the proudest day in the history of Merthyr . . . The elevation of the district into a municipal borough is regarded by the inhabitants as a very high honour, and the people were, naturally, disposed to rejoice at the distinction conferred upon it after years of arduous struggle in the endeavour to secure the charter.[124]

D. W. Jones, the high constable, in his speech thanking the king for his 'gracious act', echoed these sentiments in language that was redolent of earlier debates about Merthyr's position as the old metropolis of Wales:

> Their struggle to secure this had been a long and memorable one, but great difficulties had been overcome by the pluck and perseverance of the promoters, and this made the victory all the greater (Cheers). He felt sure they all rejoiced that the old town which the geography books used to teach them was the most important town in Wales was now raised to the dignity of a municipal borough.[125]

The journey from urban to civic had, it seemed, been finally completed.

VI.   CONCLUSION

This chapter began by considering the tendency of many Merthyrians to think about their home town in terms of stagnation and even decline. Late Victorian Merthyr, so the argument ran, was 'behind the times'. This backwardness displayed itself most notably in an almost total lack of civic accomplishment. When compared with other urban settlements in the region, the absence of public buildings and open recreational spaces in Merthyr was indeed striking. As a town originally

---

[124] *WM*, 11 July 1905.
[125] Ibid.

created to meet the exigencies of the iron industry, it may have grown at a rapid rate but it had hardly developed into a centre of urban civilization.

In explaining this civic backwardness, historians have pointed to the underdeveloped nature of the district's middle class. Such was the predominance of the ironmasters in local affairs during the first half of the century that the relatively small numbers of tradesmen and professionals who made Merthyr their home found it difficult to establish themselves as a force for civic reform. But, as we have seen, as the century wore on, and as Merthyr's middle classes began to register their presence in the public sphere, so they took the lead in debating the virtues of all manner of civic schemes. To this extent at least, the bourgeoisie, even in a town like Merthyr, were to the fore when it came to preaching the civic gospel. Yet this is not to say that the civic project was simply an expression of their class interests. For it is important to note that when it came to the language employed in the debates about civic improvement, contemporaries were as likely to mobilize concepts such as 'public spirit' and 'public duty' as they were to invoke a class discourse. The good 'public' life was one that could be – indeed, should be – lived by all (male) members of the social élite. Thus it was expected that the great ironmasters and land-owners also had a role to play in effecting the civic trans-formation of the district. Some, like Wimborne, were to prove a disappointment. Others, like Charlotte Guest in earlier days, had shown themselves to be among the district's more useful 'friends'.

It might be objected that 'the public' was simply another way of referring to the bourgeoisie, be they involved in com-merce, the professions or in industry. Hence, the civic project, as described thus far, was really a class project, even if con-temporaries often dressed it up in a non-class-specific language. If we were to stop our analysis at this point, this might indeed seem a reasonable conclusion. And in any case, it is not being suggested here that class should be written out of the equation. But in terms of the dynamics underpinning the project, we have already begun to catch glimpses of ways in which the civiliz-ing power could be directed against the social élite, instead of being merely wielded by them. The discourses of 'public spirit'

and 'public duty', as deployed by the newspapers and other
such 'technologies of rule', carried with them a disciplinary
charge; shame could be administered no matter how wealthy or
important a figure was or – in the case of E. P. Martin – had
been. In fact, the more important the figure, the greater the
expectation that they would act in the interest of their town,
and the greater the shame if they failed to act accordingly.
Through the newspapers, they – along with other members of
the reading public – were encouraged to examine their own
conduct and subject themselves to the 'gaze of the inner eye'.[126]
In short, when it came to the promotion of all things 'civic' and
'civilized', power operated along lines that were never simply
shaped by the exigencies of class.

The rest of this book examines these themes through a study
of the ways in which the civic boosters – those 'public' men
drawn largely from the ranks of the social élite – were required
to accommodate the rest of the citizenry within their blue-
prints for a civic Merthyr. For the most part this is done at the
level of the streets. These were special 'public' spaces that were
freighted with notions of freedom yet which had to be regulated and watched over at all times in the interests of urban
civilization. They were also frequently made to stand for
the town itself; in certain respects a town was its streets.
Merthyrians of all social classes entered those streets on a daily
basis and for all manner of reasons. The pursuit of a raft of
popular cultural pursuits was one such reason and is singled
out for special attention here. Either as members of recreational crowds, or as lone individuals moving between places
of entertainment, pleasure-seeking urbanites using the public
thoroughfares found themselves confronting 'civilized' expectations. They could conform to or disrupt the tenets of civilized
street etiquette, but either way their civility was under public scrutiny. If the streets of a town were sites of civilized
behaviour, then the town itself was a civilized one. The obverse
also held true.

Given this ability of non-élite citizens to play a part in the
construction of a town image, those who saw Charter Day,

---

[126] This evocative phrase is used by Nikolas Rose in his 'Assembling the modern self',
in Roy Porter (ed.), *Rewriting the Self: Histories from the Renaissance to the Present* (London,
1997), p. 234.

1905, as the end of a process were mistaken. 'Civic Merthyr' could never be 'made'; it could only be aspired to, despaired of and fought over.[127] As the following chapters show, the same could be said of the truly 'civilized' street.

[127] For a general discussion of the relationship between the built form and urban meaning, see Mike Savage and Alan Warde, *Urban Sociology, Capitalism and Modernity* (Basingstoke, 1993), pp. 123–8. David Harvey emphasizes the multiple meanings that can accrue to a single piece of architecture. See his study of the Sacré-Coeur in his *Consciousness and the Urban Experience: Studies in the History and Theory of Capitalist Urbanization* (Oxford, 1985), ch. 4. For another example, see Denis Cosgrove, 'The myth and the stones of Venice: an historical geography of a symbolic landscape', *Journal of Historical Geography*, 8, no. 2 (1982), 145–69.

III

CIVILIZING THE STREETS:
SPACE, SURVEILLANCE AND SHAME

Sidewalks, their bordering uses, and their users, are active participants in the drama of civilization versus barbarism in cities. To keep the city safe is a fundamental task of the city's streets and its sidewalks.

Jane Jacobs[1]

[W]e map the city by private benchmarks which are meaningful only to us ... I hardly ever trespass beyond those limits, and when I do I feel I'm in foreign territory, a landscape of hazard and rumour. Kilburn, on the far side of my northern and western boundaries, I imagine to be inhabited by vicious drunken Irishmen; Hackney and Dalston by crooked car dealers with pencil moustaches and goldfilled teeth; London south of the Thames still seems impossibly illogical and contingent, a territory of meaningless circles, incomprehensible one-way systems, warehouses and cage-bird shops. Like any tribesman hedging himself in behind a stockade of taboos, I mark my boundaries with graveyards, terminal transportation points and wildernesses. Beyond them, nothing is to be trusted and anything might happen.

... It is the visitor who goes everywhere; to the resident, a river or railway track, even if it is bridged every few hundred yards, may be as absolute a boundary as a snakepit or an ocean.

Jonathan Raban[2]

A number of collective identities were located at the very centre of the nineteenth-century civic project. 'Class' was, of course, one of them, and has been extensively commented upon by historians. Thus, the various schemes undertaken to sanitize, order and civilize the Victorian town and city have often been understood in terms of the middle class attempting to write its own values into the urban landscape. It is certainly possible to point to many initiatives which appear to have had the aim of charging numerous urban spaces with 'bourgeois' meanings. The erection of statues commemorating the lives of city fathers, the construction of imposing town halls and libraries, the laying

---

[1] *The Death and Life of Great American Cities* (New York, 1961), p. 30.
[2] *Soft City* (London, 1988 edn), pp. 166-7.

of public parks and the naming of streets and squares can all be
interpreted in such a way, although we need to be aware that
defining precisely what those bourgeois meanings were can be a
highly problematical exercise. Similarly, some of the strategies
employed in the regulation of behaviour in and around the
built form of the nineteenth-century town have often been conceived of as elements in a wider 'class' project. For instance, an
earlier historiography of leisure viewed the 'rational recreation'
movement as an example of the urban middle class endeavouring to eradicate a raft of 'demoralizing' working-class cultural
practices from the public spaces of the town and city.[3] Likewise,
the new police were often singled out as standard-bearers of a
middle-class morality which they took right into the heart of
working-class districts. These arguments capture certain truths.
Nevertheless, other truths can be obscured by an over-reliance
upon class as a category of analysis. As noted earlier, while it is
helpful to see class as an attribute of the civic project, it is
misleading to assume that it constituted its essence.

This chapter attempts to uncover some other attributes
through a consideration of the regulation of behaviour in
Merthyr's public spaces, and, more particularly, in Merthyr's
streets. Contemporaries loaded such spaces with multifarious
moral meanings, and, in so doing, elevated the thoroughfare to
a position of great importance. Streets were made to speak
eloquently about the civility of their users; some were considered to be sites of 'safety', while others were declared to
be 'dangerous' containers of vice and immorality. Still others
defied easy categorization and posed real problems for respectable urbanites. Their efforts to ascribe meaning to the streets
require careful consideration. First, they alert us, once again, to
the significance of 'the public' as a collective identity.[4] Streets
were 'public' spaces which, theoretically, were open to all
members of 'the public'. Such a term turned around notions
of inclusivity, and had the potential to transcend boundaries
of class. (It would certainly be an unsophisticated analysis of

[3] For an excellent survey of the historiography of leisure, see Peter Bailey, 'The
politics and poetics of modern British leisure: a late twentieth-century review',
Rethinking History, 3, no. 2 (1999), 131–75, especially 141.
[4] A classic work which explores aspects of 'the public' is Jürgen Habermas, *The
Structural Transformation of the Public Sphere: An Inquiry into a Category of Bourgeois Society*,
tr. Thomas Burger with Frederick Lawrence (Cambridge, 1989).

urban space that presented the streets of the Victorian town simply as 'middle-class' spaces.) Nevertheless, 'the public' could be put together in ways that excluded as well as included. This leads to the second (and closely related) point; as 'civilized' inhabitants strolled through the 'public' spaces of their town, they necessarily carried with them expectations that stemmed from their rights as citizens. These expectations were invariably framed by the notion of 'freedom', a central concept in the political rationality that was nineteenth-century liberalism. But just as 'the public' could be structured in ways that undercut its democratic, all-embracing potential, so the freedom which ran through ideas of public space was a highly regulated one; it had to be if the streets were to remain 'safe'. By considering some of the ways in which Victorians attempted to resolve this apparent paradox – the regulation of these 'free' spaces that were so important to the civic project – we need to look beyond analyses which rely only upon class as an explanatory category, or which conceive of power as a relationship that only, or even ultimately, was shaped by the master concept of class.

I.   UNDERSTANDINGS OF 'THE PUBLIC', UNDERSTANDINGS OF PUBLIC URBAN SPACE

In January 1883, the *Merthyr Express* looked forward to one of the high points in the town's social calendar, the 'Calico Ball'. An annual event held in the Drill Hall and staged to raise funds for local charities, the Ball had a number of striking characteristics. According to the paper, one of its most noteworthy features was its inclusive quality. Readers were reminded that the fancy-dress ball

> differs in almost everything from an ordinary ball ... There are no 'sets', no cliques, no parties, no exclusiveness, but a general and thorough admixture . . . In fact, the fancy dress ball becomes a grand democratic republic, where liberty, equality and fraternity are practised with a great deal nearer approach to the reality than any so-called republic in Europe or America. Of course, it wouldn't do to throw the doors open to all the world indiscriminately. The committee and stewards exercise a wise discretion in the admission of guests, and nobody would be tolerated at the ball whose presence was objectionable on public grounds. There is,

therefore, substantial security that the company shall be irreproachable in point of respectability, and that has been one of the principal elements of the success of the previous balls. The best members of local society are at the head of it, and they take care that while extending the hand to left and right, nobody will be admitted whom the proudest lady or gentleman in the land need object to meet.[5]

Such a glowing report may well have aroused the interest of Edwin Hunt, a junior plumber from Merthyr, who, after imbibing a few pints in some of the town's drinking-places, determined to see for himself this grand democratic republic. On the way he was intercepted by Acting-Sergeant Evans, who was strategically placed on the steps of the Drill Hall. Deciding that Hunt was indeed 'objectionable', Evans reminded him of the price of admission. Upon learning this information, 'Hunt started to swear – he wouldn't pay that "b—sum"' and struck the officer in the mouth. The dénouement was played out in Merthyr Police Court where the bench observed that 'under the circumstances' he should really be imprisoned, but on this occasion leniency would be shown; he was required to pay a fine of £2 or face one month's hard labour.[6]

We could conclude that the confrontation between plumber and policeman was a straightforward example of discrimination based on class considerations. Hence, the Ball could be presented as a middle-class social event which was, by definition, out of bounds to a member of the working class. Alternatively, concepts such as 'rough' and 'respectable' could be mobilized as a means of understanding the exclusion of the intoxicated Hunt. Yet another approach may involve the interaction of both class and respectability. But while all are legitimate lines of enquiry, for present purposes it is interesting to ponder the role of 'the public' in this incident. After all, according to the *Express* it was on 'public grounds' that individuals such as Hunt were to be refused entry. The newspaper's description of the Ball alerts us to the complicated relationship that obtained between notions of 'freedom', 'the public' and, to borrow a phrase from Foucault, 'the conduct of conduct'. Rather than simply dismissing references to 'grand democratic republics' and 'liberty,

---

[5] *ME*, 13 January 1883.
[6] Ibid., 27 January 1883.

equality and fraternity' as hyperbole, it is productive to tease
out the implications of a paragraph which at once celebrated
the virtues of inclusivity and then shifted effortlessly, with the
introduction of 'the public', into a mode of analysis based on
the principle of exclusivity; clearly not all Merthyrians were
members of this particular public. Meanwhile, those who were
potential patrons of the Ball were presented with a picture of an
event in which freedom was everything, and in which social
barriers were broken down, all the while being reassured that
this was a freedom that was to be policed in their interests.

These ideas – of a structured public, and a policed freedom – are worth bearing in mind when we turn our attention
to the public spaces of the late Victorian and Edwardian town,
not least because they go much of the way towards explaining
the great significance contemporaries invested in the humble
street. We should not be surprised to learn that late Victorians
worried about their thoroughfares. After all, this was still an age
in which examples of the 'walking city' persisted.[7] At least up
until – and probably well beyond – the introduction of the
tram in Merthyr in the early years of the twentieth century,
'Shanks's pony' was by far the most common means of moving
around the built form.[8] But such practical concerns cannot, on
their own, explain the way in which the street found itself
occupying an important place in the discourses of nineteenth-
century liberalism. As Patrick Joyce has noted, the city and its
spaces featured prominently in the production of 'understandings of the social order', understandings charged with
notions regarding 'culture' and 'civilization'.[9] By the later years
of the century, this preoccupation with the town and city
resurfaced in the 'cult of the civic' as local élites celebrated 'the

---

[7] Many nineteenth-century British settlements fit the 'walking city' model, a paradigm developed originally to describe a common feature of the American urban
experience. See A. M. Warnes, 'Early separation of home from workplace and the
urban structure of Chorley, 1780 to 1850', *Transactions of the Historic Society of Lancashire
and Cheshire*, 72 (1970), 105–35; David Ward, 'Victorian cities: how modern?', *Journal of
Historical Geography*, 1, no. 2 (1975), 135–51; David Ward, 'Environs and neighbours in
the "Two Nations": residential differentiation in mid-nineteenth century Leeds',
Journal of Historical Geography, 6, no. 2 (1980), 133–62.
[8] See the letter from 'Pedestrian' in *Merthyr Times* (*MT*), 10 January 1895. For more
on Merthyr's trams, see Cardiff University Library, J. Hathren Davies, 'The tramways
of Merthyr Tydfil' (n.d.).
[9] Patrick Joyce, *Democratic Subjects: The Self and the Social in Nineteenth-Century England*
(Cambridge, 1994), p. 163.

urban' through the elaboration of all manner of rituals, symbols and representations.[10] In the process, they fashioned civic landscapes – complete with town halls, named streets, statues, parks and memorials – in urban settlements up and down the country. And as James Vernon has put it, such public spaces and buildings were not simply inert backdrops against which civic events took place; rather 'they were increasingly politicized themselves . . . [;] the civic landscape represented the town to itself'.[11]

The street ran through the heart of these civic landscapes, and was as politicized as any town hall, park or memorial. Moreover, it could produce its own understandings of the social order. In large measure, this was because it was one of the most 'public' – and therefore 'freest' – of all public spaces. A number of urban historians have made this point. Peter Goheen, for example, writing about mid-Victorian Toronto, has argued that public space was – amongst other factors – defined by 'the generality of its use'. The fact that land 'was available to the whole population which assumed a right of access without discrimination' was crucial in defining its 'public' quality, and in shaping the negotiations which accompanied competing claims to the streets.[12] In a similar vein, James Winter has remarked upon 'the tradition about the freedom of the King's Highway', a tradition which retained its vitality throughout the nineteenth century. 'In theory at least, the street was a democratic island in a sea of privilege and stratified authority.'[13] And the assumption of 'freedom of access' also underpins Martin Daunton's argument that 'space which remained in the public sphere rather than assigned to a particular function was declared neutral and anonymous'.[14] This then was space over which citizens had 'perceived rights to its use and enjoyment'.[15]

---

[10] Ibid., p. 176; Patrick Joyce, *Visions of the People: Industrial England and the Question of Class, 1840–1914* (Cambridge, 1991), pp. 182–3.

[11] James Vernon, *Politics and the People: A Study in English Political Culture, c. 1815–1867* (Cambridge, 1993), pp. 49ff.

[12] P. G. Goheen, 'Negotiating access to public space in mid-nineteenth-century Toronto', *Journal of Historical Geography*, 20, no. 4 (1994), 430–49, 432.

[13] James Winter, *London's Teeming Streets, 1830–1914* (London, 1993), p. 10.

[14] M. J. Daunton, 'Public place and private space: the Victorian city and the working-class household', in D. Fraser and A. Sutcliffe (eds), *The Pursuit of Urban History* (London, 1983), p. 219.

[15] Goheen, 'Negotiating access', p. 433.

Yet, given the experience of Hunt, the drunken plumber, it should come as no surprise to learn that the very freedom that helped define public space was heavily regulated. All manner of codes and conventions were in place to distinguish between civilized and uncivilized public behaviour, although there was always room for disagreement about whether certain practices were more acceptable than others. When the codes were broken, the police were charged with the duty of dealing with the transgressors. It was this regulation of 'free' public space that freighted the nineteenth-century street with political meaning, bound it so tightly to the civic project and situated it at the heart of the relationship between public urban space and urban identities. For any conflicts over the use of public spaces were crucial in the production of a town's identity. As private individuals exerted their claims to Merthyr's public space, or attempted to deny others access to those spaces, so 'the public' itself was problematized. More precisely, the very idea of there being 'public' spaces helped to constitute a number of 'publics' made up of private citizens publicly debating what constituted acceptable behaviour in those spaces. The public sphere was a contested one in which 'ratepayers', 'chapel-goers', 'civilized' townsfolk and others did battle with those who used public spaces for activities that had been deemed to be 'inappropriate'. These debates about street usage were necessarily debates about the nature of Merthyr society itself, for all attempts to deny access to urban spaces involved the exercise of power; thus, various definitions of 'Merthyr' were continually fought over in the public sphere.[16]

When it came to gauging the appropriateness – or other-wise – of particular practices, civilized Merthyrians were guided by a street etiquette which had, by the late Victorian period, marked out a town's thoroughfares as sites of move-ment, of silence and of safety. These principles demanded more than a modicum of restraint from urbanites. While the police

[16] M. P. Ryan argues that public urban space is 'a historical location which, rather than concentrating social problems, distills possibilities for cultural exchange, social creativity, and political ingenuity ... [creating] not just problems of governance but potential for reading new meaning into the term public', in her *Women in Public: Between Banners and Ballots, 1825–1880* (Baltimore, 1990), p. 175, cited in P. G. Goheen, 'The ritual of the streets in mid-nineteenth-century Toronto', *Environment and Planning D: Society and Space*, 11 (1993), 127–45, 128.

were always on hand to impose restraint where necessary, 'self'-control was also of the utmost importance and a whole technology of surveillance and shame was in place to encourage such a virtue. For an indication of what a breakdown in 'self'-discipline could mean in terms of public interactions we need look no further than the public drunk. Alcoholic excess – and in many sad cases, alcoholism – sometimes placed town dwellers beyond shame; in the process it allowed them to break the codes of civilized street behaviour in an often quite spectacular fashion. Indeed, the very offence of public drunkenness was little else but an unalloyed contempt for respectable street etiquette. It threatened the freedom of more sober users to enjoy the public spaces of their town on a regular basis, and demanded that action be taken. As we shall see, power relations were enacted in the name of the civilizing project which can only partially be understood by reference to 'class' alone. However, before examining the attempts to reimpose order, we need to ponder some of the assumptions which informed the civilized street etiquette of the late nineteenth-century town.[17]

II. The Principles of Civilized Street Etiquette

When it comes to evaluating shifts in the codes and conventions which governed civilized street usage, urban historians are in a state of some disagreement. Martin Daunton, for instance, has argued that the Victorian era witnessed a redrawing of the boundaries that separated public from private space. In a paper which deserves greater attention than it has attracted thus far, he concentrated on changes in the spatial configuration of working-class districts in some of Britain's towns and cities. After noting the general move away from the courts and alleys of the early Victorian urban settlement towards more 'open' streets, he concluded that the cultural life of the open-ended street was a pale reflection of the boisterous and vibrant culture

[17] Its everyday qualities make it a potentially more interesting object of study for our purposes than the somewhat extraordinary civic rituals and parades which have attracted the attention of historical geographers and urban historians. See, for instance, Peter Jackson, 'The politics of the streets; a geography of Caribana', *Political Geography*, 11, no. 2 (1992), 130–51; Vernon, *Politics and the People*, especially chs. 2–3; Goheen, 'The ritual of the streets'. Goheen, 'Negotiating access', does give some consideration to the problem of public drunkenness.

of the enclosed court.[18] This has been questioned by Bill Bramwell in his study of Birmingham. Bramwell has discovered the persistence of a lively street culture in working-class areas of that city right up until the end of the century.[19] Writing of the same period, James Winter has concurred, remarking that it would be misleading to suggest that sociability and entertainment had been completely erased from the 'good' street.[20] And these doubts seem justified in the light of the recent findings of Andrew Davies and others.[21] Davies's work on early twentieth-century Salford paints a vivid picture of the street as a major centre of working-class sociability.

Notwithstanding the important qualifications introduced by his critics, Daunton's contentions repay careful consideration, for once again we are returned to the idea of 'the public' with all the connotations of a regulated freedom that the concept carries. While in practice the streets of the late nineteenth-century town may never have become the 'socially neutral' sites that Daunton would have us believe, there can be little doubt that he has successfully identified a distinct current of urban thought which held that they *should* be socially neutral.[22] In order to bring about this move, silence became elevated into a virtue, a means of protecting oneself from unwelcome interactions with the crowds of strangers who pulsed through the thoroughfares.[23] At the same time, darkness was to be banished from the public spaces of the towns and cities. The first serious experiments in permanent systems of public lighting may have been introduced in seventeenth-century Amsterdam,[24] but it

[18] Daunton, 'Public place and private space', pp. 214–17, 219.
[19] Bill Bramwell, 'Public space and local communities: the example of Birmingham, 1840–1880', in Gerry Kearns and Charles W. J. Withers (eds), *Urbanising Britain: Essays on Class and Community in the Nineteenth Century* (Cambridge, 1991).
[20] Winter, *London's Teeming Streets*, pp. 100–1.
[21] Andrew Davies, *Leisure, Gender and Poverty: Working-Class Culture in Salford and Manchester, 1900–1939* (Buckingham, 1992), pp. 96–108, chs. 5 and 6; Andrew Davies, 'Street gangs, crime and policing in Glasgow during the 1930s: the case of the Beehive Boys', *Social History*, 23, no. 3 (1998), 251–67; Stephen Humphries, *Hooligans or Rebels? An Oral History of Working-Class Childhood and Youth, 1889–1939* (Oxford, 1983, paperback edn), ch. 7. For the importance of the street for working-class women, see Melanie Tebbutt, 'Women's talk? Gossip and "women's words" in working-class communities, 1880–1939', in Andrew Davies and Steven Fielding (eds), *Workers' Worlds: Cultures and Communities in Manchester and Salford, 1880–1939* (Manchester, 1992).
[22] Daunton, 'Public place and private space', pp. 222–3.
[23] Richard Sennett, *The Fall of Public Man* (London, 1993, paperback edn), p. 27.
[24] Jonathan I. Israel, *The Dutch Republic: Its Rise, Greatness and Fall, 1477–1806* (Oxford, 1995), pp. 681–2.

took the sensibilities of the nineteenth century to illuminate large swathes of the British urban landscape after nightfall. The effect was to increase the 'public' qualities of these public spaces; no longer would the night be able to claim back the streets, temporarily turning them into semi-privatized pockets of space in the process. Meanwhile, the belief that the streets should be sites of continuous movement caught hold of the urban imagination of respectable society. This, more than anything else, was to have implications for the sorts of gatherings – and the sorts of popular cultural practices – that were deemed appropriate by civilized opinion.

These principles resurfaced repeatedly during the century. Take as examples just two Acts of Parliament which reached the statute books in the late 1840s, the Town Clauses Act of 1847 and the Public Health Act of the following year. The former contained numerous injunctions concerned with cleaning, lighting, ordering, naming and rationalizing the public spaces of the towns and cities. It even laid down guidelines detailing the dimensions of all new streets.[25] The assumption throughout was that users of the civilized thoroughfare should be able to move through it safely and easily; anything that militated against this basic principle was to be removed. Similar impulses informed the Public Health Act of 1848. This act, concerned as it was with sanitizing the mid-Victorian town, explicitly targeted a variety of public urban spaces. No longer were they to be clogged with miasma-producing excrement; instead, the civilized town was one in which pure water circulated through its spaces and waste products flowed harmlessly away.[26] Free and easy circulation, whether of detritus, of goods or of people was now an unalloyed 'good'.[27]

Just how firmly embedded these beliefs had become by the later years of the century can be gauged by an exchange that took place during a Royal Commission of Inquiry set up in 1897 to consider Merthyr's claims to the status of borough.

[25] PP, Town Clauses Act, 1847 (10 and 11 Vict., cap. 34).
[26] For a discussion of the values held by one representative sanitary reformer, see Andy Croll, 'Writing the insanitary town: G. T. Clark, slums and sanitary reform', in Brian Ll. James (ed.), *G. T. Clark: Scholar Ironmaster in the Victorian Age* (Cardiff, 1998), pp. 33–5.
[27] Richard Sennett, in his *Flesh and Stone: The Body and the City in Western Civilization* (London, 1994), traces the history of these principles.

During the course of the inquiry, the district surveyor, Thomas H. Fletcher, was questioned about various aspects of the built environment. The condition of the southern end of the High Street was singled out for special attention. The commissioner asked whether the sharp curve in the vicinity of the parish church wall and the Carmarthen Arms and Blue Bell Inn was 'consistent with the wants of the public'.[28] After learning from the surveyor of the delays in straightening the road, the commissioner discoursed on the need for improvements and set about asking Fletcher a series of rapid-fire questions:

> Is it not of vital importance to a young or an old community that the access to it should be made as broad and wide as is conducive to public interests? – [Fletcher] Yes. – [The Commissioner] For a town to progress you know it must have the main entrance to it open and free? Yes. – And you have neglected to set free what I might call the 'throttle valve' of this place. Is it not calculated to suffocate the traffic of a district like this when you have the main entrance road in such a condition as this. – Yes.[29]

In his edition of the proceedings of the inquiry, John Astle – that keen supporter of the civic project – felt the exchange important enough to highlight it by including a photograph of the offending stretch of road.[30]

The commissioner's willingness to measure the progress of Merthyr in terms of the ease with which traffic could circulate through its streets is notable. Goods, vehicles and citizens should all be able to travel safely, and without hindrance, around the public thoroughfares. If roads were designed in such ways as to impede this free and safe passage then they should be reconfigured. Indeed, the district surveyor subscribed to such views himself. Far from taking umbrage at the line of questioning, he was in perfect agreement with the commissioner. He informed the inquiry that he too regretted the Council's slowness in dealing with the problem of the 'throttle valve', and looked forward to the day when work could begin on straightening and widening the entrance to the town. As a man trained in the

[28] John G. E. Astle, *Illustrated Report of the Merthyr Tydfil Incorporation Inquiries, 1897 and 1903* (Merthyr, 1903), p. 30.
[29] Ibid., p. 32.
[30] Ibid., p. 31.

basic principles of nineteenth-century urban design, perhaps
we should expect no other response from Fletcher.[31]

Yet one did not have to be an expert in the configuration of
urban space in order to distinguish a good street from a bad
one. There were, it seems, plenty of observers in the Merthyr
district who were only too aware when civilized codes had been
transgressed. Complaints were frequently levelled at streets
clogged by mud, waste products and detritus of all descriptions.
In 1852, for instance, a deputation from Dowlais drew the
attention of the Local Board to the 'wretched condition' of the
town's thoroughfares. 'The scenes witnessed at funerals were
painful in the extreme. The roads were covered with cinders,
and were full of deep ruts. The bearers frequently fell into these
ruts, and the bier was often very near falling to the ground.'[32]
In an editorial in 1876, the *Merthyr Telegraph* simply stated:
'The wretched condition of the Merthyr thoroughfares has long
been a disgrace to the town.'[33] Similarly, in 1895 the chair of
the Merthyr Council 'called attention to the state of the High
Street. It was in a very bad state, and it was a shame that they
could see crowds of people walking through the mud. It would
not cost much to improve the street, and it would benefit the
whole people.' He ended with a charge by now familiar to most
Merthyrians: 'He was bound to say that they were very much
behind the times as regards the streets.'[34]

If the accumulation of detritus in the streets was unacceptable to many, so was the layout of the thoroughfares. Any
scheme which could make easier and faster the transport of
goods or persons was encouraged by those motivated by notions
of the 'public good'. Sometimes this involved reconfiguring the
street and its environs. A petition that had been 'numerously
signed' by those living in the vicinity of Castle Street and the
Glebeland was presented to the Local Board asking for a
'dangerous obstruction' to be moved on the grounds that it 'has
always been an eyesore and an inconvenience to the general
public'.[35] In other cases, opening up new routes through the

[31] Fletcher, the surveyor and engineer to the Merthyr Urban District Council, was a
member of the Sanitary Institute and an associate of the Municipal and County Engineers (ibid., p. 26).

[32] *CMG*, 14 February 1852.

[33] *MTl*, 4 February 1876.

[34] *MT*, 6 June 1895.

[35] Ibid., 20 October 1893.

built environment achieved the goal of free movement. The news that there were plans afoot to build a bridge at Caedraw was warmly welcomed by the *Merthyr Times* in 1893. It would ease the flow of goods, of school children, the Volunteers and workmen coming from Abercannaid.[36] A like response had been elicited from the *Telegraph* in 1879 when the Local Board of Health determined upon two bridge-building schemes in the district. After praising the Board, it urged members to go further and construct a new structure at Ynysgau. 'There cannot be two opinions about the necessity of taking this step . . . the old cast iron bridge is in anything but a safe condition, and many persons are absolutely afraid to go on it when a load is being drawn over.'[37]

The problems presented to Merthyrians by such dangerous and dirty public spaces were compounded by the way in which so many of the streets were shrouded in darkness. From at least the 1840s, right-minded inhabitants had acknowledged the importance of street lighting. T. E. Clarke, author of a town guide, noted in 1848 that, along with good pavements and covered drains, 'public lights are among the *desiderata* (things to be desired) in Merthyr Tydfil',[38] and a similar point was made in 1850 by T. W. Rammell in his official report on the sanitary condition of the town.[39] A start was made that year when the newly constituted Local Board of Health decided to install fifty gas lamps. In December 1851 the first lamps were lit in Merthyr High Street, while a few weeks later areas of the Glebeland were also illuminated.[40] Nevertheless, there remained much to be achieved. In 1872, for example, inhabitants of Pentrebach and Abercannaid sent a memorial to the Local Board of Health, 'praying for the erection of public lamps at certain points on the Cardiff Road between Merthyr and Troedyrhiw',[41] while in 1874 the secretary to the Number Three Dowlais Building

[36] Ibid., 20 January 1893.
[37] *MTl*, 14 February 1879.
[38] T. E. Clarke, *A Guide to Merthyr Tydfil* (Merthyr Tydfil, 1848, reprinted 1894), p. 45.
[39] T. W. Rammell, *Report to the General Board of Health into the Sewerage, Drainage, and Supply of Water, and the Sanitary Condition of Merthyr Tydfil* (London, 1850), p. 48. Rammell's observations were supported by the *Cardiff and Merthyr Guardian*, 20 April 1850.
[40] *CMG*, 13 December 1851, 31 January 1852.
[41] *MT*, 9 November 1872.

Society requested lamps for streets containing over 120 houses that were all 'entirely without gas lamps'.[42] The *Merthyr Telegraph* picked up the issue, and made explicit the link between illuminated urban spaces and safety. An editorial noted the 'deficiency of gas lamps in various quarters of the town', and continued by observing that 'it has long been a scandal to the place that many quarters should be so badly lighted as to make it by no means safe to traverse them after dark, and a close attention to this matter in the future will greatly enhance the convenience of the community'.[43] And the idea of public lighting bringing with it alterations in the behaviour of urbanites was reiterated in 1876 by Daniel Williams, who suggested that the Local Board of Health 'adopt an existing lamp in Pottery Lane, belonging to the proprietors of the Drill Hall, as a public lamp, with the view of preventing nuisances occasioned by persons resorting there for improper purposes'.[44] Progress was made, although, in keeping with other civic ventures in Merthyr, it was slow. By 1880 there were some 230 lamps in the town, whilst neighbouring Dowlais was lit by 98 lamps.[45] Yet, six years later the *Merthyr Express* was still complaining that the town was 'in the shade' compared with Aberdare, Pontypridd and Tredegar.[46]

III. Constructing Moral Geographies of Merthyr's Public Spaces

Given the existence of these dirty and dark spaces within the built form of Merthyr, it was imperative that respectable inhabitants planned their journeys carefully in order to avoid such uncivilized sites; to make matters worse, they also had to take into account the possible presence of all manner of 'undesirable' fellow townsfolk. Reconstructing any mental maps that late Victorians may have taken with them as they stepped into the highways and byways of the town is a challenging exercise

[42] *MTl*, 20 February 1874.
[43] Ibid., 27 February 1874.
[44] Ibid., 21 January 1876.
[45] Ibid., 21 May 1880.
[46] *ME*, 18 September 1886.

doomed to only partial success at best. However, it is at least possible to uncover some of the 'private benchmarks'[47] which served to mark out the more notorious of Merthyr's public spaces.

Some areas of the built environment had, by the 1880s and 1890s, earned themselves reputations as permanent zones of vice and crime. For example, the Ynysfach Coke Ovens, situated on the outskirts of the town, became renowned as a meeting place for some of the poorer Merthyrians who were attracted by the heat and light thrown out by the fires. The denizens of the ovens periodically impressed themselves upon the public consciousness of the town during these years as a result of a number of 'outrages', including the murder of a labourer in 1890. 'Polonius', the gossip columnist in the *Merthyr Express*, used the event to remind readers of the dangerous nature of the place: 'The disclosures made in the recent murder case showed that there congregated nightly at this place the lowest scum of the town, to the terror of those who live in the neighbourhood of the ovens.'[48] Three years later this assessment was confirmed by the local stipendiary magistrate who proclaimed that the ovens were a 'perfect nest of iniquity' and a place 'where crimes of the most serious character were hatched'.[49] The ovens were clearly neither for the faint-hearted nor for the respectable. Similar observations could be made about 'the Cellary' or 'China', as it was better known. A mere five-minute walk from the High Street, this district still possessed the ability to frighten civilized urbanites notwithstanding the fact that its heyday as a resort of a hardened 'criminal class' had long since passed. And it was not only gullible outsiders who were susceptible to the scare stories; even Merthyrians found it difficult to erase the terrible memories of mid-Victorian China. Thus, when the *Express* sent a reporter into the neighbourhood in 1894 to detail the insanitary conditions of the houses, a policeman accompanied him. According to the journalist, this piece of slum-land was 'as bad, if not worse, than the rookeries of Whitechapel', a place which had burned itself into the imagination of civilized Britain less than

[47] The phrase is Jonathan Raban's. See the epigraph at the beginning of this chapter.
[48] *ME*, 26 April 1890.
[49] *Merthyr and Dowlais Times* (*MDT*), 5 May 1893.

six years earlier with the arrival of the most horrific of all urban nightmares, 'Jack the Ripper'.

Permanent centres of danger such as the Cellary and the ovens acted as markers which allowed Merthyrians to carve up the urban landscape into areas of safety and danger in much the same way as inhabitants of great urban centres – such as London – imagined their city as being divided into distinct geographic zones (most notably through recourse to the binary opposites of a civilized West poised against a barbarous East).[50] But, given the more compact nature of Merthyr's built environment, it was much easier to stray from a safe space into a dangerous one. The God-fearing town dweller had to exercise extreme caution; a wrong turn and one might find oneself in these less-than-salubrious areas. A correspondent to the *Express* explicitly commented upon this important feature of life in Merthyr in 1884:

> In London, Liverpool, and also nearer home, in Cardiff say, you do not jump from Elysium to Hades at a bound, but in Merthyr you pass from among the paint and plate glass of the front street, to the filth and squalor, the rottenness and decay of the slums at a step![51]

The local newspaper was well placed to alert its readers to the location of some of the fine lines that separated the 'dangerous' slums from the safer streets. Its depictions of Merthyr's poorer areas, combined with the graphic accounts of outrages in areas like the coke ovens, provide us with a glimpse of some of the features that respectable citizens included in their 'moral geographies' of the town.[52] It is possible to glean other clues about the shape of such mental maps. For instance, it is clear that one of the most significant of all spatial divisions was that

[50] An interesting discussion of London's 'imaginary landscape' can be found in Judith R. Walkowitz, *City of Dreadful Delight: Narratives of Sexual Danger in Late-Victorian London* (London, 1992), especially ch. 1. Also see Griselda Pollock, 'Vicarious excitements: *London: A Pilgrimage* by Gustave Doré and Blanchard Jerrold, 1872', *New Formations*, 4 (1988), 25–50.

[51] *ME*, 9 August 1884. Inhabitants of other smaller towns – such as Worcester for example – appear to have had similar experiences. See Croll, 'Writing the insanitary town', p. 32.

[52] The concept of 'moral geographies' is discussed in P. Shurmer-Smith and K. Hannam, *Worlds of Desire, Realms of Power* (London, 1994), pp. 173–6. For more on the ways in which spaces were freighted with moral meanings, see Teresa Ploszajska, 'Moral landscapes and manipulated spaces: gender, class and space in Victorian reformatory schools', *Journal of Historical Geography*, 20, no. 4 (1994), 413–29.

between the 'main' streets and the 'back' streets. This distinction was often made throughout the period. Thus, a number of the witnesses who appeared before the Royal Commission into the operation of the Welsh Sunday Closing Act in 1889 remarked upon the differences that obtained between the 'principal' thoroughfares and the 'back' streets.[53] Meanwhile, the newspapers are full of letters and editorials which point to this most basic of imagined boundaries.

The 'main streets' included the High Street and those adjoining thoroughfares which together comprised the commercial centre of the town. Behaviour that threatened the peace and civility of these spaces was severely condemned by defenders of urban civilization. When, for example, a tradesman in the town complained of a fight that took place on Mabon's Day (the colliers' monthly holiday) in May 1890, he was as much distressed by the fact that it could take place in a main street as he was by the unedifying spectacle itself. This was a bruising affair,

> with wooden-legged men, rolling and tumbling in the mud; also a woman amusing the onlookers (for there being many) a long time. No police were to be seen; but there were drunken men by the dozen honouring Mabon of course. Then on Tuesday . . . men were stopped, even taking their shirts off fighting and bleeding for upwards of an hour. This too in the High Street.[54]

In a similar vein, 'Polonius' took umbrage at the all-too-public nature of the funerals that were still troubling some inhabitants on the eve of the new century. In 1899 he complained of recent scenes witnessed in Merthyr's main street:

> Funeral displays are too common, and the resulting 'unusual eating and drinking' are not the least of the evils connected therewith, but this excess usually takes place, I believe, after the obsequies; when a large walking procession proceeds up the High Street with men unsteady owing to intoxication, as I saw in this case, the scandal is greatly aggravated.[55]

This sensitivity over the condition of the principal streets was rooted in the uses to which those particular urban spaces were

---

[53] *Royal Commission of Inquiry on the Operation of the Sunday Closing (Wales) Act, 1881,* 1890 (C. 5994), XL (I) Report (hereafter *SC Report*), QQ. 4197, 4083.
[54] *ME,* 10 May 1890.
[55] Ibid., 6 May 1899.

put. Different groups of influential urbanites all had good reasons to hope that these streets would be well regulated. When viewed from the point of view of the district's 'shopocracy', the importance of the main thoroughfares is obvious. As the streets that dissected the commercial heart of the town, they were the carriers of goods and potential customers. Any obstacles in these spaces were especially troublesome. And the fact that these inhabitants were amongst the ratepaying class of the town merely served to bolster their concerns. More than once was the assumption articulated that the principal thoroughfares of the town were, in a special sense, the property of the ratepayers. This feeling of ownership could be widespread; as we shall see, correspondents to the local papers regularly employed the pseudonyms 'Tax Payer' and 'Ratepayer' when complaining about disorder in the High Street. One such letter-writer put the question in 1890: 'What do we pay rates and taxes for? Is it to allow dirty and dusty streets to be the scene of fighting, drunkenness and disorder unrestrained?'[56] Yet it was never only the well-heeled of the town who worried about these streets. Working-class, respectable men, women and children also used the main thoroughfares on a daily basis, and clearly had their own sense of what constituted unacceptable behaviour. The call for 'quietness in the streets' was as likely to be made by such individuals as it was by the local notables.[57] As members of Merthyr's civilized public, they too could desire peaceful public spaces.

IV. DISRUPTING THE CODES: THE UNPREDICTABILITY OF PUBLIC DRUNKENNESS

The compact nature of the town's built form amplified the difficulties confronting these 'civilized' pedestrians. Because of the manner in which the slums of the back streets were directly adjacent to urban spaces such as the High Street, inhabitants had to tread extremely carefully through the urban landscape. Yet, even if they were assiduous in their efforts to avoid permanent danger areas, there was always the chance that the

---

[56] Ibid., 10 May 1890.
[57] The phrase was used by a miner, George Evans. *SC Report*, Q. 3678.

forces of disorder would spill into the 'safe' streets. There were certainly more than enough individuals who were capable of inverting the norms of civilized street behaviour. Prostitutes broke the codes which constructed women in public as demure and fragile creatures, members of street-corner gangs could obstruct, insult and threaten innocent pedestrians, while public drunks – as evidenced in the report on the operation of the Welsh Sunday Closing Act – had the potential to challenge almost every assumption which informed respectable street etiquette.[58] So adept were the drunks at bringing disorder to the public spaces of the mid- and late Victorian town that it is worth discussing them further.

The first point to note is that it was the public quality of the drunkenness, as much as the state of inebriation itself, that caused civilized street users so much offence. The real crime lay in the blatant disregard for the codes that were supposed to govern public behaviour. While precise numbers of Merthyrians who were willing to experiment with the conventions in such a way are impossible to gauge, there can be little doubt that the public drunk was an all-too-common feature of the district's street-life. Certainly the Merthyr authorities appear to have been kept busy throughout the period in processing cases of public drunkenness.[59] In a sitting of the police court on a Saturday in June 1872 there were no fewer than fourteen cases of 'drunken and riotous conduct in the public streets', with some £1 9s. being paid by the guilty in costs alone.[60] By August of that year the situation in the town had begun to try the patience of the stipendiary magistrate, who acted to stem what appeared to be a rising tide of street drunkenness. When confronted with George Price, who was charged with being drunk

[58] The place of the prostitute in the urban landscape of the late Victorian city has been discussed by Walkowitz, *City of Dreadful Delight*, pp. 21–4. Important themes in the history of the street-corner gang can be found in Humphries, *Hooligans or Rebels*, pp. 174–208.

[59] For general discussions regarding rates of drunkenness, see W. R. Lambert, 'Drink and work-discipline in industrial South Wales, *c*. 1800–1870', *Welsh History Review*, 7, no. 3 (1975), 289–306; D. J. V. Jones, *Crime in Nineteenth-Century Wales* (Cardiff, 1992), p. 89; A. E. Dingle, 'Drink and working-class living standards in Britain, 1870–1914', *Economic History Review*, 2nd series, 25, no. 4 (1972), 608–22. For figures relating to such rates in the late 1880s in Glamorgan generally, and Cardiff, Neath and Swansea in particular, see *Returns for England and Wales of the total number of convictions in respect of drunkenness, 1885–89*, 1889, LXI (363), p. 7.

[60] *MT*, 29 June 1872.

and fighting in the streets on a Saturday evening, 'His Worship
addressed [the] defendant, remarking that this drunkenness
and fighting in the street must be put down'.[61] Notwithstanding such resolve on the part of the Bench, in 1899 magistrates
were still declaring that 'something ought to be done to stop
the reign of drunkenness which was so prevalent of late in
Merthyr'.[62] Fifty-four drink-related cases were heard in just
one day at the police court in December of that year.[63] Perhaps
the only obvious good to flow from this state of affairs was the
high level of fines collected for drunkenness. One temperance
supporter claimed that in 1894 the fines for drunkenness and
assault in the Merthyr and Aberdare district amounted to some
£3,000.[64] Understandably, on the extremely rare occasions
when there was no public drunk in the dock during a court
session, it was a cause for celebration.[65]

The ease with which the public drunk could invert the
various codes that made up 'rational' street behaviour is
noteworthy. Take, for example, the idea that the thoroughfare
should be a site of continuous, free movement. There are numerous instances of this basic tenet of civilized street-life being
honoured in the breach by drunkards. Thus, according to one
witness in December 1892, Ball Court Lane was taken over by
'a rushing, drunken gang' comprised of 'over a hundred people
all drunk and calling out beastly names'.[66] Another recalled the
condition of the streets in the days before the Welsh Sunday
Closing Act: 'Drunken men going from public house to public
house would meet females in the street, push them about, going
in gangs together, and it would be almost impossible for respectable people to pass the street with them.'[67] A 'respectable
resident of Ivor Street', in Dowlais, complained to the *Merthyr
Express* about a fight which took place on a Sunday evening

[61] Ibid., 17 August 1872.
[62] *ME*, 18 March 1899.
[63] Ibid., 16 December 1899.
[64] Ibid., 9 May 1896.
[65] Thus, in 1871 the *Merthyr Times* informed readers that 'It is a pleasure to be able
to omit our usual "drunkards' list", there not being a single charge entered for
hearing, which circumstance, His Worship stated, was most creditable to the town'
(*MT*, 18 November 1871). Merthyr was frequently placed above comparable settlements in 'league tables' of convictions for drunkenness. For examples, see *The Brewers'
Almanack and Wine and Spirit Trade Annuals* for the years 1912, 1913 and 1914.
[66] *ME*, 10 December 1892.
[67] *SC Report*, Q. 3279.

between two drunken men in September 1888. It was estimated that at least a dozen more were drunk, whilst the street was crowded with 'hundreds of persons' intent on viewing the spectacle.[68] Similarly, in Merthyr in March 1876 the activities of Mary Anne Welsh, who was 'quite drunk, and using language such as was simply detestable', caused a crowd to gather which, in the words of the arresting officer, 'crammed the street'.[69]

The public drunks were especially skilled at bringing 'danger' and 'disorder' to the streets, challenging the right of sober, respectable Merthyrians to enjoy the public spaces of their town. This refrain was heard throughout many of the testimonies to the Royal Commissioners in 1889. Thomas Williams, a strict teetotaller, spoke of the 'good deal of disorder and turmoil' which prevailed on Merthyr's streets in the days before the Act was introduced.[70] There was much fighting and 'obstruction on the pavements by men drunk lying on the pavement'.[71] William Jones, a self-confessed 'hater of drunkenness', sketched a vivid picture of the 'scenes of disturbance' which occurred outside his house, two miles from Treharris. He described the influx of gangs of 'very indecent and defiant' men who 'terrorise[d] the neighbourhood'. 'I have had fights, free fights, exactly opposite my front door. I have seen them denude themselves, run naked up and down the towing path, and then jump in the canal to bathe ... They are the terror of the inhabitants.'[72] Another total abstainer, W. L. Daniel, informed the Commissioners of the manner in which those who abused the Act 'prowl[ed] about from one public house to another seeking a drink wherever they can find it'.[73] Nevertheless, there had been a great improvement. In the years before 1882 'it was actually dangerous' for children attending Sunday school to return home, 'owing to the fact that they were insulted and sometimes molested by people in a drunken condition'.[74] Discussing the same years, Sergeant Price talked of an urban landscape in which 'scores of drunken

[68] *ME*, 8 September 1888.
[69] *MTl*, 10 March 1876.
[70] For more on Williams, see W. R. Lambert, 'Thomas Williams, J.P., Gwaelod-y-Garth (1823–1903): a study in nonconformist attitudes and action', in Stewart Williams (ed.), *Glamorgan Historian*, Vol. 11 (Cowbridge, 1975).
[71] *SC Report*, Q. 2558.
[72] Ibid., Q. 17929.
[73] Ibid., Q. 2769.
[74] Ibid., Q. 2787.

men' were 'patrolling the streets more or less drunk and disorderly'.[75] Other witnesses also felt moved to remark upon the
'dangerous' condition of the streets.[76]

In addition to bringing danger to a town's public spaces,
drunkards – with their inhibitions liberated by the drink –
could also break the silence that had become such an important
attribute of civilized street life. Thus, in April 1872 Thomas
Malins managed to shatter almost every code of respectable
behaviour possible. He was discovered by PC Jenkins in a
'drunk and riotous' condition in Bridge Street, 'quite naked,
and standing before some houses and challenging anyone to
come out and fight with him'. Not only was Malins breaking
the silence, but through his nakedness he was also breaching the
boundaries which separated the private from the public, and he
was inviting others to break their silence too. He was punished
accordingly. The stipendiary magistrate described his behaviour as 'disgraceful in the extreme', gave him a sound lecture
and fined him the largest sum possible for such an offence, 40s.
plus costs.[77] Others, devoid of Malins's exhibitionary streak,
could still break the longed-for public silences. In 1874, for
instance, a number of prominent Merthyrians petitioned the
stipendiary magistrate and complained of the scenes which
plagued the streets outside their houses on Christmas Eve, as a
consequence of the granting of an extension of closing time.
'[N]oisy and riotous characters' crowded the streets in the early
hours of the morning, shattering 'the peace of the town'.[78] Such
outbursts were all the more troublesome because they made it
difficult to protect more 'vulnerable' inhabitants from their
demoralizing effects. This helps to explain the distress felt by
Thomas Beavan, a cashier in the Ferndale colliery, Rhondda.
Recalling his experience of walking to chapel with his family in
the days before the Sunday Closing Act, he remembered the
'indecent way' in which people would leave the public houses,
'so that it was not nice to take one's wife or daughters at those

---

[75] Ibid., Q. 3273, 3271.
[76] See the evidence of D. Robert Lewis (ibid., Q. 3229) and Mr Bowen, a
commercial traveller. He referred to the way in which it had been 'almost dangerous to
come down from Dowlais to Merthyr, there being so many drunkards' (ibid., Q. 4894).
[77] MT, 13 April 1872. For more on the scale of fines, see Intoxicating Liquor
(Licensing) Act [35 & 36 Vict.], ch. 94, 10 August 1872.
[78] MTl, 16 January 1874.

times'.[79] His role as a protector of blushing females had been severely challenged by the drunks and their insulting language and behaviour.

In the pantheon of public drunks, those who caused greatest consternation amongst the sober users of the streets were invariably women. For, no matter how able the fighting, crowd-attracting, obstructive, noisy male inebriate was at shocking civilized inhabitants, the sight of a drunken woman was guaranteed to provoke a special kind of outrage. Indeed, the female drunk was regularly singled out for especial opprobrium throughout the period. The epithets hurled at her by members of respectable society serve to illustrate the doubly heinous nature of her crime. She was not only guilty of drunkenness, but she also broke the conventions which constructed women in public spaces as delicate and virtuous individuals who required male protection.[80] As a consequence, it was common to see the female drunk defined in terms of her supposed sexual immorality. In 1909 the chief constable of the Merthyr Borough articulated this assumption most explicitly when he casually informed the Watch Committee that most women drunkards were prostitutes.[81] Newspaper journalists and magistrates were also keen to view inappropriate street behaviour in such terms. The *Merthyr Times* described Ann Brayley as 'a disgrace to her sex' in 1871 because she had been charged with being drunk and disorderly in Dowlais High Street.[82] And the same label was applied to Martha Jenkins one week later, after she had been discovered in a state of drunkenness, behaving in an 'indecent' fashion in Commercial Street. She had been charged with sixteen other like offences in the past. The Bench reminded her of how abnormal her conduct was: 'no one of sound mind would be brought up so many times, and if she were brought up again she would be placed under medical examination.' As it was, she was sent to prison for three months.[83] Almost forty

---

[79] *SC Report*, Q. 3571.
[80] For more on the relationship between women and urban public space, see, for example, Walkowitz, *City of Dreadful Delight*, especially pp. 46–52; Lynda Nead, 'Mapping the self: gender, space and modernity in mid-Victorian London', in Roy Porter (ed.), *Rewriting the Self: Histories from the Renaissance to the Present* (London, 1997).
[81] *ME*, 6 February 1909.
[82] *MT*, 30 September 1871.
[83] Ibid., 7 October 1871.

years later, the situation had altered little. Under the title 'Two Viragos', the *Merthyr Express* carried the case of Emily West and Mary Greeney, who had been charged with disorderly behaviour in Castle Street, Merthyr. According to the paper, 'The evidence against them was that they spoke to men in the street, and went to public houses with them'.[84] This was inappropriate behaviour indeed in spaces where personal silence was deemed essential for the preservation of civilization.[85]

What made both male and female drunks even more unwelcome was the fact that they served as a constant reminder that the forces of barbarism were never far away.[86] While it was always possible to avoid – and, in doing so, forget about – the Cellary or the coke ovens, intoxicated pedestrians could stagger into view at any time, in any street. They were mobile 'dark spaces' who made it almost impossible to construct a meaningful moral geography of the built environment. Even users of the High Street – the most prestigious of all of Merthyr's 'main' thoroughfares – could not be protected from the drunks, given the distribution of public houses throughout the town. Whilst no 'drink maps' exist for the Merthyr district, by consulting the trade directories it is at least possible to point to the wide dispersion of licensed premises throughout the built form.[87] Not surprisingly, in addition to the public houses located in the working-class districts, there were also a number of drinking places situated near, or on, the main streets. In the mid-1890s, there were some twenty public houses and seven 'beer retailers' fronting onto the High Street.[88] To these outlets one can add the off-licences. In the early 1890s there were some thirty grocers' licences within 300 yards of Market Square alone.[89] Any one of these had the potential to contribute to the

[84] *ME*, 3 July 1909.
[85] It is, of course, likely that they were prostitutes, charges of 'disorderly behaviour' under the Vagrancy Act of 1824 being regularly applied to streetwalkers.
[86] For a lengthier discussion of this theme, see Andrew J. Croll, 'Civilizing the urban: popular culture, public space and urban meaning, Merthyr *c*. 1870–1914', Ph.D. thesis, University of Wales (Cardiff), 1997, pp. 163–73.
[87] Brian Harrison discusses two such drink maps for London. See his 'Pubs' in H. J. Dyos and M. Wolff (eds), *The Victorian City: Images and Realities*, 2 vols. (1973), Vol. 1, pp. 162–9.
[88] *Kelly's Directory of Monmouthshire and the Principal Towns and Places in South Wales* (London, 1895), pp. 507–17. There were six places of worship.
[89] *ME*, 1 October 1892.

problem of public drunkenness that plagued more sober users of the town's main street.[90]

The chances of a respectable Merthyrian confronting an abusive drunkard were increased by the manner in which places of worship, like the public houses, were also located throughout the built environment. Indeed, there were instances where chapels were surrounded by drinking places. Thus, within a few yards of Ynysgau Chapel could be found two of the most notorious beershops in the town, the Parrot and Patriot Inns.[91] In like fashion, there were thirty-two pubs within 300 yards of Merthyr Parish Church in the early 1890s.[92] As a consequence, chapel- and churchgoers were frequently brought face to face with less 'civilized' townsfolk. In 1889 David Davies remembered the situation that obtained in the town before the passing of the Sunday Closing Act. 'Previous to the passing of the Act very often on a Sunday afternoon when I came home from Sunday school, from half-past three to four, we could see people out by the hundreds; large throngs quarrelling and fighting. That was a very common occurrence.'[93] Another inhabitant, D. Robert Lewis, painted a vivid picture of the condition of the streets in Dowlais on Sundays before the Act:

> Previously to September 1882 [when the Act came into force] it was perfectly dangerous to walk through some of the streets. I experienced this myself more particularly in the evenings, and by going through Bryn Zion Street, Union Street, Brecon Street, and High Street, Dowlais, which I passed through from my residence to go to Hermon Chapel, which I attend. The service at the chapel was disturbed on several occasions by rows and fights outside. Within a radius of about 150 yards of the said chapel there are no less than 13 public houses.[94]

Even after the passing of the Sunday Closing Act, as we have seen, the public drunk could still be found causing mayhem in

[90] The reports of proceedings in the local police court point to the large number of individuals who were charged with being drunk and disorderly in the main streets of Merthyr during these years. Whether there were more drunks to be found in the principal streets than in the back streets is doubtful. Rather it appears that the former were more rigorously policed, in line with respectable sensitivities. For more on this, see Croll, 'Civilizing the urban', pp. 195–6.
[91] For evidence of the criminal reputation of the Parrot and Patriot, see *ME*, 31 December 1887, 31 March 1888, 7 April 1888, 30 March 1907.
[92] *MDT*, 23 September 1892.
[93] *SC Report*, Q. 4368.
[94] Ibid., Q. 3229.

the district's streets. By bringing such danger and disorder to the streets, these inebriates continued to challenge the right of sober, respectable citizens to enjoy the public spaces of their town. In so doing, they problematized the idea of free access which characterized the very notion of what a truly 'public' space should be. Little wonder that they were often referred to as the 'disgrace' or 'curse of Merthyr'.[95]

V. REGULATING THE FREE SPACES

Contemporaries were not content simply to chronicle and condemn these challenges to their perceived right of access to the streets. On the contrary, condemnation of the drunk (as well as condemnation of the street-gang member, the prostitute and other such figures) was accompanied by a bundle of measures which attempted to discipline those who had transgressed, and, importantly, to dissuade other individuals from transgressing in the first place. Surveillance was the key to securing these spaces of freedom. Historians have for long recognized the important role played by the police in this surveillance project. They were professionals in matters of urban surveillance, and their regular walks through the built environment were an essential means of placing the spaces of the Victorian town under the 'gaze of civilization'.[96] These spaces included the semi-public ones that were the drinking places which played such a part in the production of public drunks. In 1912, for example, over 40,200 visits were made by members of Merthyr's police to public houses.[97] However, while there is no wish here to gainsay the significance of the police as surveillance agents, we should not overstate their role. There was always a very real limit to what they could achieve. The sheer scale of the task that faced them ensured that the gaze of the police was at best an extremely partial one. On the eve of the First World War, for instance, there were still only ninety-one officers in the Merthyr force,

---

[95] See, for example, the *Reformer and South Wales Times*, 29 November 1861; *ME*, 16 December 1899.
[96] The phrase is Nikolas Rose's. See Nikolas Rose, *Towards a Critical Sociology of Freedom* (Inaugural Lecture, Goldsmith's College, University of London, 3 May 1992), reprinted in Patrick Joyce (ed.), *Class* (Oxford, 1995), p. 217.
[97] *ME*, 8 February 1913.

and this at a time when the population of the borough stood at just under 84,000.[98]

Given these limitations, it is instructive to direct attention to other important players in the surveillance project, namely the citizens themselves. Throughout the late Victorian and Edwardian periods there were many in the ranks of the townspeople who were keen to watch over the various public spaces of the town. Some were undoubtedly more assiduous supervisors of urban space than others. To the fore were members of the temperance movement. In Merthyr they frequently took it upon themselves, either collectively or individually, to observe the spaces outside the district's drinking places in an effort to gather information about illicit drink shops or unscrupulous publicans. Statistics were considered a powerful weapon in the struggle to get, and keep in place, the Welsh Sunday Closing Act, and these needed to be collected. Careful observation was vital. Thus, on a Sunday evening in November 1881, teetotallers sat outside fourteen public houses in Merthyr and Swansea, counting the number of patrons who entered the houses between 8.30 p.m. and 9.30 p.m. Their figures were subsequently incorporated into an article written in defence of the Act.[99] A meeting of temperance advocates in Merthyr in March 1891 was also concerned to gather information on the drink trade. After a long discussion it was proposed:

> That vigilance committees be formed in the town of Merthyr and in the several other districts represented in this conference to watch and take cognizance, so far as possible, of infractions of the Public Houses Sunday Closing Act, to keep a record of the same for utilisation, and to aid the police in any effort they may put forth to enforce the said Act with greater stringency . . .[100]

However, it was as individuals that opponents of the drink trade were most likely to engage in surveillance. There were

[98] Ibid., 8 February 1913; J. W. England, 'The Merthyr of the twentieth century: a postscript', in Glanmor Williams (ed.), *Merthyr Politics: The Making of a Working-Class Tradition* (Cardiff, 1966), p. 83.
[99] The seven pubs in Merthyr were visited by 264 persons, while the Swansea pubs attracted some 329. Extrapolating from these figures, the author calculated that for all England and Wales some five million individuals spent some of their Sunday evening in a public house. See John Coke Fowler, 'The Sunday Closing Act for Wales', *The Red Dragon*, I (1882), 49–56, 53.
[100] *ME*, 21 March 1891.

more than enough willing to answer the *Merthyr Express*'s call on those 'honest to the cause of temperance' to help the police in eradicating the shebeens in Dowlais and elsewhere.[101] Numerous letters were sent to the local newspapers detailing abuses of the Welsh Sunday Closing Act. As a result, those willing to flout the law had to avoid not only the gaze of a limited number of police officers, but also the attention of a potentially large number of ordinary citizens keen on making visible all irregularities. One self-styled 'Eye Witness' made this very point when s/he asked readers the question, 'What are the fifteen police doing at Dowlais?' The vigilant observer supplied them with information on some of the *cwrw bachs* (illicit drinking places) that were 'trading to a great extent' in Cross Street, Upper and Lower Erin's Row, Lower Union Street and Castle Street.[102] 'Abstainer' shared intelligence on offending pubs in Penydarren gleaned whilst walking to evening service on a Sunday evening.[103] And in April 1890 'Pro Bono Publico' offered the Dowlais police some help in the form of information regarding the forthcoming pay day. The concerned letter-writer predicted that a number of 'topers' would be looking to take advantage of the traveller's clause in the Act and suggested that police officers pay close attention to the pubs on the road between Dowlais and Rhymney on the Sunday.[104] Another correspondent alerted the police to the scenes that occurred on Sundays in the Ynysgau area of Merthyr. On the road leading from lower Castle Street to the iron bridge, prostitutes could be seen plying their trade, as well as 'a number of intoxicated men staggering from one den to another'.[105]

Letters such as these alert us to the presence of a number of town dwellers willing to play an active part in the surveillance of urban space. They also point to the importance of the local newspaper in such surveillance. By the later years of the nineteenth century, the paper had become an efficient means of extending the civilized gaze over the urban landscape. This was in part the result of its rise to a dominant position in the print culture of Britain. The repeal of many of the various newspaper

[101] Ibid., 13 June 1885.
[102] Ibid., 10 December 1892.
[103] Ibid., 25 July 1885.
[104] Ibid., 5 April 1890.
[105] Ibid., 23 May 1885.

taxes and duties, together with the presence of a sizeable and
growing reading public, combined to have a massive impact
on the newspaper industry. The number of daily papers in
circulation trebled in the five years between 1855 and 1860,
and then doubled in the following decade. In 1855 alone, some
seventeen new provincial papers appeared, although it was the
twenty years leading up to 1890 that saw the real transformation of the provincial press.[106] Certainly, by the 1890s every
self-respecting town possessed its own local paper; many could
boast two, three or even more. At the same time, local newspapers became increasingly *local* in focus. Whereas it had been
common for papers in the mid-Victorian years to fill their pages
with syndicated news dealing with international and metro-
politan affairs, editors were becoming more proficient in the
gathering of local news. Amateur enthusiasts joined forces with
that new species of professional journalist, the local reporter, to
reshape the content of the provincial paper.[107] Articles detailing the latest political machinations at Westminster, or the
vagaries of the international markets, could still be found, but
they were ever more likely to be swamped by 'local intelligence'
columns and editorials that were as often concerned with happenings in the town hall as they were with affairs in the House
of Commons. Meanwhile, details of cases heard in the local
police courts – for long a staple ingredient of the local paper –
were still included, while correspondence columns became an
important site in which town dwellers could voice their
opinions on a diverse range of local matters. As a consequence
of these twin developments – the expansion of the provincial
press and its increasingly local focus – the local newspaper took
on the characteristics of both a piece of surveillance technology
and a shaming machine.[108]

The arrival of the truly local paper presented citizens concerned about misbehaviour in the public spaces of the town with
a medium through which they could produce and circulate

[106] For more on the growth of the press, see Raymond Williams, *The Long Revolution*
(Harmondsworth, 1965), pp. 195–236.
[107] For a discussion of the professionalization of journalism, see Aled Jones, *Press,
Politics and Society: A History of Journalism in Wales* (Cardiff, 1993), especially pp. 40–55.
[108] See John Garrard, *Leadership and Power in Victorian Industrial Towns, 1830–80*
(Manchester, 1983), pp. 26–7, for more on the intimate relationship between the local
newspaper and the Victorian town.

local knowledge. They could publicize any incidents of street disorder which had come to their attention, most notably in the correspondence columns. In these columns disgruntled inhabitants frequently informed the police of dangerous spaces that needed to be made safe. A few examples of letters written by observant Merthyrians will suffice. In 1892, 'Pro Bono Publico' pointed out the 'rowdy district' of Bethesda Street, where, between the hours of eleven and twelve o'clock 'almost nightly', 'respectable people are molested by women and men in a most objectionable way'.[109] Likewise, 'A Taxpayer' complained: 'It was not safe for respectable females to walk down the High Street between 8 and 10 o'clock. Only last Sunday week a lady was knocked down and considerably injured by two or three ruffians running up against her.' The letter ended with a common question, where were the police?[110] In November 1901, 'An Old Resident' asked, 'Where are the Plymouth Road police?' and continued to describe the antics of 'half-drunken men' and street gamblers.[111] And, in the same issue of the *Express*, 'Citizen' voiced disgust at the street betting that was occurring in Merthyr High Street. Bookmakers could be seen 'openly taking bets'. 'Is it possible that the police are innocent of these practices; and if it be so, may I hope that they will take this hint?'[112] 'Penydarren Ratepayer' similarly urged the police to be more vigilant in 1895. Superintendent Thorney

> should occasionally see that the pavements of the district are kept so that they may be used for the purpose that they were made for, and not monopolised by gangs of impudent rowdies, who hustle ladies who have occasion to be out in the evening. The High Streets of Merthyr, Dowlais and Penydarren are really impassable after the shops have been closed.[113]

Through their correspondence columns, the late nineteenth-century local newspapers augmented existing networks of communication and made them more efficient and far-reaching. Information about individual transgressors – as well as institutions such as badly run public houses or illicit drink shops –

[109] *MDT*, 26 August 1892.
[110] *ME*, 12 March 1892.
[111] Ibid., 23 November 1901.
[112] Ibid., 23 November 1901.
[113] Ibid., 5 October 1895.

could now be circulated more widely throughout the urban settlement.[114] One was being watched not only by friends and family, nor even only by those whom one passed in the streets; now a whole reading 'public' were potential surveillance agents, ready to inform their fellow citizens of misdemeanours and offer instruction regarding more appropriate modes of public behaviour. All urbanites, rich and poor, found themselves caught in this anonymous, 'faceless gaze', never sure exactly when they were being observed, nor by whom. A situation obtained, as described by Foucault, in which surveillance tends to become 'permanent in its effects, even if it is discontinuous in its action'.[115] Individuals were encouraged to regulate their own behaviour for fear of having any transgressions publicized; control of the 'self' was essential.

The practice of using pseudonyms when corresponding with the editor not only served to protect the identity of the informants, but also positioned them on the right side of the line that separated the civilized from the uncivilized, the respectable from the rough. Particular visions of the social order – sometimes complementary, sometimes contradictory – were constructed. As illustrated above, correspondents frequently appeared as 'citizens', 'old residents' or 'ratepayers', all writing 'pro bono publico' or, more specifically, for the good of their own public, however that was defined. Certainly the gaze of power, as refracted through the lens of the local paper, could have a number of different characteristics. For instance, as the *nom de plume* 'ratepayer' suggests, it could be put together in such a way as to underline class distinctions. Often workingclass youths were being watched, and their activities noted and reported to the police, by urbanites who chose to emphasize their own credentials as citizens of some standing, who were paying for the services of the local police and expected them to respond to their concerns. There can be little doubt that while middle-class inhabitants could, and did, fall foul of the by-laws forbidding the blocking of pavements, it was the town's

---

[114] 'Gossip' was one well-established way of administering shame, and Melanie Tebbutt has remarked upon the 'surveillance aspect of gossip'. See her *Women's Talk? A Social History of 'Gossip' in Working-Class Neighbourhoods, 1880–1960* (Aldershot, 1995), pp. 76–86, 120.
[115] Foucault, *Discipline and Punish*, p. 201.

working-class population who suffered most from the drive to clear the streets, simply because of the importance of the street as a site of working-class sociability and pastimes.[116] Practitioners of 'pitch and toss' ran the risk of being moved on or arrested if they made the mistake of taking the game into the thoroughfares, as did juvenile street footballers.[117] Men who gathered at street corners or on bridges for a smoke and a chat with friends were liable to be branded as 'loungers' by the shapers of respectable opinion, and heavily fined by magistrates who felt the need to educate the townsfolk in more civilized ways; for, as one member of the local bench put it in 1881, 'people must be taught that the pavements were not intended for a lot of young men to lounge and stand about upon'.[118] Time after time, those 'young men' were drawn from the ranks of the working class.[119]

Yet, the gaze of power was never merely a manifestation of class power. For example, it was also heavily gendered. Letters were usually written in such a way as to suggest that they were constructed from a male point of view. Correspondents discoursing about the antics of drunks or street gangs would often imply that they were writing to protect the interests of 'respectable ladies' rather than merely acting on their own behalf. Nevertheless, the anonymity of the authors meant that in theory women as well as men were given the opportunity to take part in the surveillance of public space; the gaze could be a female, as well as a male, one. There can be little doubt, however, that by simply being out in public, women were often subjected to the disciplinary gaze in ways that men were not. Take, for example, a letter sent to the *Aberdare Times* in 1885:

> Some young ladies (at any rate who wish to be considered so) are very fond of resorting to the corner of one of our squares, at the lower end of

---

[116] For examples of shopkeepers and traders being charged with obstruction, see, for example, *Aberdare Times* (*AT*), 8 October 1881, 29 October 1881.

[117] *MTl*, 23 January 1874.

[118] See the comments in the *Cardiff and Merthyr Guardian* which accompanied the news that renovations to the Morlais Bridge had transformed it from a 'lounging place' to one in which it was impossible for 'the philosophers of Pontmorlais' to sit comfortably and converse (*CMG*, 29 May 1852); *AT*, 17 September 1881.

[119] Not surprisingly, the 'class' dimension to the gaze of power was not lost on working-class inhabitants. See Andy Croll, 'Street disorder, surveillance and shame: regulating behaviour in the public spaces of the late Victorian British town', *Social History*, 24, no. 3 (October 1999), 250–68, 262.

one of our streets named after an ecclesiastical dignitary, for the purpose of gossiping and passing remarks upon any young man who may happen to go by. Such conduct to say the least is very unseemly. It would also be more to their credit were they to envelop their upper extremity with some suitable headgear. I hope this hint will be accepted favourably and acted upon.[120]

While it cannot be said with certainty that this letter was penned by a male writer, there is no doubt who the intended targets of this piece of withering observation were. And there is evidence to suggest that some late Victorian women were all too aware of their status as objects of the gaze of power. One Aberdarian who signed herself 'Alice' wrote to the local paper complaining about a report that had appeared in the 'Jottings by the way' column a few days earlier. In that report, readers had been told how a young woman had been spotted waiting in the streets for her sweetheart. Because he was late, she had gone off with another man who happened to be passing. 'Alice' informed the editor that she was the woman in question and that the facts of the situation had been inaccurately presented. 'I was merely standing for a few minutes at the corner – which it seems can't be done now-a-days, without provoking remarks from such as your correspondent.' Apparently conceding that some urbanites deserved such attention, 'Alice' concluded by urging that more discrimination be used when publicizing an individual's behaviour. 'Things have surely come hard to pass if *everybody*'s conduct is going to be remarked upon.'[121]

This letter demonstrates the discomfort that could follow from having one's activities publicized in the pages of the local paper. How much worse the experience could be for those whose names and addresses appeared in reports covering proceedings in the local police courts can be gauged by an announcement made by the editor of the *Merthyr Express* in February 1899. He went to the trouble of explaining to readers that details of all cases were published, and that his reporters were not open to bribes. This pronouncement was necessary because

There seems to be a quite settled belief in this district that newspapers have a scale of fees that can be paid by delinquents who dislike the

---

[120] *AT*, 6 June 1885.
[121] Ibid., 30 May 1885 (emphasis added).

publicity of our police court reports . . . There is a preposterous notion
abroad that 1s. is the figure at which a common or garden drunk case can
be 'kept out', and the sum rises in proportion to the seriousness of the
offence or the quality of the offender's conscience. Times out of number a
defendant has gone round to the press box at the Merthyr Police Court
and laid a shilling on the desk with the same effrontery that he has
planked down the fine, and with a knowing wink to the occupants, as
much as to say 'that's all right' . . . Another class still more modest to
approach us openly, send this style of missive to our weary scribes on the
morning of the court.

DEAR SIR – i rite to arsk if you will keep out my case today – drunk and
disorderly at Troedyrhiw. i am told the fee is a shilling, so enclose twelve
stamps.[122]

We need to exercise some caution at this point. Notwithstanding the indignant tone adopted in this editorial, there is
reason to doubt the implication that the newspapers were
completely impartial in their treatment of offenders. Not
enough is known about the criteria for composing the reports of
proceedings in the local police courts, but it is clear that editors
could choose which offenders to include, as well as the manner
in which they, and their misdemeanours, were to be represented. Certainly, newspapers lavished more attention upon
some of Merthyr's drinking class than on others. Thus, habitual
drunks could find themselves transformed into household
names. Bridget Dacey was one such, courtesy of her large
number of convictions – seventy-two by December 1897.[123]
Another was Redmond Coleman, pugilist, notorious drinker
and general thug. Every time he reoffended, editors ensured
that their readers were reminded of his previous record. By
November 1898 he had chalked up his forty-fourth appearance
in court.[124] In April 1903, on being charged with living off the
proceeds of prostitution, the *Merthyr Express* précised the life
story of 'the terror of the Iron Bridge'. He had been sleeping
out for much of the last two years, and had earned some
money through boxing. For the previous four years he had been
unable to get a steady job, claiming that the Cyfarthfa Iron

[122] *ME*, 25 February 1899.
[123] Ibid., 18 December 1897.
[124] Ibid., 19 November 1898.

Works would not employ him after he had assaulted a policeman. He had committed approximately fifty offences by this
date.[125] By August 1905 this figure had risen to eighty-six.[126]

Most offenders were not accorded the column-inches that
were devoted to the likes of Dacey and Coleman. Nevertheless,
for those who were unfortunate enough to find even the bar-
est details of their transgressions discussed in the papers, there
was clearly the potential for much embarrassment. And life was
made even more difficult for them in 1903 with the introduction
of another piece of civilizing technology, the blacklist. In the
wake of a new licensing act, habitual drunkards could be placed
on a blacklist and banned from public houses for a period of
three years. Their names, as well as photographs of the condemned drinkers, were then circulated to all local publicans.[127]
In addition, a new offence – that of supplying a blacklister with
alcohol – was introduced as a means of encouraging publicans
to remain vigilant. The ranks of the observers had once again
been augmented.

VI. 'REVOLTS AGAINST THE GAZE':[128]
EVADING, INVERTING AND BREAKING
THE GAZE OF CIVILIZATION

Thus far the analysis has drawn freely upon many of the insights
contained in the work of Foucault and 'neo-Foucauldians' such
as Nikolas Rose. While Foucault spent most of his time in
Discipline and Punish considering the workings of the diabolical
'panoptic machine', and very little on how the targets of this
all-seeing system of power could resist it, he did at least recognize that resistance was a possibility.[129] Certainly any serious
attempt to write the history of the surveillance of public urban
space needs to consider the various strategies employed by
urbanites intent upon escaping the disciplinary power of the
civilized gaze.

[125] Ibid., 11 April 1903.
[126] Ibid., 19 August 1905.
[127] For an example of a photograph of a 'blacklister', see Andy Croll, ' "Naming and
shaming" in late Victorian and Edwardian Britain', *History Today*, 47, no. 5 (May
1997), 3–6, 3.
[128] The phrase 'revolts against the observing gaze of power' is used by Michel
Foucault. See Sylvère Lotringer (ed.), *Foucault Live* (New York, 1989), p. 238.
[129] Ibid., pp. 239–40.

One tactic was to shroud public space in darkness. For example, the introduction of street lights (yet another piece of technology with the potential to civilize) could be followed quickly by an outbreak of lamp-smashing. The response of the Merthyr authorities was always swift. Within a month of the introduction of gas lamps in the town, news broke that a stone had been sent through a lamp opposite St David's Church. Immediately the surveyor responded by offering a reward of £1 for the discovery of what the local paper termed 'the evil-doer'.[130] In this case, the transgressor turned out to be a young boy who broke the lamp apparently 'by accident'.[131] Nevertheless, other incidents of lamp-smashing occurred during the first year,[132] and by 1893 the manager of the local gasworks could write to the Local Board of Health informing members that during the previous seven years some £40 had been paid out in rewards for information that had led to convictions for this crime.[133] Of course, such incidents could be seen as acts of simple vandalism. Yet it is worth pondering the possibility that in some cases at least they represented conscious attempts to 'erect a wall of darkness'.[134]

A more common strategy, and one that could be highly effective, was to invert the gaze altogether. By such means, the watchers became the watched. The deployment of networks of spies to look out for the police and other unwanted observers seems to have been a favourite tactic of those who wished to subvert the Welsh Sunday Closing Act. Shortly after the introduction of the Act, an efficient system had been established to protect the patrons of certain drinking places in Dowlais. In 1884 the *Merthyr Express* directed readers' attention to the manner in which 'the culprits are always on the watch for the police, and their approach is notified in an astonishingly quick space of time'.[135] One inhabitant of Troedyrhiw explained the mechanics of the 'spy system' in 1890. 'They have their sentries

---

[130] *CMG*, 10 January 1852.
[131] Ibid., 17 January 1852.
[132] See, for example, ibid., 23 October 1852.
[133] *MDT*, 6 January 1893.
[134] The phrase is Wolfgang Schivelbusch's. See his *Disenchanted Night: The Industrialisation of Light in the Nineteenth Century* (Oxford, 1988), p. 106. For his discussion of lantern-smashing in France in the early and mid-nineteenth century, see pp. 97–106.
[135] *ME*, 22 November 1884.

on guard, and when opportunity arrives the signal is given by so
many raps or a whistle; then the back door is opened and in go
two or three, and the door is immediately shut and bolted. If a
noise comes to the door and gives an unfamiliar sign the inmates
are seen scampering in all directions like a lot of frightened
rats.'[136] A year earlier, when a local Catholic priest, the Revd
Wade, tried to collect information on pubs evading the Act on
Brecon Road – again situated in the 'back part of the town' –
he was unable to get past the look-outs.

> At the corner of the streets there are always scouts, and immediately a
> policeman puts in an appearance it is at once telegraphed down to the
> keepers of the public houses, especially the lower class public houses,
> who derived I may say much benefit from the passing of the Act,
> because all these houses of which I was speaking, as I was told by men
> and others who knew them well, practically did not serve anything
> during the week, and on Sundays were selling three or four barrels.[137]

Meanwhile, in Caedraw, another working-class district of
Merthyr, there were reports that in one particular spot it was
'not uncommon to see . . . from twenty to thirty men and
women lounging about, waiting their turn to be served, while
someone acts as sentinel'.[138]

This inversion of the gaze was practised on both police and
non-police observers alike. In 1889 one enthusiastic member of
the temperance organization, the Good Templars, single-
handedly embarked upon a surveillance project of Merthyr's
public houses as a means of collecting information on publicans
who were contravening the Act. In so doing, he became the
victim of the 'uncivilized' gaze. Becoming a well-known figure
amongst publicans and their patrons, one Sunday afternoon he
found himself 'surrounded by a large number of men in the
vicinity of the High Street, who would have dealt cruelly and
unmercifully with him had he not providently escaped to the
police station'. After leaving the station, 'the unseemly conduct
was continued . . . and he had to escape around some back
premises to arrive home in safety. Even then he was pursued,
and *carefully watched* by a gang of men at the approaches to his

[136] Ibid., 3 May 1890.
[137] *SC Report*, Q. 4210.
[138] *ME*, 29 September 1883.

house.'[139] In like fashion, in 1903, Isaac Walters, a street organ player, was suspected by two Merthyrian women, Mary Cahill and Jane Davies, of being a police informer. They did their best to impair his powers of vision. On spotting him in the Ynysgau area of the town, 'Mary Cahill shouted, "Here's the spy for the blacklisters," and struck him in the eye, breaking the gause [*sic*] of his glasses, and the other woman pushed him'.[140]

Similarly, the effectiveness of the newspaper and the blacklister's photograph could be severely limited. For instance, the values that readers brought to the papers could have the effect of diluting the civilizing messages contained in them. A number of historians have commented upon the popularity of literature dealing with the seedier side of life in Victorian Britain.[141] That there was a class of Merthyrians who were captivated by police court proceedings is revealed by a story recounted in the *Merthyr Times* in 1893. A man 'who disported a stand-up collar of snowy whiteness, with cuffs to match, and appeared to be altogether faultlessly dressed', walked into a newsagent's in Dowlais asking for a copy of the *Express*. When informed that it was sold out, he inquired of the shopkeeper:

> 'Do the *Times* give an account of the trials at Merthyr?' . . . 'Yes,' was the reply, 'all the trials are reported except the dirty ones.' 'Have it got anything about the gel swearing the child on Wednesday?' 'No.' 'Then 'tis no good for me; 'twas only for that did I want the *Express*.'

With that, he walked out of the shop. The editor could not help berating such individuals:

> We have nothing but the strongest loathing for a thing, calling itself a man, who openly declares that he buys a paper only to read the revolting details of filthy crimes – that he expends his penny only to gloat over woman's shame and man's abuse of trusting confidence.[142]

It seems that the truly 'civilized' reader was supposed to be shocked by such 'filthy crimes', not titillated.

[139] Ibid., 8 June 1889 (emphasis added).
[140] Ibid., 29 August 1903.
[141] See, for instance, David Vincent, *Literacy and Popular Culture: England, 1750–1914* (Cambridge, 1989), pp. 196–227; Patricia Anderson, *The Printed Image and the Transformation of Popular Culture 1790–1860* (Oxford, 1991), pp. 98–110; J. Springhall, '"A life story for the people?" Edwin J. Brett and the London "low-life" penny dreadfuls of the 1860s', *Victorian Studies*, 33, no. 2 (1990), 223–46.
[142] *MT*, 10 February 1893.

If the world-view of the audience could interfere with the disciplinary intent of the civilized gaze, then so too could the attitudes of the transgressors. For all those urbanites who had been shamed as a result of unwanted publicity, there were others who enjoyed the notoriety. Blacklisters were particularly immune to the civilizing power of the public gaze. They were often alcoholics who were without many of the inhibitions that restrained more sober citizens; as a consequence, they frequently displayed their contempt for any effort on the part of respectable society to reform them. Nora Booth, making her fifty-sixth court appearance in Merthyr police court, responded in a feisty fashion to the threat that she would be placed on the blacklist. ' "That's no good," ' she informed the magistrate, ' "Blacklisters get drunk more than anybody else, and if you put me on the list, the others will sneak beer out for me." ' After this declaration, she and her half-dozen female companions in crime were all sent to prison. As they were taken down the High Street, 'the women danced and shouted so noisily that a crowd collected, and on the way down the . . . street the prisoners lustily sang "Fall in and Follow me." '[143] There were some, it appeared, who were beyond shame.

As the activities of Nora Booth and her fellow blacklisters demonstrate, there were real limitations to the effectiveness of both surveillance and shaming as techniques for regulating behaviour in public urban spaces. In the case of the former, the point of view from which the gaze was constituted was all-important. Certainly, the Good Templar whose house was watched by disgruntled drinkers was left in no doubt about the power of surveillance. And whilst the newspaper with its correspondence columns can be seen to have possessed both a surveillance and a shaming function, we should note that its disciplinary magic extended only as far as the reading public itself. Those urbanites who either chose not to, or could not, read the paper were insulated from its shaming power to a large degree. Even more significant perhaps were individuals who were to all intents and purposes without shame. Fortified by the effects of alcohol, the habitual drunks appear to have been one group of town dwellers who experienced public urban spaces more as sites of freedom than as spaces of regulation.

[143] *ME*, 14 October 1911.

VII. CONCLUSION

In 1896, 'Joe Hammersmith', gossip columnist for the *Merthyr and Dowlais Times*, drew his readers' attention to a spatial practice which he felt to be an affront to civilization. On Mondays and Thursdays groups of prisoners destined for Swansea Gaol were marched through the main streets on their way from Merthyr police station to the railway station. More often than not, the unfortunates were accompanied by 'a crowd of sightseers'. In Hammersmith's opinion this procedure was wholly unsatisfactory. 'To subject the prisoners to such indignity cannot be right. The judgements passed upon them are in themselves sufficient punishment, without making them the objects of general public curiosity in the open thoroughfares.' He continued:

> The prisoners, it may be argued, are not worthy objects of sympathy. They must abide by the consequences of their acts, and suffer public shame as well as the penalties of incarceration. I do not agree with that view, and maintain that even criminals should be treated in a humane manner. But even granting the contention, there are the public themselves to be considered. If you have seen the crowd of riff-raffs that follow the prisoners, and surround them on the railway platform, you would readily admit, I think, that such a thing should not be permitted. It cannot possibly do any good, and may work a great deal of harm.[144]

Hammersmith was, of course, not alone in feeling uneasy about the role of publicity in the punishment of offenders. Earlier in the century similar impulses had led to the abolition of public executions, a point that he went on to make to his readers. But, as we have seen, the administration of shame still had an important part to play in the disciplining of many miscreants. The late Victorian local newspaper, replete with its correspondence columns, editorials and detailed reports from the police court, had become a shaming machine which appears to have embarrassed at least some of the Merthyrians who found themselves up before the Bench. Nevertheless, Hammersmith's worries about the lack of humanity shown to convicted criminals alert us to a profound change in the focus of disciplinary publicity. For, by the later years of the nineteenth century, it

[144] *MDT*, 9 January 1896.

was hoped that the fear of falling under the judgemental gaze of 'the public' (however it was defined) would deter potential offenders rather than heap further punishment upon the heads of the convicted. Publicity and shame had become significant elements in the regulation of 'the self'.

We have explored these themes through a consideration of some of the attempts to regulate behaviour in the public spaces of Merthyr. These spaces were particularly important to all defenders of 'civility' and 'civilization'. They were sites of freedom, sites which spoke eloquently about the civilized – or otherwise – nature of a settlement and its inhabitants. Because of the sensitivities which had accrued to them, these free spaces were heavily regulated, and it is at this point that the argument put forward here has departed somewhat from an older historiographical orthodoxy. That orthodoxy, generated by historians of crime and of popular culture, tended to invoke the concept of 'social control'. Hence, the efforts of the police to bring order to the streets have often been taken to be mani-festations of a 'class' project to civilize the urban. While accepting that there is much that is of value in such an analysis, it has been suggested that such complex social processes should not merely be interpreted as evidence of class power in opera-tion. By pondering the role of surveillance in the regulation of public behaviour, and by noting how the citizenry itself took part in the supervision of urban spaces, other understandings emerge. The gaze of power could certainly be a 'bourgeois' one, but it was always more than that. Thus, it could be simultan-eously a 'male' gaze, a 'female' gaze, a 'temperance' gaze, and even a 'working-class' gaze. All urbanites could be constituted as subjects and objects of the 'observing gaze of power'. This is of significance, not least because it meant that the police themselves were also under surveillance. Their activities, and absences, were as likely to be commented upon as those of any other group of town dwellers, as revealed by the frequency with which the familiar question 'Where are the police?' was asked.

Finally, it needs to be emphasized that the civilizing gaze was at its strongest when targeted at those who most believed in its values. Certainly, the local newspaper's ability to apply shame was severely curtailed when dealing with those who stood outside the values of respectable society. If this was power enacted along purely 'class' lines, it seems that it was extremely effective at disciplining bourgeois respectables, whilst being peculiarly ill-equipped to deal with the misbehaviour of the lumpenproletariat. A life lived in an alcoholic haze was one that could remain untouched by many of the social 'norms' that Foucault suggests we all internalize. At any rate, as long as Redmond Coleman, Norah Booth, Bridget Dacey and their drunken companions continued to enjoy the freedom of Merthyr's public spaces in their own distinctive fashion, the civic projectors were provided with disturbing reminders that 'civilization' needed all the time to be maintained, defended and policed. In their more gloomy moments they may be forgiven for thinking that they were engaged in a hopeless venture. Yet just as respectable, sober pedestrians never had it all their own way, neither did the inebriates who, all too regularly, brought about the 'disgrace' of Merthyr. Other equally noisy, if altogether more welcome, groups of urbanites collected in the public spaces of the town, writing their own meanings into 'Merthyr' as they did so. It is to these more virtuous citizens that we must now turn.

IV

CONDUCTING SOCIAL RELATIONS:
THE CIVIC DISCOURSE, CROWDS AND
POPULAR MUSIC

Merthyr is a town so void of aesthetic graces of any kind, that it is a matter of profound surprise that so many men of artistic capacity should have emanated from it. It seems as though nature had made an effort to convince the world that she at least is not responsible for the almost repulsive outward aspect of the place . . .

'J.H.', 1882[1]

That music refines man is incontestable. Where no melodies are heard cruelty characterizes the people. Brutality grows in inverse ratio to musical feeling, for music is as natural to gentle natures as perfume is to violets. Is this gentleness the cause, or the effect of the art? Both, I think. If my conclusion is just, music, then, may be made a potent factor in civilization, because the tenderest feelings of man, cultured or uncultured, can be awakened by it. But this result may be obtained more easily when the heart alone is enlisted because the more exercised are our analytical faculties, the less agitated become our emotions.

British Musician, 1893[2]

The language of crowd description enabled observers effectively to use the same people for different ends. Those in power, and those who reported crowd events, wished to be able on occasion to claim thousands of the town's population for their cause, and, at another time, to be able to damn the masses for their incorrigibility, contrariness and autonomy. Language enabled them to square this circle, since it made possible the creation of groupings and sub-classifications, the separation of difficult subjects and the invention of scapegoats, all at the commentator's convenience.

Mark Harrison, 1988[3]

[1] 'Reminiscences of Merthyr Tydvil', *The Red Dragon*, 2 (August–December 1882), 337–43, 342.
[2] *British Musician*, 6, no. 65 (February 1893), 41–2.
[3] *Crowds and History: Mass Phenomenon in English Towns, 1790–1835* (Cambridge, 1988), p. 191.

Charter Day, 10 July 1905, saw the gathering of large crowds at various locations in the Merthyr district. The streets of Merthyr town 'were nicely decorated, shields and flags being attached to the standards of the Merthyr Electric Traction Company and to Venetian masts'. The town hall, according to the *Western Mail*, presented 'a particularly affective picture', bedecked as it was in bunting.[4] Most of the tradesmen closed their shops and the managers of local collieries and steelworks allowed their workers to leave early so that they might participate in the celebrations. Many availed themselves of this opportunity with the result that 'a huge concourse of many thousands of people' had assembled in front of the hall by the time the members of the incorporation committee and various public bodies took to the stage. Colonel D. Rees Lewis, that untiring proponent of civic improvement, led his detachment of the Volunteers, and, in co-operation with the local police force, was charged with the task of 'controlling the crowd'. But, in perfect keeping with the ethos of the day, all the crowds were highly civilized and united in their cheering and singing. Indeed, song featured prominently in this civic ritual, with a number of local musical societies involved at various points in the proceedings. After the charter of incorporation had been read, the Merthyr and Dowlais Philharmonic Society (under the leadership of the talented Harry Evans),[5] in concert with the Cyfarthfa Band, struck up the hymn, 'O God, our help in ages past'. Once a number of local notables had made speeches, there was a rendition of the old favourite, Handel's 'Hallelujah Chorus'. The ceremony was rounded off with the obligatory performance of the 'National Anthem', which was 'sung right lustily'. At this point the Cyfarthfa Band followed the Charter mayor and his acolytes on their journey around the borough in a charabanc so that the inhabitants of Merthyr Vale, Troedyrhiw and elsewhere could enjoy the benefits of their musical offerings.[6]

This coincidence of the 'civic', urban space, crowds and music had a long tradition in Merthyr. Of the numerous recreational crowds that wandered through the streets of the district

[4] *WM*, 11 July 1905.
[5] Harry Evans (1873–1914): after leading a number of Dowlais choral societies, in 1913 he became the resident choral conductor of the Liverpool Philharmonic Society. David Morgans, *Music and Musicians of Merthyr and District* (Merthyr, 1922), pp. 175–9.
[6] *WM*, 11 July 1905.

during the late Victorian and Edwardian periods, few were as easily harnessed to the civic project as those called into existence by musical events. In part this was because music was thought to be one of the most civilizing of all pastimes. It also stemmed from its remarkable popularity. The civic projectors made great play of music's ability to bring different social constituencies together and to unite them in harmony. The musical crowd was the embodiment of this harmony, and when it appeared in the pages of the local newspaper (the prime vehicle for the civic projectors' vision) it was invariably interpreted as symbolizing the whole community or town. Nevertheless, as we shall see, 'musical Merthyr' was, at best, an unstable construct that could be undermined from within. For the moment, however, we need to direct attention to the streets in order to ponder further the nature of the representations civilized society applied to the musical crowd.

I. Describing the Musical Crowd

The nineteenth-century crowd has exercised a powerful pull on historians. In the vanguard were the scholars Eric Hobsbawm, George Rudé and E. P. Thompson, all of whom largely focused upon the more riotous of gatherings.[7] In contrast, recent work has tended to concentrate on other types of crowds including those assembled in the shadow of the gallows, in front of the hustings, or at fairs and other places of amusement.[8] Contemporaries would have approved of this burgeoning historiography, for throughout the century urbanites paid close attention to crowd activity in their towns and cities. The reasons for their interest stem largely from the significance invested in public urban spaces; the 'freedom' inscribed in such spaces was never under greater threat than when boisterous gatherings of

[7] E. J. Hobsbawm and G. Rudé, *Captain Swing* (London, 1970); George Rudé, *The Crowd in History: A Study of Popular Disturbances in France and England, 1730–1848* (New York, 1964); E. P. Thompson, 'The moral economy of the English crowd in the eighteenth century', *Past and Present*, no. 50 (1971), 76–136. For an important later study of the riotous crowd, see David Smith, 'Tonypandy 1910: definitions of community', *Past and Present*, no. 87 (1980), 158–84.

[8] V. A. C. Gattrell, *The Hanging Tree: Execution and the English People, 1770–1868* (Oxford, 1994); Peter Linebaugh, *The London Hanged: Crime and Civil Society in the Eighteenth Century* (London, 1993); Harrison, *Crowds and History*.

rowdies moved around the built form. Contrariwise, collections of well-behaved citizens were taken as indications of the civilized nature of the population. Yet, as Mark Harrison has argued, while crowds may have been singular features of the urban landscape, they were always understood in multiple ways. One person's 'mob' may have been another's lively gathering of the common people.[9] In short, the crowd was a mirror within which different visions of the social order could be perceived, depending upon one's point of view.

Mid- and late Victorian Merthyrians needed little reminding of the potential power of the crowd; indeed, some may have been youthful participants in the rising of 1831. But, while the district was never to see such tumultuous crowd scenes again, there were still occasions when the riotous crowd declared its unwelcome presence. Political meetings and elections were some of the most common triggers for crowd disturbances throughout the period.[10] Election day, April 1880, sparked off riots in a number of settlements in the Merthyr parliamentary boroughs. In Mountain Ash a crowd moved through the main streets of the town smashing the windows of public houses owned by known or suspected supporters of the Conservative candidate, W. T. Lewis. Meanwhile, in Aberdare, the police enjoyed little success in dispersing the crowd. 'The mob was very turbulent, and when they cautioned some of the worst-behaved, and ordered them to desist from their riotous conduct, a volley of stones was in several instances directed at them, and some members of the police force were struck and hurt.' A few days later, the stipendiary magistrate declared that the crowd had been composed of 'wicked persons' and that he would not allow the police to be molested 'by a lot of ruffians'.[11] Later, in 1888, Ffoulkes Griffiths, the Liberal nominee, was accosted by a 'mob' of about 1,000 supporters of W. Pritchard Morgan, as he made his way home from a meeting in Cefn. Sand and stones were hurled, and 'he was violently hustled about and forced into a corner'.[12] Inhabitants of Dowlais were advised to remain indoors during the weekend leading up to the election because

[9] Harrison, *Crowds and History*, ch. 7.
[10] Donald Richter, 'The role of the mob-riot in Victorian elections, 1865–85', *Victorian Studies*, 15, no. 1 (1971), 19–28.
[11] *MTl*, 16 April 1880.
[12] *ME*, 20 October 1888.

of the threat of rowdyism.[13] Four years later, the right of Dowlaisians to enjoy the freedom of their public spaces was again
challenged, this time as a consequence of a major clash between
the police and a 'huge crowd of some thousands of people' that
gathered during a meeting held by local Conservatives. Frequent rushes were made at the police, and stones, mud, eggs and
flour were hurled at the officers. In addition, Edward and
Henry Martin, both involved in the management of the Dowlais
Iron Works, were attacked. According to the *Merthyr Express*,
the crowd was 'composed mainly by the riff-raff of the Dowlais
slums, reinforced by some of the same element from Merthyr'.[14]
Meanwhile, the *Merthyr and Dowlais Times* informed readers that
the 'horde of savages' was made up of 'reptiles', 'cut-throat
hirelings', 'rowdies' and 'ruffians'. Their very presence marked
a dark day indeed for Dowlais:

> [I]t is a disgrace to the humanity of the people of Dowlais that it did not
> revolt against the cowardly and dastardly doings of the unmanly herd.
> That less than a score of poor fellows, whose duty called them there,
> should be stoned and kicked by hundreds, if not thousands, of ruffians,
> suggests a queer commentary upon our so-called civilization.[15]

That respectable opinion was outraged by such scenes is, of
course, no surprise. Nor is it surprising that reporters saved
some of their most withering epithets to describe members
of the riotous crowd. A rich vocabulary of terms – including
'reptiles', 'ruffians', 'hobble-de-hoys' and 'vicious scum' – was
applied to such urbanites as a means of emphasizing their
distance from the rest of civilized humanity. By a careful use of
language these individuals were positioned both beyond the
pale of civilization and outside the 'imagined town'. But
language could not banish them from the geographical reality of
Dowlais. On the contrary, after the riots, these 'reptiles' and
'hobble-de-hoys' carried on their daily life amongst their fellow
citizens. Indeed, it is more than likely that, on occasion, they
found themselves in the ranks of an altogether different type of
gathering, the 'musical crowd'. When they did so, they were
understood in profoundly different ways.

---

[13] Ibid., 27 October 1888.
[14] Ibid., 25 June 1892.
[15] *MDT*, 1 July 1892.

For an example of the musical crowd in action we could do no better than to return to the streets of Dowlais, this time in the company of the Dowlais Harmonic Society (DHS), the premier choir in the district.[16] When the DHS returned to Merthyr after its first ever victory at a National Eisteddfod Choral Competition in Aberdare in August 1885, the singers encountered huge crowds, all united in celebration. 'In the streets [of Aberdare] a great crowd had assembled, and ringing cheers were called for and given again and again . . . At Abernant station there was a renewal of the demonstration, and several thousands of people were congregated here', all intent upon giving the competing choirs a fitting send-off.[17] These demonstrations, while notable enough, pale in comparison with the reception awaiting the Harmonic Society back in Dowlais. News of their success had reached the town courtesy of a telegraph message. This was the signal for a popular invasion of the public streets. Merthyr was the first port of call. The High Street had been blocked for over an hour with expectant supporters, waiting for a glimpse of the singers. '[W]hen at last they did arrive, there was an outburst of enthusiastic cheering, which was renewed again and again all the way up the principal street.'[18] The Dowlais Volunteer Band led the way, 'playing "See the conquering hero comes", an enormous crowd of people following until the streets became almost impassable'. Dan Davies, conductor of the choir and a remarkable figure in the musical world of south Wales, was carried by the crowd which by now had begun singing 'Auld Lang Syne'.[19] In upper Penydarren the singing was augmented by the crack of fireworks, discharged by ironmonger Mr John Thomas. As the choir and the crowd entered Dowlais they were again treated to a pyrotechnic display. Here the procession was swelled as enthusiastic supporters stood in their doorways waving handkerchiefs and cheering. Light poured onto the streets from shops which had been specially illuminated. On its march to Davies's house the procession made its way through the High

[16] Gareth Williams, *Valleys of Song: Music and Society in Wales, 1840–1914* (Cardiff, 1998), pp. 92–4.
[17] *ME*, 29 August 1885.
[18] Ibid., 29 August 1885, 5 September 1885.
[19] Dan Davies (1859–1930) was only twenty-five when he led the DHS to victory at Aberdare. Between 1882 and 1898 Davies and his choirs pocketed £3,185 in prize money. For more, see Morgans, *Music and Musicians*, pp. 155-8.

Street and Bethania Street, spirits undampened by the falling rain. With an eye upon the classical, the residents of Castle Street had hastily erected a number of 'triumphal arches' under which the jubilant crowd passed. The 'Conquering hero' was sung for a final time, and 'three lusty cheers' were raised as Davies entered his home.[20]

What is so striking about musical crowds such as these is the way that local newspapers invariably made them stand for the whole of society, rather than any specific subset. This is not to say that different individuals or groups within the social order went unrecognized in these descriptions. Some figures occasionally emerged, whether it be heroes of the moment like Dan Davies, or firework-discharging ironmongers. Similarly, mention was often made of the role played by the 'tradesmen', or the 'labouring classes' in the celebrations. However, individuals and groups were quickly subsumed back into the larger, homogeneous mass of singing and cheering citizens. All the time, the emphasis was on the socially inclusive nature of the gathering.

This theme can be illustrated further by considering a rather different type of musical crowd, that which gathered together for the funeral of a local musician. For just as music could seemingly unite a whole community in celebration, so could it in grief. Once again, when it came to representing these funereal assemblies, the newspapers – those tireless promulgators of notions of urban civilization – produced visions of the town's social order that evoked ideas of a truly harmonious community. The funeral of thirty-year-old Meta Scott in January 1892 is typical in this respect. The eldest daughter of a local grocer, Meta enjoyed a bright and brilliant, if abbreviated, musical career. After studying the piano and then the violin, she gained entrance into the Royal Academy of Music in 1884, where she received bronze and silver medals for her achievements. Elected as an associate in 1888, she returned to Merthyr and helped establish the Merthyr Orchestral Society.[21] The *Merthyr Express* noted that this highly respected musician had been 'an honour to her parents, her town, and her country . . . [a loss] shared by the whole community'.[22] At her

[20] *ME*, 5 September 1885.
[21] Morgans, *Music and Musicians*, p. 161; *Cardiff Times*, 23 January 1892.
[22] *ME*, 23 January 1892.

funeral, it was the social mix of the crowd which caught the eye of a local reporter:

> [T]he most affecting feature of the mournful event was the long line of sorrowful spectators, men in their working clothes, women with little children in their arms, not gathered together out of morbid curiosity, as their falling tears too well showed, but assembled to pay, in their humble way, their . . . respect to one who, during her brief but brilliant lifetime, had done what she could by gratuitous and willing service to ameliorate the condition of the class to which the large majority of the spectators belonged.

Notably, the working-class mourners were joined on the streets by their social superiors, all united in sorrow. Three ministers from different chapels headed a procession that was over a quarter of a mile in length, and included a number of 'leading townsmen' such as Mr W. Morgan, the high constable, and solicitor John Vaughan. Even denominational differences were overlooked as singers from various Nonconformist chapels came together to form a choir which sang excerpts from Handel's *Messiah* after the Cyfarthfa Brass Band's rendition of the 'Dead March'.[23]

II. MUSICAL MERTHYR: A SOCIAL BREAKDOWN

There can be little doubt that on one level such descriptions of the musical crowd moving around the streets can be interpreted as straightforward reflections of a social reality. Music, and especially choral music, appealed to a number of different social constituencies during this period.[24] Indeed, such was its popularity that many believed musical talent to be a feature of the Welsh national character. Whether in the pages of a learned journal, a book or a local newspaper, references were frequently made to the supposedly innate musical ability of the Welsh.

---

[23] Ibid., 30 January 1892. The *MDT* also emphasized that 'all grades of the community were represented' at the funeral (*MDT*, 29 January 1892).

[24] See Rhidian Griffiths, 'Musical life in the nineteenth century', in Prys Morgan (ed.), *Glamorgan County History, Vol. VI: Glamorgan Society, 1780–1980* (Cardiff, 1988), especially pp. 371–3; John H. Davies, 'Rhondda choral music in Victorian times', in K. S. Hopkins (ed.), *Rhondda: Past and Future* (Rhondda, 1975); Peter Stead, 'Amateurs and professionals in the cultures of Wales', in J. Beverley Smith and Geraint H. Jenkins (eds), *Politics and Society in Wales, 1840–1922: Essays in Honour of Ieuan Gwynedd Jones* (Cardiff, 1988); Williams, *Valleys of Song*.

Once again, all depended on the notion of social harmony. Thus, in 1896, Frederic Griffith, the solo flautist at the Royal Opera House, could argue that

> Music seems to come to her children as instinctively as speech. Singing is the natural gift of the Welsh man; it is his amusement, his consolation at all times. There is no village, however small, but has its choir or its male voice party; there is no gathering, whether of pleasure or sorrow, where singing, and mostly of a rare quality, is not heard.[25]

In similar vein, the editor of the *Western Mail* pondered the relationship between the Welsh and music in 1882:

> Wales claims to be, in an especial sense, a 'land of song'. The Welshman's ideal of social blessedness, if we may trust the ancient triad, is: 'A virtuous wife, his cushion in his chair, and his harp in tune.' . . . All over the Principality, in large towns and small, even in villages and hamlets, there are choral societies and singing classes that boldly attempt, with no small measure of success, to master the intricacies of the concerted music of Handel, and Haydn, Mozart and Mendelssohn.[26]

Both writers followed the same procedure when discussing the musicality of the Welsh; they deployed a discourse emptied of all but the vaguest terms of social description. When it came to understanding the Welsh love of music, the 'hamlet', the 'village' and the 'town' were the social units into which Wales was divided. More precise terminology was considered unnecessary. Of course alternative descriptors – such as 'the people' – were available for use. Thus, when Harry Evans, the talented conductor from Merthyr, sat down to write his contribution to *Wales: Today and Tomorrow*, his opening gambit comprised the simple observation that 'The love of "singing in parts" amongst the Welsh people is proverbial'.[27] In the same volume the teacher, composer and adjudicator, J. T. Rees, could liberally use the concept of the Welsh 'people' in his analysis of 'Music in the land of song'.[28] Whichever terms one chose, the powerful idea that a love of music resided in the nature of the Welsh themselves was frequently reinforced.

[25] Frederic Griffith (ed.), *Notable Welsh Musicians* (London, 1896), p. xi.
[26] *WM*, 13 March 1882.
[27] Harry Evans, 'Welsh choral singing', in T. E. Stephens (ed.), *Wales: Today and Tomorrow* (Cardiff, 1907), p. 323.
[28] J. T. Rees, 'Music in the land of song', in Stephens (ed.), *Wales*, pp. 326–30.

We do not need to fall for the myth of Welsh exceptionality in matters musical to acknowledge the sheer vibrancy of the musical culture of the region, particularly during the 1880s and 1890s, the golden age of Welsh choral music. Recent work by Gareth Williams has shown conclusively that communities throughout industrial south Wales supported a vast range of musical organizations; Merthyr was no different.[29] By the latter years of the century inhabitants of the district could look back over a long history of musical endeavour. Moreover, they could take pleasure in the knowledge that some of the most influential of south Wales's musicians had either been born in the Taff Valley or had made Merthyr their home.[30] And, given the emphasis that the civic projectors placed on the social harmony that sprang from such musical endeavour, it should be recognized that musical ventures were peculiarly successful at bringing together different groups within Merthyr society.

Take, for example, the position occupied by organized religion – and particularly Nonconformity – within this musical culture. As is well known, by the late Victorian years, members of the Free Churches often found themselves at odds with much that was unfolding in the realm of leisure.[31] While not all chapelgoers approved of the passionate manner in which some amongst their ranks embraced popular music, the fact remains that in choral music large numbers of Nonconformists found themselves participating enthusiastically in a leisure pursuit that stood at the centre of urban popular culture. Throughout most of the second half of the nineteenth century, many of Merthyr's numerous places of worship had been the venue for an impressive variety of musical events. Eisteddfodau were held in chapels from at least the 1850s,[32] while later the *cymanfa ganu* (or congregational singing festival) was developed as a means of encouraging musical excellence.[33] In this they had

[29] Williams, *Valleys of Song*, chs. 4 and 5.
[30] They were celebrated in the 1920s by David Morgans. See his *Music and Musicians*.
[31] For more on this see ch. 6.
[32] *Cardiff and Merthyr Guardian*, 1 January 1853.
[33] Although congregational singing festivals were held from the early 1860s onwards, it was not until the 1870s and 1880s that the *cymanfa ganu* proper appeared. Morgans, *Music and Musicians*, pp. 16–18. See also Rhidian Griffiths, 'Welsh chapel music: the making of a tradition', *Journal of Welsh Ecclesiastical History*, 6 (1989), 35–43, especially 41–3.

been extremely successful, and by the 1880s and 1890s the congregational choir had established itself as one of the most important of all choral organizations. From the pews of the chapels emerged talented individuals who were to cast long shadows over the cultural landscape. In Merthyr, much-loved figures, including Abraham Bowen, Rosser Beynon and Rees Prosser, had gained their musical education in such choirs and went on, in turn, to train the next generation of hopefuls.[34]

The experience of Prosser neatly illustrates both the vitality of this congregational musical tradition, and the willingness of musicians to place their art above denominational divisions. He had first become interested in choral music as a young lad after falling under the influence of the leader of the Merthyr Church Choir – known to his contemporaries as 'the Welsh Jew' (the first example of religious differences being overlooked). According to Prosser's daughter, 'This man had a great repu-tation as a reader of music, and being intensely partial to musical studies, my father joined the . . . Choir, remaining a Churchman throughout his life', notwithstanding his upbring-ing as a Methodist. He went on to lead the singing at the Welsh Church at Dowlais. During these years he became renowned as a fine teacher and ran classes that often numbered 'a couple of hundred at a time'. Faced with the practical problem of not having enough space in which to teach such large groups, the churchman once again displayed an unwillingness to be constrained by denominational considerations and obtained the use of the school room at Libanus chapel. From this more spacious environment graduated the likes of 'Caradog'[35] and

[34] Abraham Bowen (1817–92), shoesmith, butter merchant, then grocer. Leader of the Bethania Chapel choir, and a music teacher in Merthyr (Morgans, *Music and Musicians*, pp. 50–2; *MTl*, 26 January 1861); Rosser Beynon ('Asaph Glan Taf') (1811–76), an ironworker, became a notable musical commentator, composer and adjudicator (Morgans, *Music and Musicians*, pp. 38–49; *Dictionary of Welsh Biography* (London, 1959), p. 37).
[35] Griffith Rhys Jones ('Caradog'; 1834–97). A musician born in Trecynon, Aberdare, Jones was apprenticed to a smith in the local ironworks. At the age of nineteen he led his first choir in an eisteddfod, and went on to achieve much recog-nition as a conductor. He is best remembered for leading 'Y Côr Mawr' to victory at Crystal Palace in 1872 (*Dictionary of Welsh Biography*, p. 465). For more on Y Côr Mawr, see G. P. Ambrose, 'The Aberdare background to the South Wales Choral Union: Y Côr Mawr, 1853–1872', in S. Williams (ed.), *Glamorgan Historian*, vol. 9 (Barry, n.d.).

'Eos Morlais'.[36] Such towering musicians were followed by a whole host of lesser known, but equally committed, individuals, all of whom had cut their musical teeth in Prosser's congregational choirs.[37]

Just how profound organized religion's contribution was to the musical culture of south Wales becomes clear when one ponders the relationship between these congregational choirs and the large choral societies. It was so close that it may be unwise to distinguish between them; they shared personnel, conductors, sacred music and audiences. Ministers frequently addressed choral societies during rehearsals, wishing them luck in forthcoming competitions and reminding singers of the noble cause in which they were engaged.[38] The compliment was invariably returned with the choral societies turning to the chapels in search of vocal talent. Hence, when the committee of the DHS met to consider forming a choir to enter an eisteddfod in London in January 1887, the first move was to send a circular to the churches and chapels in the town 'in order to obtain their advice and co-operation in the formation of a very good choir worthy of the occasion and of the town'.[39] Within a week it was agreed that all potential members would have to satisfy an examination committee that included Dan Davies, William Edwards (Church of England), Dan Sweet (Wesleyan), William Hughes (Independent), John Davies (Baptist) and Father Bruno (Roman Catholic). It was hoped that the involvement of all the principal sects of the town would ensure that 'a thoroughly representative town choir' was established.[40] By March it was announced that not only had such a choir indeed been assembled, but that a new committee 'representative of the different religious denominations in the town' had been appointed.[41] Similarly, in 1891, 'a very strong committee,

---

[36] Robert Rees ('Eos Morlais' 1841/2? 92). Rees was born to parents who originally hailed from Machynlleth. His father was killed whilst working in a coal-mine in Dowlais when Robert was seven or eight, and his mother died shortly afterwards. He was working in the mines himself by the age of nine. A prodigious singer and a respected adjudicator, he was also an accomplished choir trainer, taking over control of David Rosser's Temperance Choir when Rosser resigned (Morgans, *Music and Musicians*, pp. 109–13).

[37] *WM*, 30 March 1911.

[38] *MDT*, 27 May 1892.

[39] *ME*, 8 January 1887.

[40] Ibid., 15 January 1887.

[41] Ibid., 5 March 1887.

representative of the various denominations in the town [i.e. Merthyr]' agreed to form a united choir which would compete in the National Eisteddfod.[42]

This desire to form choirs that were 'representative' extended beyond denominational considerations. Other social divides were also crossed, including those of class and gender. At a time when so much of popular culture in south Wales was structured along these lines, musical organizations stand out as remarkably 'open' institutions. In part, strictly musical concerns demanded that this be the case. As long as soprano and contralto parts were to be sung, women were guaranteed a place in the choral societies. Notwithstanding the paucity of evidence, we can be sure that at least well-to-do women availed themselves of the opportunity. When, for example, the Merthyr Philharmonic Society appeared at the Drill Hall in January 1892 to perform *Messiah*, amongst the sopranos were to be found Mrs Wills (wife of Vincent Andover Wills, chemist and dentist), Miss B. Hansard (daughter of mineral-water manufacturer, Henry Hansard), Miss A. Harrap (daughter of the brewer, Richard Harrap), and Miss N. Southey (daughter of Harry). The contraltos were similarly graced with female representatives from the families of solicitors, medical men, jewellers and publishers.[43]

When these bourgeois women took to the stage they did so in the company of working-class singers. Such was the popularity of choral music amongst the lower orders that it appears that some of the district's choirs were dominated by working-class singers. A working-men's Harmonic Society was formed in November 1891 in order 'to provide a resort where working men may hear some good songs, and be able to participate in providing an evening's enjoyment for themselves'.[44] And, according to the *Merthyr Express*, the 'majority' of the Merthyr and Orpheus Glee Society was 'composed of working men'.[45]

---

[42] Ibid., 7 February 1891. On occasion, denominational differences carved up Merthyr's musical culture. In the 1880s a temperance choir was established in which all members had to belong to the same denomination (ibid., 15 September 1883), and in 1888 an Anglican was expelled from the St David's choir because she had appeared at a Nonconformist concert (ibid., 7 April 1888).

[43] All this information can be found in *Kelly's Directory of South Wales and Monmouthshire* (London, 1895), pp. 507–17. Cf. Dave Russell's analysis of the chorus roll books of the Huddersfield Choral Society in his *Popular Music in England, 1840–1914: A Social History* (Manchester, 1987), pp. 200–10.

[44] *ME*, 7 November 1891.

[45] Ibid., 11 June 1887 and 25 June 1887.

A similar impression was conveyed by 'Taffy' in a letter to the *British Bandsman* in 1908. Thinking back to the days of 'Y Côr Mawr' (that is, the 1870s), the correspondent was struck by the humble social origins of the singers:

> [E]ven the girl members were working lasses from the 'tips' of Dowlais and elsewhere, and their conductor was a working blacksmith. Later, look at the choirs of Dowlais and Merthyr. Their conductor was then, as I believe he is now, a cattle merchant, and nearly all the choir conductors of Wales were drawn purely from the working classes.[46]

Apart from these general descriptions, it is only very occasionally – and usually in tragic circumstances – that we catch glimpses of the individual working-class singer. Thus we learn of David Davies, 'one of the most faithful members' of the Dowlais Harmonic Society who was killed whilst working in the lower ironworks.[47] In a like fashion, the name of John Harris, a young collier who 'was not particularly well known beyond the sphere in which he turned', came to the public's attention in April 1888 when he fell to his death from a train while travelling back from the Neath and Swansea eisteddfod with the Dowlais Philharmonic Society. The 'awful manner of his death' occasioned a funeral procession that was one of the largest that had been held in the town for some years.[48]

In contrast with the choral societies, brass bands were more exclusively 'working-class' in character, although, as the patronage of the Crawshay ironmasters demonstrated, an appreciation of brass band music could extend well beyond the ranks of the workers.[49] In 1885 observers of the musical scene reported an upswing of interest in instrumental music in Dowlais, with the town's labouring classes in the van: 'Among the workmen the love of instrumental music is spreading at . . . an alarming rate. The masons in the works have for some time been saving a part of their wages every week with a view of forming a brass band', while a drum and fife band – with an exclusively

---

[46] *British Bandsman*, 21, no. 307 (18 January 1908), 77.
[47] *ME*, 27 June 1885.
[48] Ibid., 7 April 1888, 14 April 1888.
[49] See J. O. Hume, 'A chat on amateur bands', *British Bandsman*, 12, no. 142 (1 July 1899), 185; Trevor Herbert, 'Introduction' and 'Nineteenth-century bands: the making of a movement', in Trevor Herbert (ed.), *Bands: The Brass Band Movement in the Nineteenth and Twentieth Centuries* (Buckingham, 1991), pp. 1, 22–3.

working-class personnel – had been established and was thriving.[50] Such humble social origins sometimes resulted in commentators adopting a dismissive attitude towards the whole movement. This was certainly the feeling among members of the South Wales and Monmouthshire Brass Band Association (SWMBBA). It had been established in April 1891 with the aim of producing 'not a body of well-trained parrots, but a body of intelligent musicians, capable of undertaking works of varied character and requiring varied treatment'.[51] From the outset it appears as if they had to contend with indifference and snobbery. As T. C. Edwards, a prime mover in the brass band movement in south Wales, put it in 1892,

> Some people seem to imagine that the music of a brass band must of necessity be barbarous, and the behaviour of its members ditto. I know not why this idea should prevail, but the fact remains that many people who have nothing but praise for the veriest parody of a 'military band', look with horror and disgust upon anything bearing the title of 'brass band'. But we have this past year shown them, and trust we shall continue to do so, that not only is a brass band capable of producing music 'which even the most highly-refined musician may enjoy, but also that although mainly recruited from the ranks of toil, we are capable of bearing ourselves as gentlemen should. But there is really nothing strange in this, for where is there a greater refiner and elevator of its devotees than the divine art of music?[52]

He was not alone in suggesting that music possessed the ability to civilize and uplift. Such beliefs had become a commonplace of Victorian social theory.[53] That the vibrant musical culture of south Wales brought so many different social groups together, apparently in harmony, was not lost on social reformers and those promoters of all things civic; that the working class was so prominent in such ennobling events as the eisteddfod was especially encouraging. During the Merthyr National Eisteddfod of 1881, the rector of Merthyr – the Revd John Griffiths – suggested (albeit misleadingly) that 'the Eisteddfod . . . is the product, the sole product of the working men. Workmen begin them, workmen compete in them, workmen uphold them,

[50] *ME*, 31 January 1885.

[51] *Orchestral Times and Bandsman*, 4, no. 43 (April 1891), 110–11.

[52] *MDT*, 5 February 1892. For more on the SWMBBA, see the *British Bandsman*, 12, no. 148 (1 August 1899), 245.

[53] See Russell, *Popular Music*, chs. 2 and 3.

and workmen patronize them.'[54] Similarly, Henry Richard, Merthyr's venerable MP, praised the workmen and their wives and children for attending the event in such large numbers.[55] Meanwhile J. Spencer Curwen, an adjudicator, went out of his way to express his delight at the scenes he witnessed during the great choral competition.[56]

> [T]he vast audience remained standing, packed with a dense pressure, suffering evidently the greatest physical discomfort; yet orderly, eager, electrical ... Here were the common people themselves, crowding to no brutal sport, not even to clap trap or flimsy entertainment, but to genuine art. It was a consummation for which social reformers in England sigh.[57]

III. 'To the Honour of Dear Old Merthyr': Composing the Musical Town

Given the widespread acceptance of the idea that music was an inherently civilizing cultural practice, it is little wonder that Merthyr's civic projectors were keen to ally themselves to a raft of musical ventures. Part of the duties of the 'public man' involved supporting, and being seen to support, musical organizations such as choirs and brass bands. There was no shortage of such figures in late Victorian Merthyr: solicitors, bank managers, newspaper editors, MPs and councillors, not to mention managers of the ironworks, all put much time, money and effort into encouraging musical activities.[58] In an older historiography, their willingness to involve themselves in musical ventures that contained working-class singers and musicians was interpreted as a clear manifestation of attempted 'social control'.[59] Certainly the patronage of local well-to-dos was not

[54] *ME*, 3 September 1881.
[55] Ibid. Henry Richard (1812–88), Liberal MP for Merthyr, and a staunch defender of Wales and Nonconformity.
[56] John Spencer Curwen, son of the originator of the tonic sol-fa sight-singing method, John Curwen.
[57] Anon., 'The eisteddfod and popular music in Wales', *Y Cymmrodor*, 5, pt. 2 (October 1882), 285–95, 286–7.
[58] For examples, see Andrew J. Croll, 'Civilizing the urban: popular culture, public space and urban meaning', Merthyr, *c.* 1980–1914, Ph.D. thesis, University of Wales (Cardiff), 1997, pp. 125–8.
[59] Dave Russell, for instance, has written that 'the majority of support for popular music was underpinned by an essentially conservative ideology'. See his 'Popular musical culture and popular politics in the Yorkshire textile districts, 1880–1914', in John K. Walton and James Walvin (eds), *Leisure in Britain, 1780–1939* (Manchester, 1983), p. 106.

always rooted in a disinterested love of music. In 1892, for instance, the *Merthyr and Dowlais Times* suspected the motives of W. Pritchard Morgan, MP, when he attended a meeting of the DHS. The paper, always hostile to Pritchard Morgan, accused him of 'ingratiating himself' with the choir. 'Even when he was congratulating the choir on their success he could not help dragging in his own miserable personality. "He hoped," he said, "that when he came before them on his own account they would give him an equally flattering reception."' The *Times* reminded him of the Corrupt Practices Act.[60]

Nevertheless, while there can be no doubt that the involvement of a town's social élite in musical matters could carry an ideological charge, we need to extend our argument beyond that which merely points out that middle-class commentators hoped that the behaviour and morals of the working class would be improved through musical endeavour. This is a well-worn theme in our histories, as is the fact that the working class could behave in ways which confounded civilized expectations.[61] More interesting from our point of view is the way in which the civic projectors attempted to weave musicality into definitions of Merthyr. By so doing, they were fashioning an image of the settlement that was consistent with notions of a civic Merthyr; any town that could be shown to be a musical settlement, was, necessarily, a civilized settlement. Through the local newspapers, understandings of Merthyr that defined the district in musical terms were frequently circulated. We have already noted how the papers chose to represent musical crowds in ways that emphasized their socially inclusive characteristics. In addition, the town's relationship with its musicians was dramatized through rituals, confirmed through the raising of funds to support them in their chosen careers, and constantly celebrated through the turning of musical Merthyrians into the property of the town. In short, 'musical Merthyr' was a town image that was composed, and re-composed, at any and every opportunity.

One of the easiest means of fusing town and music was simply to draw attention to a settlement's musical reputation. Take, for

---

[60] *MDT*, 10 June 1892.
[61] Andy Croll, 'From bar-stool to choir-stall: music and morality in late Victorian Merthyr', *Llafur*, 6, no. 1 (1992), 17–27.

example, the case of Dowlais, a distinct settlement within the Merthyr district. Musical prowess was seized upon and turned into a characteristic of the town and its inhabitants. The *Merthyr Express* was happy to describe Dowlais in musical terms on a number of occasions. It was lauded as 'the headquarters of excellent music', praised as being a centre of 'singing, steel and cakes', and was constantly singled out as possessing a fine tradition of musicality.[62] Of course, the achievements of the Dowlais Harmonic Society during the 1880s and 1890s did much to foster such an image. As the most successful of the town's musical associations, the choir was seen by many to be a vital ingredient in the public image of Dowlais. That it did much to place the settlement on the map, and thus distinguish it from its nearby rival, the town of Merthyr, is clear. And it ensured that music lovers in south Wales and further afield could not ignore Dowlais's contribution to the musical culture of the day. In 1885 the *Merthyr Express* received a letter from a Welshman in Australia who wished to participate in a long-running debate about the choir's performance at an eisteddfod in Abergavenny.[63] Meanwhile, it was with a great sense of pride that the paper informed its readership that the manager of a large steelworks near Pittsburgh had expressed a desire to hear the society whilst on a visit to south Wales.[64] Indeed, so well known was the leader of the DHS, Dan Davies, that when he visited Scranton and Wilkes-Barre with his wife and son in 1904, 'many thousands of Welsh friends and admirers' turned out to greet him.[65]

Another common strategy employed by a town's boosters was to attract musical competitions and festivals to their settlements.[66] Here the National Eisteddfod stands out as the most prestigious of events, and great efforts were made by civic leaders throughout the region to bring the National to their home towns. That such an event would bring credit to a town,

[62] *ME*, 18 April 1885, 16 September 1893.
[63] Ibid., 12 September 1885.
[64] Ibid., 15 September 1888.
[65] *The Cambrian* (Utica), September 1904, p. 403. I should like to thank Bill Jones for this reference. For more on the musical culture of the Welsh in Scranton, see W. D. Jones, *Wales in America: Scranton and the Welsh, 1860–1920* (Cardiff, 1993), ch. 3.
[66] The Cardiff Festival was a case in point. Started in 1892, this annual musical festival continued up until 1914. As David Ian Allsobrook remarks, the Festival was a 'form of displaying civic opulence and pride, and the city's superiority over neighbours like Merthyr, Newport, and Swansea' (David Ian Allsobrook, *Music for Wales* (Cardiff, 1992), pp. 31–3).

and thus be a matter for general celebration, was taken for granted. Hence it was with some dismay that, in May 1885, the *Aberdare Times* felt the need to admonish the inhabitants of the 'Athens of Wales' for not displaying the necessary public spirit in the run-up to the National to be held there later in the year.[67] Merthyrians perhaps could not afford to be so complacent. Their town was host to the National in 1881 and again in 1901, and on both occasions the civic projectors worked hard to exploit the situation. In the vanguard was, of course, Harry Southey's *Merthyr Express*:

> If Wales is the land of song, Merthyr is the capital of that happy land, for it is a centre of a great district, thickly populated, with a large, Welsh-speaking section, where music is the very breath of life of the majority of the people, and where the eisteddfod is the most popular form of social entertainment, its methods imbibed from earliest childhood. Add to these considerations the fact that Merthyr is an unrivalled railway centre, connection being obtainable with all the valleys that run down to the sea from the mountains, and it will readily be appreciated that the town is a fitting place for the great national assembly.[68]

In order to underline the point, Southey's paper marked the return of the National with a series of articles recounting the history of Merthyr eisteddfodau.[69]

Just as musical events were promoted, so too were talented musicians. Individuals frequently found their careers turned into a public knowledge that was structured in terms of 'the town'. Through a reading of the local papers, inhabitants were continually apprised of the achievements of local musical figures. The obsession with information was such that it included in its embrace those who had left the Merthyr district altogether. For instance, the various successes of Dan Thomas, a young baritone from Dowlais, were recounted to readers of the *Express* in 1889, notwithstanding his decision to leave south Wales in 1883.[70] Those interested in the progress of another Dowlaisian, Maggie Davies, were treated to a termly report of her activities while she was studying at the Royal College of Music.[71] Meanwhile, complimentary or testimonial concerts

[67] *Aberdare Times*, 23 May 1885.
[68] *ME*, 10 August 1901.
[69] Ibid., 25 May 1901.
[70] Ibid., 6 April 1889.

were held to mark key moments in a distinguished career. When contralto soloist Catherine Morgan ('Bronwen Morlais') returned to Dowlais after an eight-month tour of America with the Rhondda Glee Society, a soirée was arranged at Hermon Church to welcome her home.[72] Similarly, Abraham Bowen – 'the greatest personality connected with music in the Dowlais of his time' – was honoured at a complimentary concert in 1890 attended by the high constable and other local dignitaries.[73] And the services of John Evans ('Eos Myrddin'), another Dowlaisian, were recognized by his townspeople at a concert held in April 1893.[74] The chair of the meeting, Mr D. H. Edwards, set the tone for the evening. After the singing of a song by Miss Nancy Evans, Edwards 'hit the nail on the head ... by claiming Miss Evans as belonging to Dowlais, and not to Merthyr'.[75] He then turned his attention to 'Eos Myrddin' himself, sketching out his musical career and his various good works. Finally, 'Eos Myrddin' had the opportunity to speak. He did so in terms that succinctly illustrate the coincidence of music, social harmony and the town. He thanked the gathering for their kindness, and was pleased with the testimonial, 'not only for its worth, but especially for the respect which had been manifested towards him by the town generally, and as it had emanated from all classes it was worth more than a fortune'.[76] Such respect was shown even in death; obituaries recounted the glories and successes of the district's musical sons and daughters, while the public funeral represented the final opportunity to dramatize the connections binding them to their home towns.

The town's possession of the musician as a cultural symbol was also expressed through other, less subtle, means. There was an expectation, encouraged by the local newspapers, that communities should nurture the talent found within their own

[71] Ibid., 18 May 1889. The musical progress of the aforementioned Meta Scott was also relayed back to Merthyr when she was studying at the Royal Academy of Music. See, for example, ibid., 4 August 1888.
[72] Ibid., 13 April 1889 and 20 April 1889.
[73] Morgans, *Music and Musicians*, pp. 50–2.
[74] John Evans ('Eos Myrddin', 1841–1905), father of Harry Evans. John Evans was born in Carmarthenshire and moved to Dowlais with his parents. An orphan by the age of nine, Evans had already been working in the ironworks for a year. Taught by such luminaries as Ieuan Gwyllt, 'Eos Morlais' and David Rosser, he became established as a conductor (ibid., pp. 106–8).
[75] *ME*, 8 April 1893.
[76] Ibid., 8 April 1893.

ranks. This could take the form of financing specialized training. When William Morgan, 'a young genius' from Broad
Street, Dowlais, was singled out for praise by an adjudicator at
the Abergavenny Eisteddfod in 1892, the *Merthyr and Dowlais
Times* picked up the theme, suggesting that 'very soon the
Dowlais people will see what can be done to raise funds to
enable him to receive the musical education which can alone
bring to perfection his undoubted talent'.[77] The following year,
a correspondent to the paper informed the public of the case of
Ellen Jones, a member of the Dowlais Temperance Choir. The
writer urged 'fellow workmen in this neighbourhood' to raise
money for her training. The fusion of musician and town would
then be complete; this act of charity would 'enable her to
develop her talents to the honour of dear old Merthyr'. In order
to underscore the point, it was noted that neighbouring Aberdarians were once again parading their surplus of public-
spirited townsfolk, and had already collected £80 for Ellen.[78]
Two weeks later the paper took up her case again. 'If the people
of Merthyr do not secure for her that best course of training that
can alone make even the best natural voice perfect from a
musical standpoint – well, then they will be neglecting to bring
honour upon their own town.'[79] Once such funds had been
raised – and they invariably were – musicians like Morgan and
Jones owed a real debt to the community that had helped them
on their way; they had become, in a special sense, musical representatives of their town.

    Musical organizations, too, could expect to benefit from the
financial support of their fellow townsfolk, both élite and non-
élite alike. Few musical endeavours were without financial
commitments. Membership of a choral society, for example,
brought with it a number of obligations. The hire of a hall, the
price of sheet music, the cost of travelling to and from contests,
all had to be paid for.[80] In large measure the venture was
financed by the members themselves. Singers in the Dowlais

[77] *MDT*, 22 April 1892.
[78] Ibid., 30 June 1893.
[79] Ibid., 14 July 1893.
[80] If a choir strayed from the standard repertoire (such as *Messiah*), the cost of the
music could be problematic. When the Merthyr Philharmonic Society staged a version
of *The Woman of Samaria*, copies were made available on loan because of the expense
(3s. 4d. for old notation, 10d. for tonic sol-fa). *ME*, 12 November 1892. For a balance
sheet of the Merthyr Choral Society, see ibid., 21 April 1894.

Harmonic Society were expected 'to pay a small weekly sub to cover expenses',[81] as well as having to meet any travelling costs.[82] Meanwhile, brass banders ran up even greater debts. In addition to all the expenses incurred by their choral-singing cousins, those intent upon forming a band had to find the money to obtain instruments. In the early 1890s, members of the Dowlais Town Band, all drawn from the ranks of the working class, had to raise £261 in order to purchase their 'Excelsior class' instruments from Messrs Hawkes and Son.[83] And downturns in trade, or protracted strikes, could spell the end of many a band.[84] Thus it was that the local newspapers did much to publicize the financial needs of such musical institutions, and encouraged the reading public to do their duty and support them whenever possible.

In 1908, these attempts to turn music and musicians into the public property of a town were taken to their logical conclusion when the Cyfarthfa Brass Band was placed under the control of the Merthyr municipal authorities. Originally the private band of the Crawshay dynasty of ironmasters, it had enjoyed a prestigious musical history, ranking highly amongst the best bands in Britain during the mid- and late Victorian periods.[85] The idea of acquiring a public band was that of the mayor, D. W. Jones, who took advantage of an Act of Parliament that had been passed in 1907 empowering local authorities 'to provide or contribute towards the expenses of any band of music to perform in . . . [a public] park or ground'.[86] After considering his offer, and insisting that 'Cyfarthfa' remain in the title, W. T. Crawshay decided to accept, giving to the town 21 music stands, 291 music books with 842 pieces of music, in addition to the 28 band instruments.[87]

[81] *MDT*, 19 February 1892.
[82] Ibid., 22 April 1892.
[83] Ibid., 12 February 1892.
[84] See the gloomy prognoses in *British Bandsman* on the news of a threatened strike by Welsh miners in 1909 (*British Bandsman*, 23, no. 380 [12 June 1909], 659).
[85] For more on the historical background of the band, see Trevor Herbert, 'The virtuosi of Merthyr', *Llafur*, 5, no. 1 (1988), 60–9, and also his ' "A softening influence": R. T. Crawshay and the Cyfarthfa Band', in T. F. Holley (ed.), *The Merthyr Historian*, Vol. 5 (Merthyr Tydfil, 1992).
[86] *Public Health Acts Amendment Act*, 7 Edw. VII c.53. See *British Bandsman*, 12, no. 143 (1 August 1899), 215, and ibid., 21, no. 307 (18 January 1908), 78, for an avowal of the desirability of municipal bands, and an enthusiastic response to this piece of legislation.
[87] *ME*, 1 August 1908, 15 August 1908.

From the outset, it was envisaged that the Cyfarthfa and Municipal Band was actively to serve the citizens of the borough. The General Purposes Committee made it clear that 'the Corporation have the first call upon the services of the Band, and that they [the band members] shall play in different parts of the Borough at least two evenings a week during the summer months'. Jones was delighted with the outcome. At the first public appearance of the 'Cyfarthfa Municipal Band', he prefaced the musical fare with a short speech in which he set out his hopes for the future:

> [T]he efforts of the players were greatly appreciated. He asked them to be loyal to the Council and to the town, and also to their veteran leader. He expressed the hope that the band, which had such a glorious past, would have a still more prosperous future as the Municipal Band. The taking over of the Band, he felt sure, would be a great advantage to the town, and would do something to improve and foster instrumental music in the district.[88]

By the start of summer 1909 it appeared as if the inhabitants of the borough were already reaping the benefits of their new acquisition. When the band played an open-air concert at Treharris Athletic Grounds, the effect upon the population appeared to at least one observer to be suitably ennobling:

> Treharris was made happy and gay for several hours. The parents and children were there in hundreds, the children gambolling on the grass to the merry strains, while the parents listened with attentive ears to every item so well rendered. The crowd was made up of all classes – ministers of religion, elders, and all who seek the welfare of the masses.[89]

Here was yet another crowd – brought together by music and interacting in a public urban space – which could only be understood by invoking the rhetoric of social harmony.[90]

V. THE INADEQUACIES OF 'MUSICAL MERTHYR' AND 'THE GREAT BETRAYAL'

Despite the obvious success enjoyed by the promoters of musical ventures in the district, the consequences regarding the civic

---

[88] Ibid., 24 October 1908.
[89] Ibid., 19 June 1909.
[90] The subsequent months were in fact difficult ones for the band. See Croll, 'Civilizing the urban', pp. 121–2.

image of Merthyr were ambiguous. There was undoubtedly much that the projectors could be pleased with, particularly regarding their efforts to incorporate musicality into the portfolio of characteristics that together amounted to 'Merthyr'. The string of victorious choirs, the rise to national prominence of such figures as Joseph Parry – a man who was always keen to link his name with the town[91] – and the continued production of a host of well-respected violinists, soloists, organists, singers and conductors were all factors which redounded well upon the public image of Merthyr. Nevertheless, this 'musical town' was an unstable compound in many ways.

Take, for example, the supposedly inclusive qualities of music. Notwithstanding the potency of the discourse which stressed music's ability to heal social divisions, it was still possible to understand music in ways that led to the exclusion of many Merthyrians. In part this stemmed from contemporaries' willingness to distinguish between different types of music. For all the general assertions regarding music's role as a civilizing agent, there was widespread agreement that some genres were more uplifting than others. Chief amongst the promulgators of this view was the Revd H. R. Haweis, author of a best-selling treatise on the relationship between music and morals. He contended that civilization, far from simply being a product of music, was itself a force that could act upon music. Hence, some music (and by implication, some music lovers) could actually be uncivilized.[92] Thus when '[n]early all the élite of the town' turned out to hear local virtuoso Maggie Davies perform with the Merthyr String Quartette, their presence was explained by reference to the high quality of musical entertainment on offer. Moreover, the absence of those musical connoisseurs normally to be found in the gallery was welcomed by one observer:

> When the gallery is crowded, the rowdy element is sure to be present in strong force, and it generally succeeds in making everybody else

[91] He referred to himself as 'bachgen bach o Ferthyr erioed, erioed' ('a little boy from Merthyr, always, always'). See Griffiths, 'Musical life', p. 372.

[92] He noted that Wales, along with Scotland and Ireland, was a place in which popular music had 'never got beyond rude national ballads'; it was a 'wild germ' that 'remained undeveloped by civilization'. H. R. Haweis, *Music and Morals* (5th edn, London, 1874), pp. 529, 531. Also see the concerns of one 'Student', in *British Musician*, 6, no. 64 (January 1893), 21.

> miserable. Their tastes do not rise above 'Ta-ra-ra-boom-de-ay' and
> 'Rosey's Sunday Out', and it is safe to say that they would not have appre-
> ciated the rich musical treat that was given on Monday evening . . .[93]

In fact, the musical taste of many working-class Merthyrians
was far more sophisticated than this analysis suggests, but it
does appear that there was a reluctance to stray beyond the
boundaries of a repertoire of favourite oratorios, cantatas and
the like. This provided plenty of opportunities for those intent
upon policing the borders between those 'in the know' and all
the rest. Certainly, some of those who made up the 'crowded
and fashionable audience' listening to a Cyfarthfa Band concert
in 1906 relished the complexities of the music on offer because of
the cachet attached to 'difficult' music. On this occasion the
band was joined by Tom Davies, who played a series of violin
solos including Wieniawski's 'Légende' and Vieuxtemps's 'Fan-
taisie caprice'. The correspondent from the *Merthyr Guardian* did
all he could to effect social closure. He emphasized the technical
aspect of Davies's performance, noting that Vieuxtemps's work
was 'teeming with difficulties, embracing all kinds of bowing,
chords, harmonies and double stopping, all of which were
played with the sure hand of a master'. Whilst he was educated
in this sort of material, he could not help remarking on the
ignorance of many of his fellow townspeople; they had yet to
appreciate anything other than the crude sounds 'of the organ
grinder's music', he solemnly declared.[94]
Even choral music, that most inclusive of all genres, could
leave a sizeable number outside its clutches. In spite of the frequent references to 'all classes' and 'all grades of the community'
attending choral events, its suspension in a particular discourse
of respectability meant that some Merthyrians were immediately cast as outsiders. For example, it is clear that, more often
than not, the urban poor were left shivering outside the choir
stalls, rehearsal rooms and grand pavilions. The possession of
smart clothes was an essential prerequisite for participation in
most choirs, and observers were quick to applaud the dress sense
of many singers. J. Spencer Curwen waxed lyrical about the

[93] *MDT*, 6 May 1892.
[94] *Merthyr Guardian*, 17 November 1906. One should not discount Merthyrians' taste
in organ grinders' music. In 1861 reference was made to 'Jacko and the organ grinder
turning out his music by Handel' in one of the town's streets (*MTl*, 24 August 1861).

'collier lads in their Sunday best of very shiny broadcloth or coarse tweeds' whom he encountered at the Merthyr National in 1881.[95] The unfortunate John Harris, the singer who fell to his death from a train, was a paragon of sartorial elegance. According to the telegram informing the Dowlais police of the accident, 'the body of a young man respectably attired in a black cloth suit, and a red and black plaid muffler', had been picked out of the river. In the pockets were a tuning fork, a keyless watch and a return ticket for Merthyr, all potent symbols of financial independence, and all beyond the reach of a sizeable number of urbanites.[96]

While this reinforcement of difference may have appeared regrettable when viewed from the perspective of the civic projectors, of greater concern was the manner in which the 'Other' was, at times, all too present *within* choral culture. Disturbingly, this presence could be registered in the form of the disruptive and unruly crowds that were supposed to have been tamed by the 'concord of sweet sounds'. Indeed, the National Eisteddfod itself was often the venue for behaviour that was far from rational. Judges were regularly the focus of much derision, especially if their decisions appeared dubious to the audiences.[97] At the Aberdare National in 1885 sections of the audience threw clumps of earth at each other while waiting for the grand choral contest to begin, while at an eisteddfod held in Pontypool a suspect decision led to a choir from Ebbw Vale storming the platform, much to the astonishment of onlookers.[98] By the 1880s it had become necessary for choir leaders to impress upon their singers the virtues of good behaviour in defeat as in success.[99] Brass banders were similarly advised of the need to desist from underhand, and unbecoming, tactics. These could range from insulting the judges to wasting time in the hope that some competitors would have to play in the semi-darkness of the early evening.[100] Occasionally there were even suggestions that more serious infringements were committed. In

[95] Anon., 'The eisteddfod and popular music', p. 286.
[96] *ME*, 7 April 1888.
[97] Stead, 'Amateurs and professionals', pp. 119–21.
[98] *ME*, 5 September 1885.
[99] Ibid., 23 April 1887. For more on unrespectable behaviour at choral contests, see Croll, 'Bar stool to choir stall', pp. 23–4.
[100] *British Bandsman*, 23, no. 371 (10 April 1909), 393.

1908, as an adjudicator from Bradford was making his way to a contest at Aberdare, he was stopped outside Cardiff railway station by a bandsman offering him a bribe of £10. When the adjudicator asked the musician if such a thing was common in Wales, he was told: 'Oh yes! . . . judges who come down here often do it.'[101]

To compound the projectors' problems, the very discourse they employed when welding music and town together could be utilized in ways that worked to undermine the notion of 'civic Merthyr'. The language of friendship and social harmony, so often used to interpret musical relationships, could be inverted at a stroke, as anything which threatened to have a deleterious effect upon the chances of victory of a choir or band was immediately isolated and subjected to castigation. The elevation of 'the town' above all else could certainly result in some inharmonious outbursts. For instance, the news that in 1885 members of the DHS and the Morlais Choral Society (also from Dowlais) had, 'for no perceptible reason, left both choirs and joined a choir whose rehearsals are held several miles away' provoked a prickly response from the *Merthyr Express*. Under the heading 'Choral secessionists', a reporter noted acerbically: 'The assistance which these people may render any choir is no doubt very little, but still it is decidedly unfair that they, after learning the good points of the Dowlais choirs, should go to rival choirs and thus betray their own townspeople.'[102] Not prepared to let the matter drop, the paper returned to the issue two weeks later when discussing the rehearsals of the DHS. They were proceeding well,

> and notwithstanding the fact that a number of splenetic individuals are endeavouring to make the people of Dowlais appear ridiculous in the face of the whole world by forming a branch of a rival choir in the town, the Harmonic Society continues to make most satisfactory progress, and it is not without reason that we look forward to the victory of our choir at Aberdare.

The rehearsals were held behind closed doors from that point on. However, in order that Dowlais people – 'who have hitherto stood by the choir' – could hear them before the big day,

[101] Ibid., 22, no. 332 (11 July 1908), 29.
[102] *ME*, 4 July 1885.

a miscellaneous concert was planned just before the competition. The journalist expressed the hope that 'on this occasion the people of Dowlais will show by the patronage they will give to the Harmonic Society how they resent the childish attempts of a discontented fraction to do an injury to the most renowned choir in Glamorganshire of which every man in Dowlais ought to be proud'.[103]

In this case, Dowlais's honour was being defended in the face of high-quality opposition from outside the Merthyr district. A more disturbing scenario was one in which all the tensions implicit in the idea of 'Merthyr' itself were brought to the surface. The distinctions that obtained between Merthyr town and Merthyr district were vital to the success or failure of a number of civic reforms. We saw in a previous chapter how the problem of the 'outlying districts' could seriously impede the 'progress of Merthyr'. In fact, the problem was actually one of the outlying 'towns'. Here, again, music could be used as a means of defining difference rather than similarity. These processes, disruptive as they were of 'Merthyr', were clearly revealed during a phase in the district's musical history known to contemporaries as 'the great betrayal'.

The reworking of Merthyr's musical identity began with the news that Dan Davies was to leave Dowlais in 1892. Had he been making the 3,000-mile journey to America, the response of his fellow townspeople might have been a rather melancholy sense of pride. The fact that he had embarked upon a trip of less than two miles to neighbouring Merthyr Tydfil was far more distressing for Dowlaisians. At first it appeared as if all would be well, with the Dowlais correspondent in the *Express* commenting: 'we are glad to think that, in regard to choral matters, Mr Davies will continue to remain, to all intents and purposes, a Dowlais man.'[104] However, warning bells could be heard in Dowlais in February 1893 when it became clear that Davies was not going to take the DHS to the National Eisteddfod at Pontypridd.[105] Worse news was to follow when the rumour was confirmed that he was to lead a Merthyr choir instead.[106]

[103] Ibid., 18 July 1885.
[104] Ibid., 7 May 1892.
[105] Ibid., 11 February 1893.
[106] Ibid., 25 February 1893.

By early March, the feeling of betrayal suffered at the hands of their erstwhile hero began to be registered. An article in the *Merthyr and Dowlais Times* by the Dowlais correspondent showed the extent to which the language of friendship was being stretched to its limits. Commenting on the prospect of a newly formed Dowlais choir meeting Davies's singers, the reporter observed that 'Dowlais will strain every nerve when the new choir [from Merthyr] is encountered, not because we have the slightest ill-feeling against our Merthyr friends – far from it – but because it is not in human nature to sit down and smile at our desertion'. The Dowlaisian proceeded to reveal the depths to which relations with those 'Merthyr friends' had slumped:

> For an outsider to sing side by side with the Invincibles [as the DHS was popularly known] was an honour. For any of the Invincibles to go and render assistance to the man who has left them as Mr. Davies has will be a disgrace. Merthyrians themselves have told me that without the aid of Dowlais the new choir cannot hope to make headway. Then let it die. It has no right to expect assistance from the people whose desertion was the foundation of its own existence. And the people of Dowlais will regard as traitors anybody who will render such assistance . . .[107]

He appealed to the sense of 'duty' of Dowlaisians, and urged townsfolk to unite behind 'a noble band of singers' being formed.

In the face of such treachery from one of Dowlais's own sons, it was with pleasure that the *Times* noted the loyalty of Katie O'Brien, an inhabitant of the town who had been approached by the Merthyr choir and asked to join. The paper was especially impressed by the 'example of patriotism' that had been set by O'Brien, given her Irish roots. 'We hear a great deal at times about Irish duplicity and treachery', the correspondent remarked, but her answer was 'worthy of a true Britisher. "No, I will not come," said Miss O'Brien, "I am a Dowlais girl, and I am not going to lend a hand to the degradation of the old town." Bravo, Katie.'[108]

The rifts in the identity of Merthyr were publicly displayed before all of south Wales at the Porth Eisteddfod in May, when the new choir competed in the grand choral competition.

[107] *MDT*, 10 March 1893.
[108] Ibid., 12 May 1893.

Its rendition of Mozart's 'Dies Irae' was enough to secure it first prize, and thus the inhabitants of Dowlais had to watch all the jubilant celebrations that usually attended a Dan Davies victory happening in Merthyr's streets instead of their own. The bitterness that had been created by the break was a remarkable testament to the power of the 'town' as a collective identity. The Dowlais correspondent was hissed, booed and subjected to bad language at the hands of the Merthyr choir as they left the platform, prompting him to justify his talk of betrayal over the previous months:

> In taking up the position which I did, I knew I had not only the sympathy of the betrayed choir but of the people of Dowlais as a whole. This was amply provided by the fact that although nearly every member of the old Invincibles was asked to join the new combination, not a score of them were so unpatriotic as to do so. What did those cultured gentlemen who demonstrated that Dean Swift's imagination had only been prophetic when it created the Yahoos, expect of us? Did they expect that we would hail with enthusiasm a combination that exists only as a memorial of our own desertion and betrayal? But after all, what does it matter what they think?
> . . . When the award had been declared Mr. Davies came to the reporters' table, and said, "Shake hands, old friend: let us make it up." "Yes," I said, "I will shake hands, and let me congratulate you heartily on your victory: but I cannot forget that Dowlais was betrayed!" These words, I expect, express the sentiments of Dowlais as a whole.[109]

It seemed that somehow, almost without anyone noticing, the uncivilized 'Yahoos' had got into musically defined 'Merthyr'.

VI. CODA

It has been argued in this chapter that the civic projectors made conscious efforts to weave music into Merthyr's identity. Such was the extent of its appeal that it was relatively easy to generate inclusive images of Merthyr society when discussing musical matters. Nonconformist leaders, the commercial élite, professionals, working-class Merthyrians, men, women, young and old could be incorporated within this identity. A much wider discourse that understood music as a potentially civilizing force

[109] Ibid., 26 May 1893.

was also in operation here, enabling the connection to be made between a musical Merthyr and an urbane and civilized Merthyr.

In many respects, the projectors were highly successful. Their vision of a musical town was clearly in tune with the visions of a great many of the district's population. The scenes in Dowlais's streets, before the 'great betrayal', on the arrival home of a victorious Harmonic Society can usefully be interpreted as demonstrations of a popular celebration of 'the town'. At the moment a choir took to the stage, it became the conduit for the expression of civic loyalties, a symbol around which one defined oneself, as either a friend or a foe. The honour of the town was taken seriously indeed, and to that extent the boosters could be satisfied. Nevertheless, there is also evidence that such conceptions of the town were inscribed with identities that had the potential to undermine the civic vision. The unruly behaviour of some of the audiences and musicians at choral competitions and brass band contests suggests a way in which the 'honour' of one's home town could be defended that did not involve genuflections in the direction of all things 'civilized'. That many of these 'ungentlemanly' participants in this popular musical culture were working class is noteworthy, although on its own this is not enough to suggest that such deviations from the civilized norm were unalloyed manifestations of class differences.

That said, it should immediately be acknowledged that the pull of class is discernible in aspects of this musical world. For example, the attitude expressed by the working-class members of the Dowlais Town Band on the question of the patronage of the town's shopocracy could well be seen as the articulation of a sense of class difference. Notwithstanding the obvious need for assistance, and indeed the willingness to accept any offered, great store was set on the maintenance of the band's independence. In the words of one of the bandsmen, the band

> was formed independently of the tradespeople of the town, and although named the 'Town Band', the members contribute weekly to raise a fund to defray expenses incidental to paying the bandmaster for his services; also in obtaining the music and whatever is required by a brass band.[110]

[110] *ME*, 7 January 1893.

Thus, there was a conscious effort to separate the 'town' from the band's identity. The band was a Dowlais band, and the members were all Dowlaisians, yet there are the makings here of a sense of Dowlais being played out in terms of difference rather than unity. Even more disturbing perhaps was the manner in which the discourse of musical and social harmony could be used to the detriment of the civic project. The language of friendship could be reversed at a stroke with 'treachery' and 'betrayal' emerging as central concepts. As a consequence, the sentiments that already constituted the problem of the 'outlying districts' were reinforced and reinvigorated. A musical Merthyr was one riven with fault-lines and weak spots.

In the final analysis, the point has again to be made that Merthyr's civic identity was contingent and in constant need of definition and maintenance. To suggest that a stable and essentially static civic identity could somehow be created by the town's boosters would be mistaken. The processes whereby identities were (and are) constructed is one that denies closure. Thus, Charter Day in Merthyr, with all its musical accompaniment, should not be interpreted as the moment when the journey from the urban to the civic had come to an end. The presence of the municipal band at the celebrations was doubtless intended to symbolize the many successes that had been registered by the civic projectors over the years. And the manner in which the band was expected to play in all the different parts of the Merthyr district can be seen as a means of encouraging the development of a consciousness that united the constituent parts of that district. Nevertheless, as we have seen, musical institutions could also result in the promotion of more parochial interests. Even the 'municipalization of music' could not bridge these divides. In 1913 an appeal for financial assistance was received by the Parks Committee from workmen's bands in Merthyr Vale, Treharris and Plymouth, prompting the mayor to observe that 'Merthyr was not a small town, but divided into extensive districts, and provision should be made to support the band in each locality'.[111] He argued that in the interest of fairness, any money should be split equally between bands from all parts of the district. Others disagreed, and a

[111] Ibid., 15 March 1913.

counter-proposal was put suggesting that the Merthyr and Cyfarthfa band should get £50 whilst lesser amounts be distributed amongst smaller combinations. In the end, the matter had to be handed over to the full council, where it was decided to give all the available money to the municipal band.[112] One can only guess at the feelings of those members and supporters of bands who were denied access to public funds on this occasion. But it is clear that discord as well as harmony marked out this 'musical Merthyr'. Certainly, through the multiplex attempts to incorporate a popular cultural pursuit into a civic identity, 'popular' (and often contradictory) understandings of what civic Merthyr might mean were constantly generated by the crowds of music-loving inhabitants as they gathered in the parks, attended concerts or simply threw clumps of earth at each other in the heat of a choral battle.

[112] Ibid., 22 March 1913.

V

MERTHYR UNITED?
SPORT, SPACE AND URBAN MEANING

An immense crowd of people is waiting for somebody, brass bands are in attendance, and when the train steams in, the hero of the hour goes triumphant down the street amidst the blare of trumpets and the cheers of thousands. It is not a Cabinet Minister coming to his constituency, nor a great soldier welcomed back to his birthplace; it is a football player...

Ernest Ensor, 1898[1]

In a previous chapter it was noted that Victorians were required to rethink their relationship with the urban environment. More precisely, and drawing upon the insights of Martin Daunton, it was suggested that the codes which governed behaviour in public spaces such as the streets were recast in significant ways. Certainly for the later years of the nineteenth century it is possible to identify a civilized street etiquette which held that the ideal thoroughfare was a site of continuous movement, safety and silence. Such a conceptualization of public space had profound effects, not least upon urban popular cuture. A number of citizens – some of them impeccably 'respectable', some of them decidedly 'rough' – discovered that their popular cultural predilections brought them into conflict with the defenders of a civilized urban *mentalité*. Sporting Merthyrians, of all ages, all classes and both sexes, found that the 'where' of popular culture was ever more important. Any sporting practice which took them into the highways made it likely that they would fall foul both of the authorities and an ever vigilant citizenry. And this was at a time when spaces set aside for recreation were at a premium in the district, and when many were forced to look to the street as the most convenient, and most obvious, alternative.

I. 'ELSEWHERE THAN IN THE STREETS':
SPORT, GAMES AND THE MISUSE OF THE HIGHWAYS

Few groups of urbanites were more reliant on the streets as a setting for games and sports of all descriptions than working-

[1] 'The football madness', *The Contemporary Review*, 74 (November 1898), 753–60, 753.

class children.[2] Yet, while it is possible to discern the persistence
of a lively 'juvenile street life' well into the twentieth century,
it is also the case that the street became an increasingly un-
friendly environment for youngsters.[3] Their noisy activities frequently blocked pavements and roads. Street football, one such
practice, was frowned upon both by the police and the local
magistrates. Thus, when eleven of the sixty 'juniors' who were
seen playing a game in a street in Dowlais in 1890 were brought
before the Bench, the stipendiary expressed the hope 'that they
would all turn out good footballers' but informed them in no
uncertain terms 'that they must practise elsewhere than in the
public streets'. A fine of 2s. 6d. was levied as a means of pushing
home the lesson.[4] Youthful foot-racers, equally obstructive and
noisy figures, were similarly treated, as were lovers of games
such as 'cat and dog'.[5] That many inhabitants resented the
interventions of the police in their street culture is clear; for
example, when a boy was summonsed for playing with a bat and
ball in Thomas Street in 1896, his mother complained to the
magistrate that 'she had herself played in the street forty years
ago, and games had always been played there, as the children
had nowhere else to play in'. The stipendiary acknowledged the
problem, lamented the lack of a recreation ground in Merthyr,
but fined her son 2s. all the same.[6]

   If games-playing children were most likely to turn the idea of
free and easy movement on its head, other sporting Merthyrians were guilty of taking the notion of free and easy movement
rather too seriously. As the cycling craze of the 1880s and 1890s
caught south Wales in its grip, so the numbers of cyclists
charged with bringing danger to the streets steadily increased.[7]
Initially, in Merthyr as elsewhere, it was the middle class who

[2] Pamela Horn, *The Victorian Town Child* (Stroud, 1997), pp. 12, 15, 154.
[3] Bill Bramwell, 'Public space and local communities: the example of Birmingham, 1840–1880', in Gerry Kearns and Charles W. J. Withers (eds), *Urbanising Britain:
Essays on Class and Community in the Nineteenth Century* (Cambridge, 1991), pp. 31–54, 46.
Daunton has identified the 1890s as a key decade in which attitudes hardened towards
children. See his 'Public place and private space: the Victorian city and the working-
class household', in D. Fraser and A. Sutcliffe (eds), *The Pursuit of Urban History*
(London, 1983), pp. 212–33, 223.
[4] *ME*, 15 November 1890. For another example, see *AT*, 5 November 1881.
[5] *PC*, 14 February 1890; *AT*, 1 October 1881.
[6] *ME*, 18 July 1896.
[7] For accounts of the popularity of cycling, see David Rubinstein, 'Cycling in the
1890s', *Victorian Studies*, 21, no. 1 (1977), 47–72; John Lowerson, *Sport and the English
Middle Classes, 1870–1914* (Manchester, 1995, paperback edn), pp. 116–21.

availed themselves of the (still expensive) machines and established fashionable cycling clubs.[8] In their hands, the bicycle was generally conceived of as a 'rational' recreational device. However, by the 1890s and 1900s it was beginning to come within the grasp of the working class. Second-hand bicycles were being sold for £2 10s. in 1903, and it was possible to hire one from as little as 2s. for four hours.[9] As the sport of cycling went from strength to strength in the region (the world championships were held in Newport in 1896),[10] and as tales of the latest epic efforts of local cycling stars, Jimmy Michael and Arthur Linton, were recounted, so the bicycle came to represent social prestige, modernity and, above all else, excitement.[11] Yet not all urban dwellers welcomed these developments. As early as 1885, the chairman of Aberdare Local Board had tried to get all bikes banned from the local park on the grounds that they were a public nuisance.[12] Although he was unsuccessful on this occasion, many cyclists were well aware of the hostility which their pastime continued to generate through the 1890s.[13] For instance, in 1897 and 1898 local well-to-dos were outraged by the 'demon kids' who turned the salubrious Courtland Terrace into a cycle-racing track.[14] As 'Chwareu Teg' saw it, this was a matter for the police; he had 'no objection to a rational use by cyclists of this or any street' but the conversion of a highway to a racing path was too much to bear.[15] More sensitive cyclists realized such antics only increased the likelihood of unsympathetic treatment in the future. As one remarked, 'If a wheelman has the misfortune to come before an average dispenser of justice he may calculate, with a pretty fair amount of certainty, that the interview will leave his pocket lighter.'[16]

In the long run, of course, cyclists became an accepted part of modern street-life. In contrast, other sporting practitioners

---

[8] *ME*, 12 August 1882.

[9] Ibid., 9 May 1903, 27 September 1902.

[10] Ibid., 27 June 1896. Less prestigious, though no less popular, events were held in Merthyr during these years. See, for example, *MDT*, 5 August 1892, 15 July 1892.

[11] See the *AT*, 11 September 1897, 30 October 1897, for reports of Michael's tour of America.

[12] Ibid., 18 April 1885, 25 April 1885, 2 May 1885. For even earlier signs of hostility, see *ME*, 10 January 1881.

[13] See the correspondence column of the *ME*, 13 June 1896.

[14] Ibid., 16 July 1898.

[15] Ibid., 5 June 1897.

[16] Ibid., 11 July 1896.

found themselves pushed out of the urban environment altogether. To the fore in this respect were foot-racers and pugilists. Foot-racing had for long been a feature of the streets of
urban south Wales. Races often took the form of informal meetings between two athletes competing for 'prizes rising from jugs
of beer to golden sovereigns', in front of crowds of gambling,
disorderly spectators.[17] By the century's mid-point, civilized
opinion was already turning against the foot-racers. In 1850 one
commentator complained about the 'racing madness' that had
seized Merthyr, pointing out that the 'mania' had 'force[d] its
way into the highways'. One event produced some particularly
unfortunate scenes; two men had been seen staging a race in
Castle Street in front of a large crowd of men and women, many
of whom were laying bets. 'One of the racers, a remarkably fine
and broad-chested fellow, had nothing on but a drawers. In the
struggle this frail covering gave way, and a highly indecent
exposure of the person was the result.'[18] By the 1880s, aggressive
policing had effectively cleared the streets of athletes, naked or
otherwise, forcing lovers of the informal foot-race to carry on
their sport beyond the boundaries of the built environment.[19]
If meetings were held within the town, they were usually organized, highly regulated and held on land specifically set aside for
such sporting events.[20]

The prizefighter was even more despised by shapers of
respectable opinion.[21] While this ritualistic 'sport' occupied an
important position in the lives of a number of working-class
men, as a direct consequence of the enforcement of the by-laws,
the prizefight was successfully marginalized, both physically
and temporally, from the main currents of urban culture.[22]
Any attempt on the part of pugilists to ply their trade in urban
public spaces was guaranteed a speedy response on the part
of the Merthyr police. As a result, prizefights were generally

---

[17] W. J. Edwards, *From the Valley I Came* (London, 1956), p. 21.

[18] *CMG*, 7 September 1850.

[19] Even this relocation was no guarantee of freedom from the charge of obstruction as witnessed by the police action against a race on Hirwaun Common. See *ME*,
9 October 1880.

[20] See below, pp. 151–4.

[21] See Dai Smith's 'Focal heroes' in his *Aneurin Bevan and the World of South Wales*
(Cardiff, 1993). For a general history, see Dennis Brailsford, *Bareknuckles: A Social
History of Prizefighting* (Cambridge, 1988).

[22] See Brailsford, *Bareknuckles*, ch. 5.

confined to 'bloody spots' – including Thomastown Tips, the
Graig woods and Aberdare mountain – and were often staged
in the early hours of the morning in an effort to evade the
unwelcome attentions of the authorities.[23] Even this did not
stop the police actively pursuing the district's fighting class;[24]
nor did it satisfy civilized urbanites who were always willing to
inform their fellow citizens, and the authorities, of any signs of a
return to the bad old days. So it was that a correspondent to the
Express wrote of distasteful scenes that occurred in a public
house on the road between Merthyr and Aberdare in May 1897:
'[A] number of young men, some of them mere boys, were seen
coming out of [the] public-house. One of them had been
bleeding considerably. The boy said he had been having a "few
rounds" of sparring upstairs.'[25] That it was still possible to see
sights of this nature was regrettable, but at least the years of
regulation and control had been successful in pushing the
pugilists to the margins. As 'Polonius' put it in 1891:

> There appears to be a revival in this district, and for the matter of that,
> throughout the country, of the old passion for prize fighting. Old inhabi-
> tants inform me that years ago, before the establishment of a police force
> in the town, it was no uncommon thing to witness a dozen fights in
> Lower High Street on a pay day. Fortunately civilization has driven
> such brutal practices from the main streets, and pugilists are now forced
> to practise the noble art (?) in mountain solitudes.[26]

II. TEAM SPORTS AND THE PROBLEM OF SPACE

Given that 'civilized' urbanites were particularly sensitive
regarding the uses to which their streets were put, it is no
surprise to discover that these were declared to be unsuitable for
a variety of sporting practices. However, it is worth noting that
the problem of finding space to play in Merthyr extended well
beyond the public highways. The lack of sufficient open spaces
set aside for games was a constant source of complaint; certainly
few late Victorian inhabitants needed reminding that it had

[23] Edwards, *From the Valley I Came*, pp. 21–5; *ME*, 28 March 1885, 15 September
1894.
[24] For examples of prosecutions, see *AT*, 23 July 1881; *ME*, 23 July 1881.
[25] *ME*, 22 May 1897.
[26] Ibid., 15 August 1891.

been the exigencies of work, and not play, which had conjured their town into existence a century earlier.

The relationship between sport and urban space was most acutely problematized with the introduction of football (of both codes) into the district. As was the case elsewhere in south Wales, rugby football first made its appearance in Merthyr in the 1870s.[27] During these early years the oval ball remained largely in the hands of a select few, with young members of the social élite – including civic boosters such as Colonel D. Rees Lewis and Harry Southey – showing a particularly keen interest in football matters.[28] Nevertheless, although the game had the patronage of a large number of 'worthies' during the late nineteenth century, this did not preclude the problem of space making its presence felt. As a cultural practice which demanded a finite but nonetheless sizeable area, it – along with the older pastime of cricket – highlighted just how little room there was in Merthyr for enthusiasts of the new model sports.[29] In the most extreme cases clubs could find themselves without any ground at all. This was the fate that befell the Treharris Saturday cricket team in 1904, whilst the Merthyr cricket team was forced to make the journey to Aberaman for 'home' games during the 1897 season because no playing field could be secured in their own locality.[30] The more fortunate clubs were merely subjected to an almost ritual scramble for territory during the close season. In 1889 Merthyr's premier rugby club was required to wrestle with the ground issue.[31] The following year, after a season playing at Penydarren Park, the club lost out to the Merthyr Recreation Company, whilst in February 1892 it was announced that the club was looking for yet another new ground.[32] In October 1894 the team kicked off the season

[27] See David Smith and Gareth Williams, *Fields of Praise: The Official History of the Welsh Rugby Union, 1881–1981* (Cardiff, 1980). Also, see Gareth Williams, 'Rugby Union', in Tony Mason (ed.), *Sport in Britain: A Social History* (Cambridge, 1989).

[28] For more on the social profile of rugby in Merthyr, see Andrew J. Croll, 'Civilizing the urban: popular culture, public space and urban meaning', Merthyr *c.* 1870–1914, Ph.D. thesis, University of Wales (Cardiff), 1997, pp. 222–3.

[29] Cricket was played in the Merthyr district during the nineteenth century although it never attracted the following of football. For more, see Andrew Hignell, *A 'Favourit' Game: Cricket in South Wales Before 1914* (Cardiff, 1992), especially pp. 36–9, 79, 94, 123–4, 127–8.

[30] *ME*, 14 May 1904, 29 May 1897.

[31] Ibid., 28 September 1889.

[32] Ibid., 30 August 1890, 27 February 1892.

optimistically by playing its first game at Gwynne's Field, Cefn, but by the annual general meeting in June players were faced with yet another obstacle, this time in the form of a proposed rent increase to £20 per season.[33] At a meeting in 1896, a gloomy retrospective highlighted the very poor season that the club had endured. At the root of the decline in fortunes was cited the uncertainty over a ground. As the club secretary, Mr W. R. Evans, put it, 'unless they tried to secure one, there was no earthly use in having a club at all'. Only after a prolonged debate was it decided that every effort should be made to keep the team together.[34]

Even when teams could find space to play, the constraints imposed by local geography were often considerable. In 1912 soccer teams involved in the Merthyr Schools' League were blessed by the directorate of the Merthyr Town club which placed a field at their disposal every Saturday morning. In addition to developing their footballing skills, it appears that the young players needed to cultivate the sensibilities of a mountain goat. Reporting on the game between Abermorlais and Twyn-yrodyn, one journalist observed:

> The pitch on which the game was played was in a very bad state for football of any kind, and the boys are to be congratulated on putting up such a good game. At one end it was a case of running down-hill, and a climb at the other; and the posts were not placed to the best advantage... It is nothing short of a disgrace that no better patch could be found to play on for our schoolboys.[35]

This acute lack of available ground was hardly conducive to the development of the sport in the district; neither did it endear the landowners and local notables to the followers of organized sport.[36] On learning about the difficulties faced by the Merthyr Alexandras who, in 1900, spent much time worrying over the ground issue, one supporter of the club was left in no doubt as to who should be blamed. 'Merthyr', he

[33] Ibid., 20 October 1894, 15 June 1895, 7 September 1895.
[34] Ibid., 22 August 1896.
[35] *Merthyr Pioneer* (*MP*), 20 January 1912.
[36] The local landlords had, of course, a determining role to play in the provision of open spaces. See Helen Meller, *Leisure and the Changing City, 1870–1914* (London, 1976), pp. 112–13.

argued, 'is a delightful(?) place for sport . . . to get a yard or two of it for a game of football or cricket is absolutely an impossibility.' He went on:

> [T]hough the members [of the Alexandras] had every confidence that this season would be one of the best ever known – a deal of new blood, good working committee men, having got together, and the financial aspect looking rosy – their hopes have been dashed through the lack of support accorded them by the people who, when opportunities occur, get upon public platforms and shout about what should be done for young men! Merthyr would years ago have come prominently to the fore in matters of recreation – football included – but for the miserable support given to the players. Even supposing that the Goitre field is obtained, can the club expect people to walk through slush and mud ankle-deep?[37]

Predictably, the correspondent ended his letter with a plea for some of the town's leading citizens to act on the matter.

The reasons for landowners' indifference to football during this period can only be guessed. It seems likely, however, that many took umbrage at the dubious reputation that the game was already developing. Certainly by the 1880s the drunken rugby player appears to have been a common enough feature of the urban landscape of the Valleys. When, in March 1885, the Merthyr Football Club (MFC) gave their neighbours in Aberdare 'a sound thrashing', the experience was traumatic enough for the vanquished 'to drown their sorrow in the flowing bowl, and about midnight a large number of them were observed trying to steer their way through Commercial Place, a feat they would never have accomplished but for the kindly help of some passers-by'.[38]

The close relationship that obtained between the district's drink trade and rugby could also be interpreted as a thoroughly undesirable state of affairs. Given the lack of suitable alternatives, the public house became the chosen headquarters of many teams. The Merthyr Thursdays operated out of the Cowbridge Arms during much of the 1880s,[39] whilst in the mid-1890s the MFC utilized the facilities – including a changing

---

[37] *ME*, 29 September 1900. 'The club expressed regret that the great landowners did not come forward and support not only football, but other movements organized for the benefit of the old town' (ibid., 1 September 1900).

[38] Ibid., 14 March 1885.

[39] Ibid., 29 September 1883.

room and a bathing area – on offer at the Nelson Inn.[40] Other, less prestigious, teams had their origins in the comradeship that was a feature of the 'local'.[41] In 1881 a club based at the Cambrian (Aberdare) played a team from the Anchor Inn (Merthyr) in front of 'a large number of spectators'.[42] And even towards the end of the period under consideration the public house was still an important institution for those who belonged to the smaller clubs. For instance, members of the Troedyrhiw Stars took the Fox and Hounds Inn as their headquarters, the ideal environment for post-match smoking concerts and other social events.[43]

If many observers suspected the drinking habits of the players off the pitch, their antics whilst on the field of play could also be seen to deviate from the standards expected by the 'rational recreationalists'. Complaints of rough play were voiced at a time when the game seemed to be most securely in the hands of the social élite. Of course, ritualized violence was a feature of rugby during the time of its invention in the English public school system. What concerned many, however, was not simply the display of 'manly' aggression, but rather the intrusion of obviously unfair and intimidatory tactics in order to gain the upper hand. Matches between Merthyr and nearby Troedyr-hiw were characterized from the outset by a finely honed rivalry which could easily spill over into unpleasantness. In 1886 a fight erupted after a referee's decision upset the Troedyrhiw players, precipitating allegations that one of the Merthyr team threat-ened to 'break the skull' of an unruly opponent.[44] Seven years later, the fixture again produced some unnecessary scenes and another flurry of letters to the *Merthyr Express*, with proponents from both sides arguing their case. According to an 'Old International Player' from Troedyrhiw, the Merthyrians were

[40] Ibid., 14 December 1895. The Dowlais Football Club met at the Canford Inn (*MDT*, 29 April 1892).
[41] Tony Mason has rightly drawn a distinction between teams that used the facilities of public houses, on the one hand, and those that actually originated from the pub's clientele, on the other (Tony Mason, *Association Football and English Society, 1863–1915* (Brighton, 1980), p. 27).
[42] *ME*, 12 November 1881.
[43] Ibid., 19 January 1907. See also Richard Holt, *Sport and the British: A Modern History* (Oxford, 1989), p. 150; Richard Holt, 'Working-class football and the city: the problem of continuity', *British Journal of Sports History*, 3, no. 1 (1986), 5–17, 9.
[44] *ME*, 16 October 1886, 23 October 1886, 30 October 1886.

to blame. 'On the first onset they marked the best three-quarter we had on the field. They rushed him like a lot of Zulus, and felled him to the ground, disabling him for the remainder of the game which was a very serious loss to Troedyrhiw.'[45] Not surprisingly, this evoked a speedy response from a Merthyr halfback who suggested that the 'Old International Player' was little more than a rowdy 'who attends football matches for the purpose of creating a disturbance'.[46] Given contemporary conceptions regarding the 'barbarity' of 'Darkest Africa', the fact that rugby players were likened to Zulus suggested that the reality of the game was a long way from being an aid to 'civilized' behaviour. Certainly such public displays of bad feeling did little to enhance the reputation of the game, and may go some way towards explaining the unwillingness of landowners to assign suitable plots of land to the footballing fraternity.

III. The Civic Project, Sport and Space

Not only did such unsavoury associations add to the problems faced by Merthyr's footballers; they also raised difficult questions for social commentators intent on evaluating the potential of organized sport to do good. One school of thought had, by the late 1880s, decided to denounce football altogether as a thoroughly demoralizing influence.[47] Another attempted to draw a distinction between uplifting physical training and corrosive 'games'.[48] Notwithstanding such gloomy prognoses, it was possible to find commentators who were far more optimistic. In 1907 a religious gloss was put on the game when Paul Roos, captain of the South African national team, made a speech in Pontypridd:

> Men could not all be ministers, but they could preach by their words and actions, and could do so in playing football, as in the everyday walks of life. There the players' actions could be seen by thousands and if their

---

[45] Ibid., 4 February 1893.
[46] Ibid., 11 February 1893.
[47] See, for example, the comments of Ernest Ensor, 'The football madness', p. 78.
[48] Eugene Sully, 'Physical training and character', in T. E. Stephens (ed.), *Wales: Today and Tomorrow* (Cardiff, 1907), pp. 289–93; W. Beach Thomas, 'The failure of games', *The National Review* (February 1907), 1003–9, 1008.

conduct was good, it would appeal to others. Let them take Christ into the football field, not only as players, but as spectators, and try to disassociate themselves from the idea that footballers and athletes were fighters and drunkards... Football was an excellent moral training, and in it were the true spirit and enjoyment of sport.[49]

It seems clear that a significant number of Merthyr notables had long been in sympathy with such an argument. In 1881, Charles Russell James, HM Inspector of Schools in the district, argued for the dissemination of 'a knowledge of field sports and athletics. He maintained that it was as necessary for them [school children] to be trained athletically as it was to be trained mentally.'[50] His views obviously found favour with the authorities at Merthyr Proprietary School who advertised the institution by noting that it was set in sixty acres of ground thus 'affording every facility for cricket and outdoor sports'. Only after this proclamation were the academic strengths of the school detailed.[51] An explicit reference to the potential of sport to work for the promotion of civilized behaviour was made by the most committed of civic boosters, Colonel D. Rees Lewis, in 1894. As president of the MFC he delivered a speech at the annual supper in which he pondered the links between temperance and sport. Although he recognized that in the past the relationship between the two had not always been of the healthiest nature, he was glad to inform his listeners that he had observed a change in the behaviour of sports lovers:

> During his early days the chief item in connection with a game was the drinking part, and unless a man got 'tight' and went home 'tight', things were not considered to have gone off properly. It was exceedingly gratifying to observe that young men nowadays were coming to the conclusion that athletics and drink didn't agree – (applause) – and if athletics were patronised more generally there would be a corresponding decrease in drink, and the manhood of their workingmen would be nobler and more vigorous.[52]

[49] *ME*, 5 January 1907. For a similarly upbeat assessment, see Hely Hutchinson Almond, 'Football as a moral agent', *Nineteenth Century*, 34, no. 202 (December 1893), 899–911.
[50] *ME*, 19 March 1881. James could turn to a number of authors in support of these views. See, for example, Edward Lyttleton's 'Athletics in public schools', *Nineteenth Century*, 7, no. 35 (January 1880), 43–58.
[51] *PC*, 10 September 1881.
[52] *ME*, 21 July 1894.

This singling out of working men as a social group that could profit morally from the game of rugby is important, especially given Lewis's relationship to the civic project. The link between the project and the ennobling function of athletic exercise was explored further by another speaker at the event, Alfred Edmonds. 'He thought that Merthyr ought to congratulate itself upon possessing a football club at all, for, unfortunately, the opportunities afforded the young men of Merthyr for indulging in manly, healthy games were of a very limited character indeed.' After remarking that the season had hardly been spectacular, Edmonds articulated the idea that it was the taking part, and not necessarily the winning, that mattered. For if the Merthyr club had not reached greatness, 'the fact that they had been able to give facilities to the young men of Merthyr to indulge in rational recreation amply justified the existence of the club'.[53]

The significance of these pronouncements is clear. They indicate the presence in Merthyr of a group of prominent individuals who wished to bring the new model sports firmly within the boundaries of the urban, as part of their drive to transform Merthyr into a civic settlement. The construction of recreation grounds would encourage such a development. Moreover, a publicly owned park in the congested sprawl of Merthyr would serve as an engine for the improvement of public health and morality. The tenets of contemporary urban liberalism demanded such an amenity, and there was no shortage of urban liberals willing to support any scheme which would further the cause.[54] For example, the news that local solicitor, John Vaughan, was about to open Merthyr's first swimming baths in 1889 was welcomed by one observer as a step in the right direction. However, private enterprise was not enough and the members of the Local Board of Health were urged to follow the example of Vaughan, 'and do something towards lifting the veil of obloquy which the absence of all rational means of recreation has deservedly brought down upon the town'.[55] And while swimming baths were useful, they were a

[53] Ibid., 28 July 1894.
[54] Colonel D. Rees Lewis argued that the whole question of a park was one that should be resolved by the Board of Health (*ME*, 31 March 1894). Also see the editorial in the *ME*, 18 June 1881.
[55] Ibid., 29 June 1889.

poor substitute for a park. Failure to reorganize the built environment along these 'civic' lines, so the argument ran, reflected poorly upon the district.[56]

Despite the supposed benefits of a park, the civic boosters had to overcome a number of formidable obstacles: hostility from the 'outlying districts', a belief that the great capitalists and landowners (and not the smaller commercial sector) should do more to help the district, together with the ever constraining 'ratepayer mentality', all conspired to frustrate the progressives. Even when some of the district's working-class parents entered the debate, petitioning the council in 1896, the labyrinthine structure of local government ensured that the matter was defused.[57] In the face of such powerful forces working for inertia it is perhaps remarkable that progress of any description was made. As with so much of the civic project in Merthyr, when it came it was speedy. In 1902 it was announced that the Urban District Council had (finally) agreed to lay a recreation ground in the town.[58] Better was to follow. In the aftermath of the elevation of Merthyr to the status of a county borough came the news that the town was to get the magnificent Cyfarthfa Park as a public park. By June 1909 the people were able to enjoy this prestigious amenity, a fact celebrated by Councillor Simons in a speech he delivered at the opening ceremony:

> If all the money expended in the town in the past had been spent in such a good way as this, Merthyr would not now have to take a back seat to her sister towns in South Wales. Merthyr, cloak it as they would, had been a disgraceful Merthyr in the past. It had nothing to recommend it. They had wretched houses and streets, and no open spaces. But he hoped that day had gone; that old Merthyr had passed away, that the new Merthyr had arrived, and as time went on the inhabitants would appreciate places like the parks, and that they would become better citizens (cheers).[59]

In keeping with all the requirements of a truly 'civilized' and 'public' space, the grounds were highly regulated. For instance,

---

[56] See the observations of one Dowlaisian in 1899: '[I]t is astonishing, in this age when all our towns cry out for more open spaces and public parks, that we have never moved in that direction. Are we so behind the times as all this?' (ibid., 1 April 1899).
[57] Ibid., 17 October 1896.
[58] See Charles Wilkins, *A History of Merthyr Tydfil* (2nd edn, Merthyr, 1908), p. 570.
[59] *ME*, 12 June 1909.

teams wishing to avail themselves of the facilities were required
to book a pitch in advance, ensuring that the space was effici-
ently utilized; this served as a reminder that the land was under
the control of the municipal authorities.[60] More importantly
perhaps, with the arrival of the park Merthyrians were at last
provided with the opportunity to play rational sports on publicly owned spaces within the urban environment. Yet another
feather in the cap of the civic projectors.

IV. COMMERCIALIZED SPORT'S INCORPORATION WITHIN THE URBAN

The municipal provision of facilities for Merthyr's sportsmen
and women marked an important stage in the process whereby
popular sport was physically reintegrated into the built form.
It could also be perceived as a victory for the town's boosters.
However, the civic projectors were only one group who encouraged the spatial realignment of sport in these *fin-de-siècle*
years. Other forces, driven by commercial imperatives, were in
operation, aiming to promote sport's position in the district.
Certainly, during the early to mid-1900s there was a general
recognition of the potential of the commercially organized
sports event to bring trade, and money, into Merthyr. As one
individual noted in 1904:

> From time to time there arises amongst the tradesmen of Merthyr a
> feeling that far more advantage ought to be taken of the excellent railway
> facilities of the town in order to promote holiday attractions for the
> immense population within easy reach of the place ... Such ideas are
> strong just now, possibly owing to the slackness of trade, and there are one
> or two schemes under consideration in order to secure a first-class athletic
> ground for the town.[61]

And only the previous year the Merthyr Chamber of Trade had
invested £150 in the organization of a Whitsun sports day.[62]

---

[60] See, for example, the County Borough of Merthyr Tydfil, Minute Book, no. 3,
9 October 1907. Also see Daunton, 'Public place and private space', p. 218.
[61] *ME*, 28 May 1904. Concerned inhabitants continued to make the connection
between sport, business and civic pride throughout the 1900s. When news broke that
there was to be an international Northern Union game between Wales and New
Zealand in 1907, one 'Tradesman' was quick to suggest that every effort should be
made to secure the fixture for the town: 'A large influx of visitors would be a boon to the
town at large, especially to us as tradesmen' (ibid., 26 October 1907).
[62] Ibid., 25 April 1903.

They were rewarded for their enterprise, for while nearby Troedyrhiw experienced a haemorrhaging of population as pleasure-seekers left for the 'various places of amusement and ... the seaside', Merthyr was augmented by 'several thousand' who converged upon Penydarren Park. As the high constable, Dr C. Biddle, remarked when opening the event, 'Years ago 8,000 and 9,000 people have been seen at sports in the park, and there is no reason whatever why Merthyr should not get back to maintain its sports days.'[63]

This invocation of a prelapsarian era during which Merthyr was a major centre of sporting entertainment was no mere flight of nostalgic fancy. During the 1870s and 1880s a number of fêtes and galas had been held at Penydarren Park under the auspices of travelling impresarios.[64] These itinerant entrepreneurs of leisure were joined by a cohort of local tradesmen, active from the mid-1870s, who made a concerted attempt to establish the town as a home of the commercialized sports day. To the fore were members of the Merthyr Licensed Victuallers' Association (MLVA). Their most telling contribution, in a town so devoid of recreational amenities, was in the provision of (often costly) facilities.[65] Take, for example, the efforts of William Scott, landlord of the Great Western public house in Merthyr High Street. A shrewd judge of market conditions, and doubtless conscious of the success of Job Davies's track at nearby Trefforest, he decided to construct a running track 'at considerable expense' on ground behind the Penydarren Iron Works in 1882.[66] The opening of his 'Merthyr New Athletic Grounds' demonstrated that his faith in the town's athletes had been justified; thirty-three hopefuls paid the 1*s*. 6*d*. to compete, and a crowd of over 500 parted with an entrance fee of 6*d*. He would have profited further had not an even larger number assembled free of charge on the nearby tips overlooking the track.

Scott's individual enterprise in Merthyr's athletic world was matched at the collective level of the local Licensed Victuallers' Association. Their various initiatives represent the most

---

[63]   Ibid., 6 June 1903.

[64]   For more on this, see Croll, 'Civilizing the urban', pp. 213–14.

[65]   For a general discussion of the resourcefulness of drink-sellers in this respect, see Brian Harrison, *Drink and the Victorians: The Temperance Question in England, 1815–1872* (2nd edn, Keele, 1994), p. 320; Richard Holt, *Sport and the British*, p. 63.

[66]   *Kelly's Directory of South Wales and Monmouthshire* (London, 1884), p. 402; *ME*, 8 April 1882, 15 January 1881; *PC*, 17 September 1881.

sustained attempt by a single body at providing commercialized sporting entertainment in the town from the 1870s
through to the 1890s. Formed in 1872, one of the first acts of the
Association was to organize a sports day and grand fête the following year.[67] Despite the inclement weather, the venture was
enough of a success to warrant repeating. From the outset the
victuallers hit upon a formula which, in its essentials, was
retained unaltered throughout the history of the event. Musical
entertainment was provided, the local police force was involved
to maintain order, while the races themselves were a judicious
mixture of amateur and professional. From 1883 the meetings
were held under the rules of the Amateur Athletic Association,
although before this date races 'Open to Gentleman Amateurs'
were included.[68] Nevertheless, the prospect of financial gain
was apparently uppermost in the minds of the average enthus-
iast. The two amateur entrants for the Champion Race in 1881
were lonely figures indeed compared with the forty-four who
competed in the 120 yards for workmen, a contest run for prize
money.[69] Such was the seriousness with which they took the
competition that in the weeks leading up to a MLVA sports day
the hills and roads around the town were colonized by training
athletes, all intent on winning the cash prizes on offer. Little
wonder that by the early 1880s the future of 'this brilliant event'
seemed assured.[70]

By staging the annual athletics, the licensed victuallers (or,
more precisely, a loose confederation of ten publicans centred
on the energetic figure of Dan Thomas), capitalized upon the
interest that already existed in the sport and helped to boost its
profile within the district. The presence of a brass band, the construction of a grand stand for 'ladies' in 1882, as well as innovations such as a telegraph board for quick relaying of results,
all served to add to the spectacle of the day.[71] They were much
helped by the good railway links with other valleys that allowed
inhabitants from other settlements easy access to the event,
which was advertised in local papers throughout the region.
Indeed, it appears that the sports were a vital ingredient in

[67] *MTl*, 5 September 1873. Also see *Merthyr Express Almanack for 1894*, p. 64.
[68] *ME*, 4 June 1881.
[69] Ibid., 9 July 1881.
[70] Ibid., 5 June 1880.
[71] Ibid., 15 July 1882.

Merthyr's growing reputation as a regional entertainment centre. Thus, in 1884, when they coincided with a Volunteers' demonstration at Llanwonno, it was reported that the demonstration 'interfered with the Rhondda Valley people who may justly be said to make the greatest contribution to every festival held in the town'.[72] Fortunately, the publicans had already staged two successful events earlier in the year: an Easter Monday Festivity and a Sports Day and Great Brass Band Competition on Whit Monday.[73] By the time of the latter, the rumour was abroad that 'the now famous "Ten Men of Merthyr" . . . are said to have made "a good pile" by both fêtes this year'.[74]

In 1890, those 'Ten Men' transformed themselves into an organization with an explicit brief, namely the Merthyr Recreation Company. The object of the company was 'to promote sports and bring people into the town on Bank Holidays', and with this end in mind Penydarren Park was acquired for ten years at a rent of £80 a year. Of the company's twenty-five shareholders, all had interests in the local drink trade with the exception of one. As with their earlier efforts, athletics meetings were their most popular offerings. Taking advantage of Mabon's Day in March 1891, a foot-race was organized under their auspices between two local men for £25-a-side. This event alone attracted a crowd of some 2,500.[75] However, notwithstanding such red-letter days, poor organization meant that by September 1892 debts started to mount and, despite struggling on for a few years longer, the Merthyr Recreation Company effectively existed in name alone by 1895. The dénouement came four years later when Dan Thomas found himself in court being sued by a local printer for non-payment of a longstanding debt of the company.[76] Thus ended the most ambitious attempt on the part of the licensed victuallers to expand the dimensions of Merthyr's sporting world.

Some inhabitants were not sorry to see the demise of the Recreation Company. The close connection between the drink trade and athletic events concerned many, not least those

[72] Ibid., 9 August 1884.
[73] Ibid., 8 March 1884, 7 June 1884.
[74] Ibid., 7 June 1884.
[75] Ibid., 7 March 1891.
[76] Ibid., 22 April 1899.

wedded to temperance ideals. In particular, the practice of setting up a 'refreshments' tent was roundly condemned. Heavy drinking was indulged in by many who made up the crowds at Penydarren Park. Hence, in 1883, the Merthyr stipendiary magistrate, whilst granting a special licence for the forthcoming MLVA sports, felt moved to discourse upon the lamentable scenes that had occurred the previous year:

> He was not in the town himself, but he had been informed that it was almost disgusting to see the drunken people rolling about the town. If it happened that he heard a bad character given to the town in consequence of these sports, any future application for a licence for the sale of beer would surely be refused.[77]

Later, in 1892, one commentator, remarking upon the 4,000 who flocked to the park to patronize the foot-races, noted sadly that 'the drunkenness in the streets was something enormous'.[78] And, as if public drunks were not enough to worry about, they were invariably accompanied by significant numbers of professional bookmakers, much to the chagrin of some.[79]

If the commercialization of pedestrianism ushered in some unsavoury associated practices to the urban arena, in other cases the process had far more profound and disturbing consequences. This is most clearly illustrated by considering the development of pugilism. As has been shown earlier, this was a cultural practice that was marginalized physically and temporally from the currents of mainstream urban life. By 1909 the situation had altered so drastically that the arrival of a certain Frederick Hall Thomas, intent upon visiting his mother, brought not only Merthyr but almost every town between it and Cardiff to a standstill. Thomas, better known to his contemporaries and posterity alike as 'Freddie Welsh', was a professional boxer who had just won the British lightweight championship. That he was a Pontypridd boy rather than a Merthyrian did not trouble the hundreds who crowded to catch a glimpse of their sporting hero. As the *Express* noted, he 'has attained a height of popularity that does not fall to the lot of

[77] *ME*, 7 July 1883.
[78] *MDT*, 10 June 1892.
[79] Ibid., 8 July 1882.

every professional boxer, and thousands of admirers on Saturday extended to him a heart's welcome-home' to Wales. After reaching Cardiff by train, this 'well-built young fellow dressed in a navy blue suit and wearing a straw hat' with a monster leek for a button-hole, headed north for Merthyr by car, passing large crowds who lined the road as he did so. *En route* Welsh stopped at Pontypridd, stood up in the car and made a 'characteristic' speech. '"I am not an orator," he said, "I am a fighting man, and I hope to put Pontypridd right on top of the world."' These few words were followed by a drive to Troedyrhiw where he was greeted by local pugilist, 'Tiger' Smith.[80] A procession was formed with the Merthyr Vale Battalion Band at the head, and Freddie slowly made his way to his mother's house in Merthyr itself.[81]

Such scenes would have been unimaginable in the south Wales of the 1870s. There were enough observers who wished to condemn them to the realm of the unimaginable in the 1900s and 1910s. For whilst Welsh may have been untypical in terms of the scale of his popularity, he was only the most prominent of a number of boxers who now openly plied their trade within the confines of the urban environment, courted by an adoring working-class public. Over 4,000 watched 'a splendid programme' of boxing at the Tonypandy Pavilion in 1914,[82] while 'Tiger' Smith himself enjoyed a warm welcome when he returned from a fight in London to decide the heavyweight championship of England in 1907. Although beaten, 'hundreds' were waiting for his arrival at Merthyr station and the streets were the venue for a celebration of all things pugilistic as 'Tiger' was carried shoulder-high to the Garth Inn.[83]

It should be noted that this was by now a modified pugilism. Commercialization and the demands of respectability had ensured that aspects of the knuckle-crunching prizefight were softened somewhat. The introduction of gloves was a concession

[80] 'Tiger' (or James) Smith: a sergeant major in the 10th Hussars who saw action in South Africa, and also did a tour of duty in India. On his return to Merthyr, he became a collier, a pugilist, and had connections in the drink trade. As a fighter he enjoyed a sizeable local following. A benefit concert was held for him in 1911 after he survived a roof fall whilst working in a local colliery (ibid., 2 March 1907, 25 January 1908, 4 February 1911, 27 May 1911).
[81] Ibid., 26 June 1909.
[82] *South Wales Worker*, 21 February 1914.
[83] *ME*, 2 March 1907.

at least to the imperatives of civilization.[84] Yet, to both practitioners and horrified observers alike, more than enough vestiges
of the older practices remained. For example, in July 1907 three
gloved fights were held in the Drill Hall in Merthyr, the promoters charging admission fees which ranged between 2s. 6d.
and 1 guinea. The main event was a fifteen-round gloved contest between Dave Peters of Treorchy and Joe White of
America for a £100 purse refereed by a representative of the
Sportsman. However, it was the encounter between the nine-
stone champion of India, Fidget Parker, and Alf Williams from
Salisbury that caught the attention of the local journalist. Any
notion that gloves sanitized the sport was exploded:

> The contest made one's blood curdle, for each man fought as for his life.
> Williams was floored soon after the first round opened, but on rising he
> attacked Parker with much fury, getting in some good 'shots'. Williams
> was the first to show blood, however, and his opponent bashed him about
> so cleverly – we suppose that's what they call it – that he 'went under'
> for a third time, and a moment or two elapsed before he could rise, and
> just then time was called. Both men now showed blood and marks of
> having been severely punched.

Williams was knocked out soon after the start of the second
round, and 'For over an hour he remained in a semi-conscious
state'.[85]

In the same month the secular and the sacred sang a
harmonious chorus of disapproval as a result of the establishment of Professor Taylor's boxing booth at the top end of the
High Street. The Merthyr Corporation received letters from
both the local branch of the Independent Labour Party and the
Pontmorlais Calvinistic Methodists, forcefully contending that
it should be closed. 'Polonius' agreed:

> The respectable portion of the community will regret this, as the booth,
> *placed in the heart of town*, is a public nuisance. Such exhibitions as are given
> there are not calculated to have any uplifting tendency, but rather the
> reverse. In the interests of the rising generation it is a pity the booth
> cannot be got rid of.[86]

[84] Gloved fights were certainly being held in the 1890s (*MDT*, 29 January 1892,
5 August 1892).
[85] *ME*, 27 July 1907.
[86] Ibid., 20 July 1907 (emphasis added).

In fact, by 1907 respectable Merthyrians had already endured at least five years of similar ventures. Boxing booths had made frequent, though mercifully short, appearances in the town, as part of the various galas and sports days held in Penydarren Park.[87] With the arrival of the 'Prince of Wales Circus of Varieties' in 1900, the town's fighters were provided with the means of pursuing their chosen sport under the guise of legitimate entertainment. Thus, while patrons of the circus could one month enjoy the antics of the 'famous tramp cyclist', Woodward, the trapeze artists 'Nana, Nano, and Nana', and the contortionist Max Merlin ('who even dislocates his neck'), the next they could see a boxing match between Billy Ross, the lightweight champion of England, and local bruiser and drunkard, Redmond Coleman.[88] The very idea that Coleman could enjoy the support of a large number of his fellow town dwellers was anathema to many; that there was a near riot involving 'hundreds of people' when Ross was deemed to have been guilty of sharp practice provoked outrage.[89] As a consequence, the Merthyr Council felt able to seize upon a report from the district surveyor which had noted that the circus building was safe for 'ordinary performances, but not for an excited and overcrowded audience'. Councillor David Evans suggested that the surveyor was referring to the fights which had recently taken place in the circus, and added that 'Those were no credit to the town'. There was general agreement that the lessee should be given three months' notice to remove the building.[90]

On this occasion at least, 'Respectable Society' had been able to enforce its values, albeit via a circuitous route. But, ominously, the Council felt unable to ban boxing matches because they were, in and of themselves, 'savage', and by January 1902 three days of scientific boxing were again being held in the circus.[91] This was an altered situation; no longer was it possible simply to charge the police with the duty of chasing the more brutalized members of the community out of the town and onto the 'bloody

[87] See, for example, ibid., 11 July 1908.
[88] Ibid., 5 January 1901, 9 February 1901. For more on the notorious Coleman, see above, pp. 95–6.
[89] Ibid., 9 February 1901.
[90] Ibid., 23 January 1901.
[91] Ibid., 4 January 1902; the 'savagery' of boxing was referred to in the ME, 5 July 1902.

spots'. The arrival of entrepreneurs of entertainment like Professor Taylor meant that the local authorities were now dealing
with individuals who, as his title suggests, were skilled in the art
of covering themselves with a patina of respectability. The
extent to which Taylor differed from the mountain-fighter of
old was revealed in 1907, when he informed his critics that he
would donate his recent winnings to charity if they could prove
alleged irregularities in his latest contest; he went on to
announce that he had already sent £5 to Merthyr General
Hospital because the fight had been so easy.[92]

V. 'FOOTBALL! FOOTBALL! FOOTBALL!' –
MONEY! MONEY! MONEY!

Mammon's influence was also evident in rugby and soccer.
Despite rugby union's amateur status, covert professionalism
appears to have been a *de facto* feature of the game in the
coalfield at least from the late 1890s onwards when large fee-
paying crowds became commonplace. In 1907 this undercur-
rent of rugby life surfaced in Aberdare with spectacular results.
Amateurism was revealed to be 'shamateurism' in the Taff and
Cynon Valleys at least. The Welsh Football Union was forced to
hold an inquiry that was conducted in such a secretive manner
that observers were left in little doubt that they were witnessing
an exercise in damage limitation. The Merthyr Football Club
was allowed to struggle on, whilst the Aberdarians were expelled from the Union altogether. Within weeks of the revelations,
Merthyr, along with Aberdare and Ebbw Vale, was experi-
menting openly with the professional Northern Union code.
And by 1912 the town had also enthusiastically embraced professional soccer, with Merthyr Town securing a place in the first
division of the Southern League and attracting the likes of
Manchester City to its home ground at Penydarren Park. An
indication of the extent to which commercialism had intruded
into that code was provided with the conversion of Merthyr
Town into a limited liability company in 1911.[93]

[92] Ibid., 20 July 1907.
[93] Ibid., 20 May 1911. For more on the economics of football, see Wray Vamplew,
'The economics of a sports industry: Scottish gate-money football, 1890–1914', *Economic
History Review*, 2nd series, 35, no. 4 (1982), 549–67; Richard Holt, *Sport and the British*,
pp. 282–6.

Such developments rested upon a rapid growth in the popularity of both rugby and association football during the 1890s and 1900s. The rise of the association code in the district is especially noteworthy, given the attention which has been lavished by historians upon its sister code.[94] The local newspapers clearly reveal an active association scene in settlements such as Merthyr Vale, Dowlais, Plymouth, Treharris, Troedyrhiw, and Merthyr town itself.[95] Treharris marked itself out as a particular stronghold while inhabitants of Dowlais could watch, amongst others, Dowlais Albion, Dowlais Wanderers, Dowlais Excelsiors, Dowlais Association Football Club, Dowlais Black Bats and Dowlais Railwaymen. Meanwhile, the game of rugby was also undergoing a similar process of popularization. By 1888 the public's preference for rugby over cricket was being noted, while on the eve of the 1889–90 season observers of the footballing scene in Merthyr were commenting upon the unprecedented levels of interest shown in the game.[96] In Dowlais so noticeable was this phenomenon that the local correspondent informed the *Express*'s readers that 'the football fever is certainly contagious just now' with four teams battling to maintain the honour of the town.[97] By 1904 it appeared as if a great swathe of the population was totally obsessed with footballing matters. As one commentator noted,

> The football season is once again upon us, and for the next eight months the dominant note will be football! football! football! One half of the week will be utilised by large sections of the community to discuss the previous Saturday's match – in a joyous and defiant mood if the favourites are successful, apologetic if defeated – and the second half in prognosticating the result of the ensuing Saturday's match.[98]

So established was the game by the 1908–9 season that it was even possible to find vicars preaching sermons based on footballing themes.[99]

[94] A start has been made. See B. Lile and D. Farmer, 'The early development of association football in South Wales, 1890–1906', *Transactions of the Cymmrodorion Society* (1984), 193–215. Also see Martin O. Johnes, 'Association football in South Wales, 1906–40', Ph.D. thesis, University of Wales (Cardiff), 1998.
[95] The most cursory glance at the local press during the late 1890s and 1900s confirms this.
[96] *ME*, 5 October 1889.
[97] Ibid., 26 October 1889.
[98] Ibid., 10 September 1904.
[99] The Revd S. S. Orpwood delivered a series of sermons with titles such as 'Offside', 'Foul play' and 'Referees' (ibid., 9 January 1909, 16 January 1909).

By this time, supporters had been presented with ever-increasing opportunities to see their favourite teams. The length of the season grew from eleven or twelve games in the 1880s and early 1890s to forty-plus by the late 1900s. And there were more teams to which they could pledge their allegiance. The numbers of clubs that were formed – and appeared in the pages of the local newspapers – in the 1880s and particularly the 1890s are impressive indeed. The number that went completely unnoticed was no doubt also large. There was a rash of works clubs, school teams, junior teams and scratch teams as well as the clubs which operated one step down from the premier sides in a town. Some enjoyed only the briefest of lives. Outfits such as the 'Rowdy Dowdy F.C.', the 'Merthyr Stars', the 'Merthyr Red Stars', the 'Merthyr White Stars', the 'United Rovers', the 'Maggie Murphy Pals', 'Paynter's Pups', the 'Lady Slavey Mashers', the 'Death or Glory Boys' and the 'Kill or Cure' team were especially prone to an abbreviated existence.[100] As junior clubs, usually set up and run with the help of an enthusiastic adult, they stayed together only until some boys were old enough to work (a factor which perhaps helps to explain the prevalence of teams made up of 11–13 year olds), or until others graduated to more prestigious sides. Teams that had their origins in the workplace were likely to enjoy rather longer careers. That butchers, ironworkers at Plymouth, Cyfarthfa and Dowlais, press men, teachers, sales assistants and policemen all had their own teams in the district is testament to the ability of rugby to appeal to a wide range of social classes, particularly during this period of growth.[101] Meanwhile, there was always a handful of clubs which took on the role of 'feeder teams', supplying the main clubs with suitable talent and even rising to take over the mantle of premier side themselves on occasion.

If the numbers playing the game increased during these years, even more were flocking to watch. Significantly, from the 1880s there was a large reservoir of spectators who were willing to pay for the pleasure of viewing a hard-fought contest. The

[100] Ibid., 16 September 1893, 19 August 1893, 21 October 1893, 18 November 1893, 30 April 1892, 13 October 1894, 22 April 1905.
[101] Ibid., 2 February 1895, 4 March 1893, 18 September 1896, 5 September 1903, 18 March 1893, 20 October 1894, 5 October 1889, 16 March 1895.

MFC felt able to introduce the policy of charging admission fees for the most popular fixtures by the 1886–7 season.[102] This was warmly welcomed by 'Gladiator', who argued:

> nobody who takes an interest in the rational amusement would begrudge the paltry threepence asked at the gate to witness a trial of skill similar to that of Rhymney v. Merthyr, or Merthyr v. Aberdare Crusaders. It is only fair that those who encourage football teams by their presence at matches should show their appreciation by stumping up their mite for the purpose of swelling the funds of the club on whose ground the contests take place.[103]

Showing a fine awareness of market conditions, the MFC carefully regulated the new scheme, not charging spectators at all when the Tredegar XV visited in October 1887, yet taking full advantage of the opportunities presented by the combination of a public holiday and an attractive fixture.[104] The Boxing Day contest of 1888 between Merthyr and Llanelli resulted in the largest take of gate money since charges had been introduced, while the local derby between Merthyr and Dowlais five years later (by this time considered something of an annual institution) drew a crowd of 500 paying spectators in addition to the extra hundred who were described either as season ticket holders or 'ladies'.[105]

By the 1900s, and as a result of an upturn in the performance of the premier union clubs in the town, the charging of admission fees was the rule rather than the exception. Football enthusiasts were generally willing to pay if there was the prospect of some high-quality action and more than an outside chance of their team winning. The Merthyr Thursdays achieved a great deal of success on the field, enjoying a particularly encouraging run in the 1902–3 season.[106] By Christmas 1906 the MFC was well placed to hold attractive fixtures. The visit of the London Irish 'was a red-letter day in the history of Merthyr football', attracting the largest paying crowd hitherto seen at a rugby match in the town.[107] In February 1907 there was another

---

[102] Ibid., 5 February 1887.
[103] Ibid., 5 February 1887.
[104] Ibid., 29 October 1887.
[105] Ibid., 7 January 1888, 30 December 1893.
[106] Ibid., 2 May 1903, 1 July 1903.
[107] Ibid., 5 January 1907.

record crowd at Penydarren Park to witness the league match against Penygraig.[108] The season climaxed at Easter with five games played over the holiday period. Of the three held at Merthyr, the contest with Swansea attracted the most interest. Yet another record crowd was entertained by some pre-match musical fare courtesy of the Merthyr Volunteer Band, followed by a closely fought game in which Swansea emerged the victors by two points.[109] Despite not winning the title, the home team could look back on 'the most successful season in its history'.[110]

Shortly after this fixture, a hairdresser from Aberdare posted an advertisement which caused a sensation throughout south Wales and had an immediate impact upon the MFC. When E. H. Rees, the secretary of the Aberdare Club, announced to the world that professionalism was rife in the game of Welsh rugby, he set in train a series of events which rapidly led to the incursion of the Northern Union code in the Valleys.[111] Immediately, observers of the footballing scene in Merthyr were fearful that if Aberdare were to be penalized by the Welsh Football Union then the MFC would not be far behind.[112] Indeed, Rees began to cite cases involving the Merthyr club in which excessive travelling expenses had been paid.[113] By the end of June the seriousness of the allegations meant that the WFU was obliged to consider the position of the club. Quite apart from the most serious charge of paying players over and above bare expenses, it was alleged that Merthyr was involved in a conspiracy with Aberdare to allow Arnold, a player banned by the WFU, to take the field under a false name. To make matters worse, it was also asserted that it was pre-arranged that if Aberdare beat Merthyr on points, the latter would protest to the Glamorgan League over two other players who were not qualified to play.[114]

[108] Ibid., 23 February 1907.
[109] Ibid., 6 April 1907.
[110] Out of a total of 43 games, the team had won 25 and lost 14 (ibid., 18 May 1907).
[111] See Gareth Williams, 'How amateur was my valley: professional sport and national identity in Wales, 1890–1914', *British Journal of Sports History*, 2, no. 3 (December 1985), 248–69.
[112] *ME*, 1 June 1907.
[113] Ibid., 15 June 1907.
[114] *South Wales Daily News*, 27 June 1907.

That the WFU dealt with Merthyr leniently seems clear. Over the matter of the large expenses demanded, the committee took the view that 'the sum was not unreasonable. It was in the nature of a guarantee, and as such was very small potatoes indeed compared with the quantities given by larger clubs.'[115] This was hardly a ringing endorsement of the club's financial policies. The decision looked all the more doubtful when it was revealed at the MFC's annual general meeting that a deficit of £20 incurred during the 1905–6 season had been transformed into a profit of £200. Gate receipts stood at £722 11s. 6d.[116] Whatever the degree to which 'shamateurism' was a feature of the MFC's operations, the episode was traumatic enough to produce some heated exchanges among the club's committee members. At a meeting held in July, a vote was taken on whether the club should remain within the amateur fold. The alternative 'found not a few supporters' and although the final decision that the status quo should be maintained was 'greeted with loud cheers', many had severe misgivings. Schoolmaster W. Harris resigned his position on the committee as a protest at the hypocrisy of the situation. He spoke out strongly in favour of open professionalism. It was becoming popular throughout the country and 'he wanted Merthyr to take the lead'. This was immediately rebutted by the secretary, D. C. Harris, who

> hoped that they would do all they could to have an amateur club. Men should play for the love of the game. Merthyr had a good record, a good ground, and they would never find difficulty in getting good men. All young fellows in the town ought to have the spirit of sport in them, and then they would hear nothing at all about professionalism or bogus amateurism (applause).[117]

The question of professionalism had fractured the club into two opposing sections and few observers were surprised when the news broke of the establishment of a Northern Union club in the town within a week of the MFC's meeting. Immediately, the promoters of the new team began the process of signing players, raising money and engaging in a war of words against the MFC. It was claimed that the majority of the old team's

[115] *WM*, 14 June 1907.
[116] *ME*, 13 July 1907.
[117] Ibid., 13 July 1907.

players had signed up for the NU club, and that there 'was plenty of money in the swim'. Ten backers had been found, and the Northern Union authorities were alleged to have guaranteed that the costs of forming a club in the heartland of rugby union would be forthcoming.[118] Games were hastily arranged with clubs in the north of England, and by the end of the summer Merthyr's first professional rugby team was in training.[119]

These developments brought a speedy response from the defenders of amateurism. At a meeting of the Merthyr Seconds, one of the committee members decried the actions of those who 'wanted to wipe the club out of existence'. They 'were traitors to football and sport in Merthyr ... What was being done was a gross insult and most unjust to the young players of the district (applause).' While the adherents of amateurism had obviously not been averse to paying more than 'reasonable expenses', to embrace open professionalism ran against all the notions of 'fair play', 'honour' and 'manliness' which had attached themselves to the amateur game from the mid-nineteenth century. Players who were paid a wage would, according to this argument, be reduced to mere 'hirelings'.[120] The secretary of the Welsh Union, Walter Rees, spoke for many when he referred to the professional code as 'the mongrel game' which would produce 'a revulsion of feeling' when the novelty had worn off. Whether such was to be the case or not, Rees sounded a note which was to characterize the relationship between the two codes from the start. 'We are confident that the Northern Union cannot live in Wales under any circumstances for long, and we are determined to kill it and its insidious influence without delay.'[121]

VI. STADIA, CROWDS AND NEWSPAPERS

The implications of the appearance of the Northern Union team in terms of football's demands upon urban space were felt immediately. Professionalism made imperative what before had only been a decided advantage, namely a field situated within,

[118] Ibid., 20 July 1907.
[119] The news that the Northern Union code had made inroads in south Wales was warmly welcomed in the north of England. See *Yorkshire Evening Press*, 12 September 1907, 27 September 1907, 30 September 1907.
[120] *ME*, 20 July 1907.
[121] Ibid., 5 October 1907.

or extremely near to, the built environment. And more than ever before, a ground's suitability was defined in commercial terms. If the professional club was to cope with the burden of having to pay its players as well as make the long journeys to the north of England, it was essential that it find a piece of land with easy access for the potential supporters.[122] The determination of their amateur rivals to kill off the Northern Union experiment merely compounded the problem. The MFC, drawing upon some powerful allies, had managed to secure the prime site of Penydarren Park for £120 per annum.[123] In contrast, those intent on furthering the cause of professionalism in south Wales found themselves with few such influential friends. The Ebbw Vale NU club was refused access to the Bridgend Field by the owner, Mr Fred Phillips. Phillips was the mayor of Newport and 'a great supporter of the Newport Club, which is being run on amateur lines, and if he lets the field to a professional club he cannot continue a supporter of Newport'.[124] The Aberdarians were also faced with a ground problem. The Merthyr side was more fortunate. It obtained the College Field for the season, which, although 'having a decided slope', was within easy reach of residential areas and the club 'realised the importance of being in town'.[125] Less than a month after the formation of the team, Merthyr possessed its own professional rugby ground, complete with a new stand, sixty yards in length.

Just as the purpose-built football ground became an integral feature of Merthyr's built environment,[126] so users of the town's streets were confronted with another new phenomenon, the large football crowd. Crowds that were measured in their hundreds (on good days) in the 1880s were more commonly estimated in the post-1907 era in terms of thousands. The novelty of the NU code and the furore which surrounded the split with the amateur game ensured that the professional club proved to be a powerful attraction. Southey's *Merthyr Express* provided readers with a crash-course introduction to the

---

[122] For more comments regarding the importance of a ground's location, see Nicholas Fishwick, *English Football and Society, 1910–1950* (Manchester, 1989), p. 57.
[123] *ME*, 3 August 1907.
[124] Ibid., 27 July 1907.
[125] Ibid., 17 August 1907.
[126] For descriptions of a new ground at Penydarren Park, see *ME*, 19 August 1905, 16 September 1905.

rules.[127] One thousand Merthyrians paid 3*d*. each to watch a pre-season trial match.[128] Despite many of the players repeatedly demonstrating their poor grasp of both the rules and the ball, and a number of crushing defeats inflicted by the northern clubs, enthusiasm for the sport remained high in the early months, and Merthyr enjoyed large gates for home games. The opening match was played in front of a crowd that had paid some £150 for the dubious privilege of seeing the home team completely outclassed, while a month later over 4,000 attended the derby game between Ebbw Vale and Merthyr.[129]

As a consequence of the commercialization of sport, new spatial practices developed in urban south Wales. The main streets of the towns, particularly those connecting the railway stations to the grounds, were now appropriated by the football supporters – and other sporting enthusiasts – on a regular basis. The arrival of the perambulating sports crowd was a particularly noteworthy event. For instance, the *South Wales Worker* was struck by the appropriation of public spaces in the Rhondda by fans of foot-racers and pugilists in July 1914:

> Tonypandy was invaded on Saturday with crowds of sportsmen, drawn together, to witness the heats for the 'Cambrian Dash'. After the events were over, the crowds poured out into the main street, and quite a large percentage wended their way to either the Rink or the New Marquee, to see a continuance of sport in the form of boxing contests.[130]

And 'Polonius' felt it worth commenting upon a scene he encountered in Merthyr High Street on Boxing Day 1893. After asking the rhetorical question, 'Are people going mad on football?', he proceeded to describe the state of the thoroughfare:

> A huge crowd was making its way down the street, and rending the air with their shouts. At first I thought that our members of Parliament had paid us a surprise visit, but on nearing the concourse of people I found perched on the shoulders of a few stalwart men a youth with a broken jersey, who had secured what is called in football phraseology a 'try' at the Goitre field. They sang the pathetic air known as the 'Rowdy

127 Ibid., 17 August 1907.
128 Ibid., 7 September 1907.
129 Ibid., 14 September 1907, 19 October 1907.
130 *South Wales Worker*, 25 July 1914.

Dowdy boys', and judging from the heterogeneous crowd which followed, I can't help thinking that the song was aptly descriptive of the singers.[131]

By the mid-1900s it was the diminutive scale of this crowd that would have been most worthy of comment. For this had become the era of the truly impressive football crowd. Take, for example, the scenes which accompanied the arrival of the professional All-Blacks team in 1907. '[T]he largest ever [crowd] seen at a football match in Merthyr' turned out to watch their team live up to all expectations and lose their tenth game in a row. The train carrying the New Zealanders into the Great Western Station was greeted by a crowd which, once again, reminded one observer of the political gatherings of the past. In this case it was 'of the time of the general election, when Pritchard Morgan was first returned to the House of Commons'. However, it was a rather different set of people's representatives who were responsible for this particular assembly:

Enthusiasm was unbounded. At every shriek of the whistle the crowd rushed to the station entrance and began to cheer. On the platform it was almost impossible to move about, and every point of vantage was occupied. People stood on boxes, hung onto railings, mounted trolleys – some fell off, but that didn't matter – and some venturesome young football enthusiasts actually stood on the sills of the parcel office. Outside the station, the high wall was converted into a grand stand, upon which youngsters swarmed like bees. Intense excitement prevailed ... and as it [the train] pulled up, and one of the New Zealanders showed his straw hat through the window, a lusty cheer was raised, which was repeated over and over again.[132]

Scenes such as this were replicated on an increasing basis, and were not dependent solely upon the Northern Union game.[133] With the rapid rise of the soccer club, Merthyr Town, the sight of supporters bedecked in their red and green scarves

[131] *ME*, 30 December 1893.
[132] Ibid., 9 November 1907.
[133] Indeed, a never-ending run of bad results, combined with the problem of distance between south Wales and the north of England, led to many inhabitants losing interest in the professional code. Nevertheless, Merthyr continued to act as a centre of Northern Union activity up until the end of the decade. For instance, 6,000 watched Australia play Wales in 1909 (ibid., 23 January 1909).

and hats, sporting pin-badges of 'Kruger' the bulldog mascot and chanting football songs as they made their way to and from the match became a common one. Over 4,000 supporters of Merthyr Town made the journey to Ninian Park in 1912 to witness a league match against Cardiff.[134] Seven thousand converged on Penydarren Park in April 1909 when Manchester City played the 'Romans'. Despite the heavy rain which the visitors brought with them, a 'large number of the public' waited at the station to greet the First Division team.[135] A few months later, some 5,000 arrived to watch the clash between Merthyr and Ton Pentre at the start of the 1909–10 season.[136] By this point, all inhabitants were forced to confront large crowds as they moved through the public thoroughfares, whether they liked the game or not.

The football crowd's appearance in the streets and public places of a town was only one way in which the followers of the sport found themselves occupying an enhanced position in urban culture. For the increasing demands of professional football upon urban space were matched by the sport's intrusion into the prime medium through which collective representations of the urban were articulated, the local newspaper. Of course the game had been a common enough feature in the *Merthyr Express* before 1907. A dedicated football column was introduced in November 1886, although in an eight-page broadsheet its impact was decidedly muted. The proceedings of the Merthyr Police Court were more prominent – and probably more widely read – than the austere football notes. During the 1890s the column was expanded somewhat. The treatment of the matches became more detailed, and some information was given about the fortunes of the local clubs. Nonetheless, these early forays into the new genre of sports journalism pale into insignificance when compared with the coverage that the sport enjoyed in the 1900s and 1910s. In-depth analyses of games, prospects for the season, lengthy league tables, information about players as well as photographs of local heroes were now the staple diet served up to the readership.[137]

[134] Ibid., 2 March 1912.
[135] Ibid., 1 May 1909.
[136] Ibid., 25 September 1909.
[137] For some general comments upon the relationship between the media and sport, see Tony Mason, *Sport in Britain* (London, 1988), pp. 46–50.

Similarly, the *Merthyr Pioneer*, a paper dedicated to the cause of labour, was alert to the popularity of both codes and reflected this in its pages. In addition to a large section of football notes by 'Earwig' covering all manner of topics of interest to the football fan, the paper also boasted a regular 'late football news' column giving vital information on last-minute team changes and the like. On occasion, the editors were keen to use rugby and soccer as points of entry into wider debates about the iniquitous nature of capitalism and industrial relations.[138] However, for the most part the column was free from polemics and full of the sort of material that presumably 'the average man who supports football' wanted to read, including résumés of individual players' performances throughout the season, their hobbies and vital statistics, as well as general debates about the standard of play.[139]

It could be argued that this increased press coverage simply reflected the fact that there was more footballing activity in south Wales during these years. It would certainly have been a foolhardy editor who ignored such a popular pastime completely. Nevertheless, it is worth noting that other journals managed to treat popular sport in the most cursory of fashions during these years. Many Welsh-language newspapers, for example, were extremely hostile right up until the 1890s and beyond, while the socialist *South Wales Worker* hardly mentioned sports at all in its pages.[140] Only when it could be construed as a political matter did the paper feel ready to make space for popular sports.[141] And the playing of games and the attendance of crowds of spectators were no guarantee of in-depth coverage (as the district's prizefighters of the 1870s were well aware). Editors always had the power to choose what to include. The point being made here is that football's increased prominence in

---

[138] See, for example, *MP*, 6 January 1912; 11 May 1912.

[139] For more on the paper, see Deian Hopkin, 'The *Merthyr Pioneer*, 1911–1922', *Llafur*, 2, no. 3 (1978), 54–64.

[140] Aled Jones, *Press, Politics and Society: A History of Journalism in Wales* (Cardiff, 1993), p. 52.

[141] See, for instance, the comments of the correspondent 'Syndic': 'We are, as is well known, no worshippers of sport as such. It is but one of the departments of life, and should be so regarded – as a part, not the whole. For those fanatics of sport who fritter their lives away, with no other ideas or desire of knowledge than that of sport we have no patience' (*South Wales Worker*, 7 February 1914). For more on the often frosty relationship that obtained between socialists and popular culture, see Chris Waters, *British Socialists and the Politics of Popular Culture, 1884–1914* (Manchester, 1990).

the local newspapers contributed to the enhancement of popular sport's position in local urban culture. It was no longer possible for the newspaper-reading Merthyrian to ignore popular sport in the way that it had been in the 1870s. The local intelligence column, still packed full of announcements of forthcoming chapel tea parties, lectures and philanthropic events, now featured snippets of information about team injuries that had arrived too late to appear in 'Linesman's' main column. And the correspondence columns, still featuring letters from Nonconformists expressing concern over the spiritual health of the population, were now as likely to include letters from football fans discoursing about their favourite pastime.

VI. 'MERTHYR UNITED'? SPORT AND MERTHYR'S TOWN IMAGE

In May 1912 the mayor of Merthyr, Alderman J. M. Berry, accompanied by the district's medical officer, a number of councillors and assorted other notables, attended a complimentary five-course dinner held at the Castle Hotel in honour of the Merthyr Town soccer team which had just been promoted to the First Division of the Southern League. The mayor proposed a toast in which he wished the team every success. Suggesting that Merthyr could now expect to see sporting crowds as large as those witnessed in Newport, Cardiff and Swansea, he went on to link the club's success with the civic accomplishment of Merthyr itself:

> If they looked back ten or twelve years they would see that everything the town had attacked she had accomplished successfully, including corporate powers, its own police force, County Borough, and Quarter Sessions, and now the Borough had the best football team in South Wales (loud cheers).[142]

The football team had become a symbol of the town itself; sport had truly become part of the cultural mainstream.

It has been argued in this chapter that commercial enterprise was an important force in bringing sport in (both physically and symbolically) from the margins of Merthyr society. The

[142] *ME*, 4 May 1912.

'Ten Men of Merthyr' played an important role in the 1880s and early 1890s with their sports days and athletics meetings. In the 1900s professionalism compelled football clubs to obtain suitable pieces of ground in or near the centre of the town. Even pugilists began to find space for their bruising encounters within the confines of the urban. Merthyr's tradesmen were also quick to see the profits that could accrue from such events. As the sports-loving crowd became an increasingly familiar sight in the town (with crowds of over 10,000 on occasion) so retailers and publicans celebrated their good fortune and implored the powers-that-be to do all they could to encourage sporting ventures.

Notwithstanding the support of such an influential section of Merthyr's population (and one closely associated with the civic project), the implications of these developments with regard to the town image of Merthyr were highly ambiguous. On the one hand, as the mayor's speech indicated, popular sport could be incorporated into 'civic Merthyr'. Not only could sporting success be seen as a metaphor for the town's progress, it could also promote more positive images of the district. One commentator saw the visit of the New Zealanders as a perfect antidote to some of the more unsavoury collective representations of the 'old metropolis of Wales'. 'Last Saturday', he wrote,

> was undeniably a date of great historical interest in the annals of this town, for once again the eyes of the West Country were attracted to good old Merthyr, the town which is at one and the same time the head and tail of Wales. Now praised! Now ridiculed! Now held up to the world as a model of industry! Again as a patch of putrescent stagnation![143]

'Polonius' agreed. He interpreted Merthyr Town's promotion as an unalloyed blessing. Inhabitants in towns and cities such as Coventry, Stoke and Southampton would now be made aware of Merthyr, 'a matter of no small importance to the town'. Thus, in the hands of some, organized sport became a tool with which to fashion a new, dynamic identity for Merthyr, one that obliterated older, less reputable town images.

Moreover, sport, in common with music, also provided an opportunity for the generation of inclusive images of Merthyr.

[143] Ibid., 9 November 1907.

This was never more apparent than on the occasions when the district's teams were pitted against old rivals. When Merthyr Town played Cardiff City (itself a poignant reminder of their respective places in the urban hierarchy of south Wales) in 1912, 'Merthyr' was the master category of social analysis. The 4,000 supporters who travelled to the 'Queen of the South' were united behind their team. They even dressed alike. 'The colours of the Merthyr team were in strong evidence, red and green ribbons being freely worn as decorations to the cards bearing words "Play up Merthyr", which were seen in all parts of the city.'[144] Similar scenes were observed when Merthyr played Aberdare that season:

> As the time drew near a huge crowd was seen wending its way down Abernant-road, and it looked as if the whole population of Merthyr were invading Aberdare. The 'enemy', however, proved to be a very good-humoured crowd, several thousands in number decorated with the Merthyr colours and carrying banners with many mottoes, all of which indicated that the Merthyr team were the champions of creation.
>
> At the Great Western Railway station the Merthyr men met a crowd of Aberdare supporters, and the latter sent up a shout of 'Are we downhearted', to which the Merthyr boys responded with 'Remember Southend'. The crowd marched right into the town [headed by a brass band], and some good-humoured chaff was the order of the day.[145]

Soccer in this instance was interpreted as the vehicle for good-natured expressions of local patriotism.

Nevertheless, if such scenes could be accommodated easily enough in 'civic Merthyr', we should note that there was the potential for alternative understandings to emerge. A sporting Merthyr was not necessarily a Merthyr united. Popular sport could not magic away the divisions that separated the old iron town from the 'outlying districts'. In this respect it had much in common with popular music. Just as choral music could lead to increased bitterness between the various towns and pit villages, so sport could work in ways that undercut the district-wide conception of 'Merthyr' upon which so many of its civic claims rested. The rivalries that flourished between Dowlais, Merthyr

---

[144] Ibid., 2 March 1912.
[145] Ibid., 23 March 1912. Aberdare had been beaten by Southend, while Merthyr had just beaten the team 5–0.

Vale, Treharris, Troedyrhiw and Merthyr town asserted themselves on the football field, and could spill over into decidedly
uncivilized behaviour. When the Merthyr Alexandras and the
Dowlais Harlequins met in October 1897 at Merthyr, the home
crowd were keen to do all they could to bring about the
downfall of the visitors. After throwing clumps of earth at them
failed to bring about the desired effect, the partisan spectators
embarked upon a well-orchestrated programme of trying to
trip them up as they ran down the touch-lines.[146] If local derby
games could occasion such disgraceful antics, it is also notable
that attempts to establish a district team in the mid-1890s came
to nothing. After the Merthyr Football Club had experienced
a particularly poor season in 1895–6, the new secretary,
Valentine Watson, urged a rethink amongst lovers of the game:

> Why should not the best players from all the teams in the district be
> drawn upon, and so form a thoroughly strong and representative team,
> to be called 'The Merthyr United District'? If Dowlais and other places
> could be made to fall in with this idea, much good would come to local
> football.[147]

The logic of his argument in footballing terms was undeniable,
but the reality of the situation in the Taff Valley made it
untenable. Needless to say, 'The Merthyr United District' team
never materialized.

Popular sport also drew attention to other lines of social
division. For while many Merthyrians accepted the developments of the 1890s and 1900s, there were those who were far less
happy to see the public spaces of the town colonized by crowds
of sports fans. Their disgust could be expressed in moral or
religious terms, although it is notable that a sense of class difference was often discernible. For example, an 'Old Boy' went to
watch an MFC match at Penydarren Park over the Easter
period, 1907. This being the first game of rugby he had seen for
many years, he was impressed by the performance on the pitch,

> but I am grieved to have to comment on the attitude of the crowd. When
> any good point occurred on the Merthyr side, all was loud hurrahing,
> but, to my dismay, every score by the visitors was booed shamefully.

---

[146] Ibid., 30 October 1897.
[147] Ibid., 3 October 1896.

> I blushed for my native town . . . Perhaps I would not have written had I
> not observed on Saturday last, as a visiting team walked up the
> Promenade to the gate, a crowd of embryo hooligans sitting on the
> railings, casting vile and offensive remarks to the players, such as made
> me long to put my stick to their backs.[148]

A similar sense of moral outrage was articulated by the Revd
J. M. Jones, pastor of Hope Chapel. He felt moved to preach a
sermon on the evils of professional Northern Union rugby.
After reminding the congregation that he had been in Merthyr
for ten years, and had closely monitored the spiritual and moral
condition of the town, he declared that matters had degen-
erated lamentably. The current obsession with boxing, he
decided, was 'foul'. Moreover, the very character of the town, as
manifest in the everyday street-scenes, had changed for the
worse. The appearance of 'loungers' and their domination of
Merthyr's public spaces was especially disturbing. Supporters
of professional sport were to blame:

> I am not an enemy of anything to which the name of sport can be
> applied, but a sport that brings into this town, that collects hundreds
> and thousands of the rottenest characters of the neighbourhood to swell
> the stream of rottenness of this town, I tell you, and I say it deliberately,
> that sport is an unmitigated curse.[149]

There were many who agreed, and who looked on in horror
as Merthyr's sporting fraternity left their imprint upon the
town's identity. Sport's decisive move from the margins to the
centre and its appropriation of space (both urban and discur-
sive) prompted many to protest. While Merthyr Town's success
could be utilized by the civic projectors, other sporting figures
were never to be accommodated within their vision of Merthyr.
The district's fighting class is a case in point. For years they had
been confined to the margins of Merthyr society, but Freddie
Welsh's visit to the town in 1909 illustrated their altered position; 'uncivilized', working-class prizefighters had come down
from the hills and made their home in the athletic and boxing
clubs that were proliferating in the towns of south Wales. That
space was found in Merthyr for them was regretted by many;

148 Ibid., 13 April 1907.
149 Ibid., 7 December 1907.

that Merthyr's name was invoked as a centre of boxing excellence was lamented by respectable inhabitants. Councillors could argue that it was 'shameful that Merthyr be made the centre for prize fights', yet by that point it was already too late; the district's pugilists had fought their way back into the town image.

The same process can be discerned in the cases of rugby and soccer. Although both games may have begun life in the Taff Valley as largely middle-class pursuits, by the start of the twentieth century their popularization was complete. The subsequent professionalization of the game alienated many. Colonel D. Rees Lewis, civic booster *extraordinaire*, made his views clear on the subject as early as 1894. At the MFC's annual supper, the president warned the players that they

> must guard against the introduction of professionalism into it. If they allowed the professional element to become paramount it would be the beginning of the end . . . They should play for the glory of the town and not for themselves, and then they would be bound to get on (applause).[150]

In the Merthyr of the late 1900s and the 1910s, the 'glory of the town' depended on the performances of a professional soccer team and a professional rugby club. As a cultural practice, football, within the space of a single lifetime, had altered dramatically. The arrival of the noisy football spectator was one that could not be ignored by any late Victorian urbanite. Whilst it was possible to include some members of the football crowd in 'civic Merthyr', the 'embryo hooligans' and the 'rottenest characters of the neighbourhood', bedecked in Merthyr's colours and intent upon claiming the streets for themselves, were strange representatives of 'civilized' Merthyr. Their cries of 'Merthyr! Merthyr!' which rang through the public spaces of the district on a weekly basis proclaimed the generation of an altogether different town image.

---

[150] Ibid., 29 September 1894.

VI
THE CIVIC SPIRIT(UAL): NONCONFORMITY AND THE 'PURSUIT OF PLEASURE'

It is clear that the amusements which will always bring together large masses of folk must be either (1) amusements, so called, which brutalise; (2) amusements, so called, which corrupt; or (3) amusements which – I find the best expression of my meaning here in tautology – amuse.
Godfrey Turner, 1877[1]

The chapels have lost all their power because they have ceased to influence the people. It would open the Revd gentleman's mind a little to the attitude of the working man if he served behind a public house bar for one evening, and heard some of the remarks which I constantly hear about some of the ministers of religion . . . The attack of the chapel people on the Church, and on every other institution that rivals them in influence, is only evidence of the deep-rooted spleen for which they are now becoming notorious.
A letter from a licensed victualler to the Merthyr Express
(12 October 1912)

Within the space of a few weeks in the summer of 1909, two inhabitants felt the need to discourse publicly about Merthyr's town image. The picture they painted was a bleak one indeed. In June the Revd J. M. Jones declared in a sermon that 'Merthyr is degenerating'. A month later the Revd W. Rowland Jones bemoaned Merthyr's morals; the town was the 'capital of slumdom' and a centre of 'boozing, gambling, and pugilism'. In explaining the town's downfall, both these prominent Nonconformist ministers pointed to the importance of organized, professional sport. J. M. Jones had been moved to speak on the subject after he had witnessed the crowded street scenes that had accompanied boxer Freddie Welsh's recent (and triumphant) visit to the town. He suggested that 'it was wrong that the town should be made to recognize blackguardism by receiving a man from the sporting world, with a brass band to

---

[1] 'Amusements of the English people', *Nineteenth Century*, 2, no. 6 (December 1877), 820–30, 822.

head the procession'. Moreover, he hoped that 'a little more discretion will be shown in the future. They must remember that there are some people who do not regard prizefighting a fit and proper qualification for hero-worship.'[2] W. Rowland Jones reached similar conclusions. After describing the slums of Merthyr and Dowlais, he went on to consider the morality of those who populated them. Spiritually they were bankrupt; non-attenders at chapel, they had fallen under the sway of some new and powerful idols. 'Who were the gods of Israel today? It was obvious to all who they were at the present moment. They were the pugilists of the country.' Pugilism, he said,

> had swept over South Wales like a fatal epidemic. It had reached the little school-children, who were heard on the streets discussing the merits and demerits of certain fighters; and one legitimately came to the conclusion that the editors of the daily papers were under its spell when they saw so much space devoted to describing such brutal contests.[3]

Both commentators agreed that recent changes in the popular culture of the district had worked to the detriment of the town. It had become both a less spiritual and a less civilized place. Merthyr may have recently gained its charter of incorporation, but in terms of its urbanity it left much to be desired.

The pronouncements of these two Nonconformist ministers highlight the manner in which Merthyr's religious leaders were well placed to contribute to the ongoing project to manufacture a civic image for the town. As public figures with a highly particular vision of what a civilized Merthyr should look like, they were in a strong position to debate publicly the desirability of all manner of local developments. This they did with alacrity, articulating their views from the pulpit, in the pages of the local newspapers, in the council chambers and through various bodies such as the Free Church Councils. Throughout the late Victorian and Edwardian periods, an increasing number of Nonconformists were keen to single out popular leisure as an especially insidious influence in the social life of the district. Whilst this form of criticism was nothing new in itself, the ferocity with which many prominent chapelgoers denounced

---

[2] *ME*, 26 June 1909.
[3] Ibid., 24 July 1909.

the various innovations that transformed popular culture during these years is worthy of note. The commercialization of leisure which proceeded apace from the 1890s onwards was a particular cause of concern for many. For not only was the 'pursuit of pleasure' seen as a threat to the idea of a spiritual and civilized Merthyr, it was also perceived as a threat to the very future of organized religion itself.

This chapter considers the difficult relationship that obtained between the Nonconformists and leisure during the late Victorian and Edwardian periods. As a highly specialized band of civic projectors, it is ironic perhaps that the chapel élite began to conceive of their own position in terms of 'Decline' at a time when all around them appeared to be dancing to the bewitching tune of civic 'Progress'. Just as popular culture played its part in enabling the generation of alternative, 'uncivilized' images of Merthyr, so it can be seen to have contributed to the marginalization of the Free Churches. The rise of commercialized leisure presented Nonconformists with a raft of difficult problems. Certainly the arrival of various leisure businesses in the town had important consequences for those keen to project an image of a spiritual Merthyr. Attention is focused primarily on two of those commercial enterprises: the theatre and the cinema. Long despised by Welsh Nonconformity, the theatre became a permanent feature of the urban landscape of the town during the 1890s. Less than twenty years later it was joined by a number of electric cinemas. These capital-intensive centres of commercialized entertainment marked a significant break with what had gone before in matters of recreational provision. It is argued here that the proliferation of such entertainments posed a number of threats to Nonconformity. Firstly, commercialized leisure had the potential to attract individuals out of the chapels. This, to an extent, manifested itself in falling congregation figures especially in the years after the spectacular success of the religious revival of 1904–5. Secondly, the inability of certain prominent Nonconformists to accommodate institutions such as the cinema within their world-view provoked much resentment, and did much to marginalize their own position. Finally, the 'pursuit of pleasure' registered some important symbolic victories over the Chapel. The respectable nature of so many of the commercialized entertainments on offer enabled them to be incorporated in the public image of towns such as Merthyr. Popular culture had not only become commercial, it had also become more acceptable.[4] As skating rinks, cinemas and theatres became centres of family entertainment, so respectable people found it easier to include them in collective representations of the urban.[5] The local and regional newspapers bear witness to this acceptance. Leisure became news, with the result that Nonconformity found itself increasingly marginalized. This is demonstrated by a consideration of the media treatment accorded to the Whitsuntide holidays during the period.

I. 'THE PURSUIT OF PLEASURE CARRIED TO EXCESS'

Those still left in their chapels in the late 1900s and 1910s could be forgiven for feeling both depressed and worried. The religious revival of 1904–5 – that intense outburst of religiosity inspired by the mystical Evan Roberts – had blown itself out, and whereas only a few years previously the newspapers had reported mushroom growth and a surfeit of spirituality, the emphasis was now on shrinking congregations and spiritual decline.[6] Estimates of the size of the problem facing the various denominations in the Merthyr district by 1911 varied considerably. Some commentators noted rather vaguely that the 'vast majority' of Merthyr's population were outside the churches;[7] others were willing to be more precise. One assessment placed

[4] One should be careful not to overstate this case. As should be clear already, in the minds of many, popular culture still posed a major moral threat. Nonetheless, when compared with the radical culture associated with the Chartists, late nineteenth-century leisure appeared tame indeed. See Hugh Cunningham's comments in his *Leisure in the Industrial Revolution, c. 1780–1880* (London, 1980), Conclusion.

[5] The move towards more family-centred patterns of leisure is noted by Gareth Stedman Jones in his article 'Working-class culture and working-class politics in London, 1870–1900: notes on the remaking of a working class', *Journal of Social History*, 7, no. 4 (1974), 460–508, reprinted in his *Languages of Class: Studies in English Working-Class History, 1832–1982* (Cambridge, 1983), especially pp. 217–20. In the twentieth century, this trend became even more pronounced. See Hugh Cunningham, 'Leisure and culture', in F. M. L. Thompson (ed.), *The Cambridge Social History of Britain, 1750–1950*, 3 vols. (Cambridge, 1990), Vol. 2, 'People and their Environment', p. 317.

[6] See R. Gill, *The Myth of the Empty Church* (London, 1993), ch. 7. For a more optimistic assessment of Nonconformity's position in Wales during the early years of the century, see Christopher B. Turner, 'Conflicts of faith? Religion and Labour in Wales, 1890–1914', in Deian R. Hopkin and Gregory S. Kealey (eds), *Class, Community and the Labour Movement in Wales and Canada, 1850–1930* (Aberystwyth, 1989), pp. 67–8.

[7] *ME*, 25 February 1911.

some 8,000 out of a possible 21,500 in the category of those untouched by religion.[8] Statistics such as these appeared all the more harrowing when compared with the halcyon days of 1905, when the Nonconformist denominations could lay claim to over 20,400 communicants and over 16,200 adherents in the parish of Merthyr alone.[9] Letters were printed in the *Merthyr Express* posing all manner of unsettling questions: 'Why are the Churches half empty?'; 'Is the Church played out?'; 'Is the pulpit in Merthyr losing its power?'[10] Others pointed to the problems encountered by inhabitants of the 'Athens of Wales'. One correspondent mused over the problem, 'Nonconformity in the Aberdare Valley – Is it a Failing Force?', and arrived at some disturbing conclusions:

> The more one moves about the Aberdare Valley the more one is convinced that all is not well with the Nonconformist churches. There is a slackness, a want of earnestness and a growing indifference . . . matters are more unsatisfactory now than they have been for a good many years.[11]

This disquiet in the localities was replicated at the highest levels. The president of a Methodist conference held in 1911 declared that 'the question of South Wales Methodism was one of the most urgent present-day problems in the Wesleyan Connexion', whilst the Revd Dr Pope, a leading expert in the matter of missions, opined that 'all the churches are more or less failing to reach the people who are crowding to the coalfields of Glamorganshire' and called for the setting up of a fund of £25,000 to be devoted exclusively to mission work in the region.[12]

In their search for the causes of this spiritual malaise, concerned onlookers repeatedly emphasized the importance of

[8] Ibid., 12 February 1910.
[9] *Report of the Royal Commission on the Church of England and Other Religious Bodies in Wales and Monmouthshire*, 1911, Cd. 5437, Vol. 6, p. 186. Also see Keith Strange, 'The condition of the working classes in Merthyr Tydfil, *c.* 1840–1850', Ph.D. thesis, University of Wales (Swansea), 1982, pp. 810–97.
[10] *ME*, 11 March 1911, 18 February 1911.
[11] Ibid., 24 June 1911.
[12] Ibid., 4 February 1911. It is worth noting that contemporaries were right to think they were living through something of a turning-point in the fortunes of organized religion. Whilst an imperfect measure of religiosity, figures regarding attendance at chapels reveal the religious revival to be a highpoint. Thereafter the trend is inexorably downward. See John Williams, *Digest of Welsh Historical Statistics*, 2 vols. (Cardiff, 1985), Vol. 2, pp. 284–5, 310–11.

leisure.[13] In 1911, a committee appointed by the Methodist Church of Wales concluded that the 'love of pleasure' was on the increase, a development widely considered to be to the detriment of the denomination.[14] In April of the same year the Revd David Jones delivered a speech at a meeting of the Welsh Calvinistic Association; 'in dealing with the spiritual aspect, [he] made an onslaught on the amusements of the day, and indiscriminately condemned what he termed the craving for pleasure and recreation amongst the young – from theatregoing down to the playing of dominoes'.[15] Two months later, the Revd Matthias Jenkins from Abercwmboi singled out Sunday concerts as prime culprits. They acted, he argued, as an unhelpful diversion. 'Even when the things themselves are not evil, they draw people away from religion. There are so many opportunities for pleasure that a thirst for enjoyment is created which kills and destroys every religious feeling.'[16] Meanwhile, one commentator saw commercialized leisure as effecting a fundamental alteration of the character of the Welsh. 'Are the Welsh people losing that earnestness which was one of their most prominent characteristics?', he asked.

> Are they becoming vain and frivolous? Are the music-halls and theatres, which are scattered about these valleys, the social clubs and other means of pleasure changing the character of the people? If so, then it is a bad day for Wales when the pursuit of pleasure is carried to such an excess as to lessen the interest in the more serious duties of life.[17]

This gloomy analysis came just two months after an Eastertide apparently dominated by recreation rather than religiosity. In Cardiff, for example, some 8,000 made their way to Ninian Park to witness the promotion clash at the top of the Southern League Second Division between Cardiff City and Reading, whilst 20,000 lovers of the rugby code converged upon the Arms Park where the home team was entertaining the London Harlequins. Meanwhile, 'theatres, music-halls, picture theatres, a

---

[13] Although other issues, such as the 'social question', were also to the fore. Robert Pope, *Building Jerusalem: Nonconformity, Labour and the Social Question in Wales, 1906–1939* (Cardiff, 1998), ch. 4.
[14] *The Times*, 4 November 1911.
[15] *WM*, 6 April 1911.
[16] *ME*, 24 June 1911.
[17] Ibid., 24 June 1911.

skating rink and a menagerie among other things' were competing for the patronage of Cardiffians as well as the 50,000 excur-
sionists brought into the Welsh metropolis by the railways.[18]
The increase in the number of amusements on offer in the city
was cited as the primary reason for the large influx of excur-
sionists over the holiday weekend. The impresarios, along with
the various railway companies operating in and out of the
Great Western Railway station, appear to have been the chief
beneficiaries of this holiday bonanza. The Cardiff Tramway
Company similarly profited. Within a few days, officials were
boasting that they had carried over 360,000 passengers during
the Easter period (80,000 more than the previous year) with a
resulting increase in takings of some 20 per cent.[19] In the face of
such overwhelming evidence, less worldly-minded contemporaries were forced to acknowledge the unwelcome presence of
Mammon on this most holy of holidays. Little wonder that by
1912 a reflective 'Polonius' observed: 'The deep things of life do
not grip men and women as they did formerly. People today
desire entertainments and amusements and the picture palaces
and other places are endeavouring to meet the public taste.'[20]

There was, of course, nothing new about Nonconformist
hostility towards entertainments. Certainly Nonconformists in
south Wales had taken the lead in condemning all manner of
worldly activities throughout the nineteenth century.[21] However, according to some historians, what was novel about this
period was the way in which entertainments were seen as contributing to 'the secularization of Sunday'.[22] Both E. T. Davies
and W. R. Lambert, for example, have portrayed commercialized entertainment as an essentially corrosive presence in
the religious life of south Wales.[23] Both historians also suggest

[18] *WM*, 18 April 1911.
[19] Ibid., 18 April 1911, 19 April 1911.
[20] *ME*, 22 June 1912.
[21] Take, for example, the hostility between the Nonconformists and the drink trade.
See W. R. Lambert, *Drink and Sobriety in Victorian Wales, c. 1820–c. 1895* (Cardiff, 1983),
especially ch. 4; W. R. Lambert, 'The Welsh Sunday Closing Act, 1881', *Welsh History
Review*, 6, no. 2 (1972), 161–89.
[22] Gill, *Myth of the Empty Church*, p. 193. Also see, for example, James Obelkevich,
Religion and Rural Society: South Lindsey, 1825–1875 (Oxford, 1976), p. 326; James Obelkevich, 'Religion', in F. M. L. Thompson (ed.), *The Cambridge Social History of Britain,
1750–1950*, 3 vols. (Cambridge, 1990), Vol. 3, 'Social Agencies and Institutions', p. 345.
[23] E. T. Davies, *Religion in the Industrial Revolution in South Wales* (Cardiff, 1965); W. R.
Lambert, 'Some working-class attitudes towards organized religion in nineteenth-
century Wales', *Llafur*, 2, no. 1 (1976), 4–17.

that the Nonconformists themselves played a part in their own decline. In Davies's words, a religion shot through with 'a rather crude Puritanism' in which '[t]he good life was still thought of in such negative terms as total abstinence' was poorly placed indeed to deal with the proliferation of music-halls, cinemas, football clubs and other similar places of amusement.[24] An oft-repeated, unbending insistence upon the sinful nature of such recreations combined with the strict temperance line to ensure that by the 1890s the failure of the chapels to respond to the problem of leisure in a positive fashion had become 'a great bone of contention' for many of the working class.[25]

A book of directions intended for leaders of a Wesleyan Sunday school in Merthyr illustrates the extent to which the simultaneous equation of the moral terms 'leisure', 'pleasure' and 'sin' still framed the Nonconformist approach to the world. After reminding incumbents of the grave responsibility they now carried – 'Immortal souls are committed to your care'[26] – the guide-book continued to warn teachers of the many potential and complex difficulties they might face in their duties as guardians. Even the socializing of scholars immediately after the class had finished was something to be avoided if the lessons they had learnt were not to be swamped by the sinful inanities of childish chatter.[27] This prescriptive document took as its ideological touchstone the rules of the Wesleyan Society which were included as an appendix for reference purposes. Of utmost importance was the question 'Of Conformity to the World', and here official Wesleyan attitudes towards leisure were revealed with clarity.

> The Rules of the Society forbid 'diversions' which 'cannot be used in the name of the Lord Jesus;' and the drinking of spiritous liquor, 'unless in the case of extreme necessity'. The obligation to 'do all to the glory of God' implies an avoiding of all questionable recreations and indulgences; in particular of such as lead into worldly company, or promote trifling, or indispose for the use of the word of God and prayer.[28]

[24] Davies, *Religion in the Industrial Revolution*, p. 173.
[25] Lambert, 'Some working-class attitudes', 12.
[26] Glamorgan Record Office (GRO), D/D Wes. MT 129, Register of Class Members and Instructions to Leaders (1886), p. 2.
[27] Ibid., p. 7.
[28] Ibid., p. 15.

Many contemporaries doubted the wisdom of enforcing such a rigid distinction between religion and recreation. As one Nonconformist put it in 1911, at its simplest the problem was that '[W]hile the churches are half empty, football matches, boxing matches, theatres and music-halls do not fail to attract the people'.[29]

Nonconformity's difficult relationship with organized, commercialized leisure was demonstrated most graphically during the revival of 1904–5.[30] The glee with which followers of Evan Roberts catalogued the declining interest in all manner of leisure pursuits spoke eloquently of their distrust of such entertainments. As might be expected, news that publicans were struggling as a consequence of the evangelist's activities was particularly well received.[31] Nevertheless, the conviction of a young schoolboy from Merthyr that 'Mr Evan Roberts is a good man sent by God to save drunkards' expressed only a partial truth about the revival;[32] Roberts was also sent to save footballers, theatregoers and musicians. Stories abounded in the press of the various casualties of the revival. Football clubs suffered as spectators and players fell under the spell of revivalism.[33] Publicans looked on as the numbers of patrons entering their establishments began to fall.[34] Former drunkards, hitherto loyal customers, found themselves converted by the simple words of 'little girls'.[35] Some licensed victuallers were forced to witness conversions on their own premises.[36] The prayer of one lost sheep suggests that he knew well enough what he had to give up if he was to be saved: 'Lord, forgive me and my old friend

[29] *ME*, 25 February 1911.
[30] For more on the religious revival, see C. R. Williams, 'The Welsh religious revival of 1904–5', *British Journal of Sociology*, 3, no. 3 (1952), 242–59.
[31] For example, in assessing the impact of the revival, J. Vyrnwy Morgan privileged statistics relating to convictions for public drunkenness. See his *The Welsh Religious Revival 1904–5: A Retrospect and Criticism* (London, 1909), p. 247.
[32] *ME*, 18 February 1905.
[33] See, for example, *Evening Express* (*EE*), 27 December 1904.
[34] For a pictorial representation of the success of the revivalists at the expense of the publicans, see the pen and ink drawing by J. M. Staniforth, 'A Result of the Revival: Then and Now' (*c.* 1905), reproduced in J. Harvey, 'The visions of the 1904–5 Revival', *Llafur*, 6, no. 2 (1993), 75–93, 77.
[35] In February 1905, in keeping with the democratic nature of the revival, it was reported that a drunkard from Troedyrhiw had been saved not by 'a man with an MA . . . but [by] a little girl' (*EE*, 11 February 1905).
[36] See the case of John Williams, a young north Walian, who was touched by the revival after reading accounts of revival meetings while drinking in a Merthyr public house (*ME*, 3 December 1904).

for neglecting other services of Thy House for so long at a time, and for going up to the mountain to play cards, pitch-and-toss, and drink beer.'[37] Even musical ventures, generally considered to be highly rational and respectable pastimes, were called off as urbanites determined to spend their leisure hours in the chapel. A report on the condition of Dowlais in December 1904 highlighted the effects that revivalism could have upon popular pastimes:

> A number of churches have resolved to abandon the customary eisteddfodau which they hold on Christmas Day, notwithstanding the fact that the programmes of the competitors have been printed and issued. A theatrical company which visited the town played to less than a score of patrons on the first night and the audience being *non-est* on the following evening, the hall doors were closed, and the members of the histrionic band shook their feet of the dust, or rather the mud of Dowlais, and betook themselves to fresh fields and pastures new. During the past fortnight the Dowlais Harlequins football club, the representative organisation of the town, have been unable to raise a team to fulfil their engagements, owing to some of the leading players having come under the influence of the revival. As a consequence it has been decided to disband the club.[38]

The cumulative effect of Evan Roberts's preaching was a civilizing of the district's streets. Indeed, Christmas 1904 was a remarkable one in the Taff Valley. At the very time when the narrative of 'Progress', so beloved of the civic boosters, appeared to have replaced that of 'Decline' as the most effective means of understanding Merthyr's recent past, its present and its future, the public spaces of the Valley seemed to proclaim the triumph of civilization over barbarism. According to the *Merthyr Express*,

> The streets [of Treharris] are deserted at night, the Public Hall is closed, amusements of all kinds are discarded, but the churches are all aglow. We have it from reliable authority that the attendance at public houses is very much less, and that the publicans are complaining of bad trade.

Similarly in Troedyrhiw: 'The streets at night are a marked improvement, and not near the number are in the public

[37] Morgan, *Welsh Religious Revival*, p. 41.
[38] *ME*, 10 December 1904.

houses. Police officers remark that the place is quite quiet at dark.' A new crowd was now to be seen in the streets, the religious crowd. Thus, 'great crowds' congregated (aptly enough) in the public spaces of Merthyr Vale, and 'people paraded the streets in groups, singing hymns'. Meanwhile, in Aberfan, colliers were to be heard offering up prayers, calling upon God to destroy all engines of demoralization and hatred: 'We ask Thee to close all the public houses and make us better men and women, neighbours and friends.'[39] It was observed that the festive season in Dowlais had passed off without incident, the 'reptiles' and 'hobble-de-hoys' who had been a notable feature of the street-life of that town in previous days now noticeable only by their absence.[40] Even in Merthyr town itself, the former 'Samaria of Wales', the forces of civilization were making their presence felt. The month leading up to Christmas had witnessed impromptu open-air prayer meetings held in the streets after chapel meetings, while the first few weeks of the New Year saw the number brought before the local police court charged with public drunkenness offences fall to an all-time low.[41]

Throughout the course of the revival, the question of Nonconformity's relationship to entertainments was hotly debated. All shades of opinion were expressed, although battle lines between two major groups were drawn early on. On the one hand there were those who argued for the need to adopt a more liberal attitude towards 'the knotty question of amusements' as a means of holding on to the new converts (or 'the babes in Christ' as one put it).[42] As a correspondent to the revival edition of the *Evening Express* eloquently reasoned, '[I]t is a mistake . . . to set out with the notion that certain forms of amusement are necessarily sinful. Under what rule of logic or common-sense is cricket cherished, bagatelle blessed, billiards banned, and football anathematised?' The letter-writer proceeded to advise the Nonconformist chapels to concern themselves with the social side of life as much as with the spiritual, bearing in mind all the while the revised idea 'that worldliness consists not in the use of things commonly called worldly, but in the allowing of such

---

[39] Ibid., 17 December 1904.
[40] Ibid., 31 December 1904.
[41] Ibid., 3 December 1904, 21 January 1905.
[42] *EE*, 25 March 1905.

things to dominate life to the exclusion of spiritual interests'.[43] Despite the regularity and force with which such views were articulated,[44] there were more than enough voices urging that a strict policy be adopted. Thus, in the very same issue of the paper there appeared the words of the Revd J. Williams from Brynmawr, who addressed a conference of the Monmouthshire Baptist Association on the question of 'How to help converts'. He left his audience in no doubt as to his position. 'His Church had the right to do as they desired, but at the same time they would never have a football club while he was a minister. They would never, also, have a billiard table or a dancing class while he was a minister.'[45] Although diametrically opposed in terms of the arguments they advanced, both the liberals and the hard-liners were agreed on the threat that the new commercialized entertainments represented to the Free Churches. Whether one saw chapel-sponsored amusements as a means of tempting a pleasure-loving people back into the places of worship, or believed that such pastimes were sinful distractions that could only undermine spirituality, the basic assumption was the same; chapels had to compete in a world of popular entertainments for the hearts, minds and (especially) souls of the population.

So sensitive were some Nonconformists on this issue that even Evan Roberts did not escape their censure. Long before the whirlwind of revivalism had blown itself out, critics charged Roberts with reducing serious religion to mere entertainment. In January 1905 the Revd Peter Price, Congregationalist minister from Dowlais, sent a letter to the *Western Mail* suggesting that there were two revivals unfolding in Wales. The first was 'a Revival which is of God – of God alone'. This was the 'real', 'true' revival. However, 'there is another Revival . . . a sham Revival, a mockery, a blasphemous travesty of the real thing. The chief figure in this mock Revival is Evan Roberts.'[46] Such a declaration provoked a violent backlash; a flurry of abusive letters was sent to Price setting him straight on a number of

---

[43] Ibid., 25 March 1905.

[44] For similar pleas for pragmatism in such matters, also see, for example, ibid., 3 June 1905, and the *ME*, 17 December 1904.

[45] *EE*, 25 March 1905. Brynmor P. Jones, rather dubiously, asserts that, during the revival, 'there was very little sermonizing of any kind' on the sinfulness of sport. See his *Voices from the Welsh Revival, 1904–5* (Bridgend, 1995), p. 222.

[46] Letter to the *WM* cited in Morgan, *Welsh Religious Revival*, pp. 141–5.

points.[47] Nevertheless, in the wake of his critique, other Non-conformists felt empowered to question Roberts's actions. 'One still in the throes of doubt' wrote to the *Merthyr Express* in March, likening Roberts to a music-hall performer. 'I have many times essayed to write on this person's extraordinary actions which savour so much of gallery trick . . . Personally, I believe him to be the perpetrator, consciously or unconsciously, of practical jokes upon a scale never before attempted in South Wales.'[48] Others felt uneasy when it was revealed that a photograph of Roberts 'comforting a female penitent' had in fact been posed for publicity purposes.[49]

Misgivings about the nature of the revival were fuelled by the scenes that accompanied the Roberts phenomenon as it toured around the region. For not only was revivalism a 'frontier sport',[50] it was also high-quality entertainment. The revival meetings certainly possessed all the characteristics of a gripping dramatic performance. Take, for example, the electric atmosphere generated by Roberts's arrival in Dowlais in January 1905. He appeared before a packed Presbyterian chapel in Elizabeth Street, 'labouring under strong emotion, tears coursing down his face as he expatiated on the wondrous love'. From this point on, spontaneity was the watchword, as the direction of the meeting switched unpredictably from prayer to song to testimony, and the focus of attention shifted rapidly from Roberts to his female helpers to the congregation. After Roberts's opening statement, 'some Welshman, overcome with glad emotion, . . . burst out with "Diolch iddo" [Thanks be to God], and this was the prelude to the singing of hymn after hymn in Welsh'. Miss Mary Davies, one of the evangelist's female companions, recited a prayer in Welsh, to which the congregation responded. Then the meeting 'suddenly reverted into English'. Another one of Roberts's helpers, Annie Davies, struck up a hymn, after which a 'champion walker' from Tredegar commanded attention. He was 'very original in his somewhat crude remarks. After referring to his achievements as a pedestrian, he remarked that

---

[47] A selection of the letters is reprinted in Morgan, *Welsh Religious Revival*, pp. 146–54.
[48] *ME*, 4 March 1905.
[49] Morgan, *Welsh Religious Revival*, p. 161.
[50] See David Smith, 'Wales through the looking glass', in David Smith (ed.), *A People and a Proletariat: Essays in the History of Wales, 1780–1880* (London, 1980), p. 225.

he had changed his course, and would henceforth "walk" with God.' The degree to which these events resembled a theatrical performance was well illustrated by the subsequent report in the *Evening Express*. After describing the excited gathering as a 'congregation' at the start of the report, the journalist (either consciously or unconsciously) went on to employ a significantly different term: 'the *audience* listened with rapt attention'.[51] This 'audience', just like a crowd drawn to the town to see an important rugby match, came from far and wide: 'The morning trains brought a big influx of visitors, the London and North Western Railway alone carrying over a thousand passengers.'[52] Indeed, so much of an attraction was it, that even Lady Wimborne was tempted back to Dowlais to watch the mercurial Roberts weave his magic.

II. MAKING A CRISIS OUT OF A DRAMA? NONCONFORMISTS AND THE BUSINESS OF PLEASURE

That the new commercialized entertainments had the potential to tempt Nonconformists out of their chapels is clear. Stephen Yeo has reminded us that at the most fundamental level, leisure was the context in which religious bodies and other voluntary organizations were forced to operate.[53] That context was ever expanding during the late Victorian and Edwardian years, and if one observer could legitimately complain in 1880 about 'the great want of good and cheap amusement in Merthyr', thirty years later such a claim would have been impossible to make.[54]

We have already noted a number of significant developments in the district's popular culture. The activities of the entrepreneurial licensed victuallers, culminating in the establishment of the Merthyr Recreation Company in 1890, did much to alert inhabitants to the possibilities of commercialized sport. The arrival of both Northern Union and professional soccer was later to demonstrate the continued willingness of Merthyrians to pay for their sporting entertainment. However, the example set by the 'Ten Men of Merthyr' had implications that

---

[51] *EE*, 23 January 1905 (emphasis added).
[52] *ME*, 28 January 1905.
[53] Stephen Yeo, *Religion and Voluntary Organizations in Crisis* (London, 1976), p. 185.
[54] *ME*, 19 June 1880.

stretched far beyond the sports ground. Certainly by the 1910s, the urban landscape of Merthyr bore witness to the proliferation of commercialized entertainments. Late Victorian entrepreneurs of leisure were encouraged in their speculative ventures by the introduction of customary holidays such as Mabon's Day (which was celebrated from 1888 to 1898) and the passing of the Eight Hours Act in 1908. With increasing hours of 'free' time at their disposal, the working men of south Wales provided such businessmen with a potentially profitable source of income. And whilst working-class women did not enjoy the same clear distinction between hours of leisure and work, it appears that at least some of them partook of the commercialized entertainments on offer.[55] Skating rinks, billiard halls, bicycle race tracks, running tracks, refreshment houses and fish and chip shops were thrown up as speculators tried to cash in on the latest craze.[56] Some lasted longer than others; all added flashes of bright colour to the social life of the Valley towns.

One of the most impressive of these leisure institutions, and one which caused many Nonconformists much anxiety, was the permanent theatre constructed in the Pontmorlais district of the town. Within a few years of the appearance of the licensed victuallers' Merthyr Recreation Company, a group of Merthyrians floated the idea of setting up a theatre in the town.[57] Under the name of the 'Merthyr Theatre Company', fifteen local men, all drawn from commercial or professional backgrounds, set about providing their fellow urbanites with high-quality entertainment. In response to 'the increasing interest displayed by the production and performance of Stage Plays, and such like performances in Merthyr', these self-appointed directors raised £4,000 by the selling of 800 £5 shares. Convinced that the population of the upper Taff Valley was large enough to support such an ambitious venture, they alerted potential shareholders to the existence of good transport links which, they argued, ensured that Merthyr 'affords a convenience to the

---

[55] For a consideration of the problem of defining working-class women's leisure, see Andrew Davies, *Leisure, Gender and Poverty: Working-Class Culture in Salford and Manchester, 1900–1939* (Buckingham, 1992), ch. 3; M. Tebbutt, *Women's Talk? A Social History of 'Gossip' in Working-Class Neighbourhoods, 1880–1960* (Aldershot, 1995), pp. 57–9; Cunningham, 'Leisure and culture', pp. 305–6.

[56] Skating rinks were particularly popular in the late 1900s and early 1910s, with a number opening in the Merthyr district. See, for example, *MP*, 6 January 1912.

[57] *ME*, 24 March 1894.

Theatre-going public which is not possessed by scarcely any other town, inasmuch as there are late trains running from Merthyr to nearly all the surrounding towns'.[58] When it finally opened in 1894 under the grandiose title 'The New Theatre and Opera House' (later renamed the 'Theatre Royal'), the brick building was one of the finest in Merthyr. Completed at a cost of some £6,000, it boasted no less than eight dressing rooms (with fireplaces) and was, at fifty feet wide and sixty feet deep, the largest auditorium in Wales. Technically it was well provided for with a scene dock enabling a carriage and four horses to be driven on to the stage.[59]

The building of the theatre was highly significant. It was a major project involving local inhabitants willing to invest relatively large sums of money in a venture whose primary *raison d'être* was to generate profits from leisure. Its sheer scale set it apart from anything that had gone before it.[60] By the 1910s it had been joined by an increasing number of commercially run centres of entertainment. As Merthyrians made their way through the urban spaces of the district, they passed through a landscape that proclaimed the close association between Mammon and amusement. In 1910 the Merthyr Electric Theatre opened its doors. The first purpose-built venue dedicated to the showing of cinematographic films, its flickering images and modern feel quickly caught the imagination of the public. In the first six months they were treated to a varied diet of films including such gems as *Carlino in Love*, *Tweedledum learns a Tragic Part* and *Tontolino as a Prize Fighter*. Sports fans were not forgotten by a management clearly in tune with popular taste; anyone who had missed the clash between the Welsh and the English rugby teams could cheer on their heroes in the air-conditioned splendour of the theatre. And for those desirous of rather more substantial fare, the entertainment always included news items in the form of 'Pathé's Gazette', the 'Warwick Chronicle', and, from March 1911, the 'Gaumont Graphic'.[61] So successful was

[58] *MDT*, 6 January 1893.
[59] Much was made of the technological dimension. Within a few months of opening, a grand water spectacular was held involving thousands of gallons of water and an indoor firework display (*ME*, 31 March 1894).
[60] For an account of the commercialization of leisure which also singles out the importance of the 1890s, see Asa Briggs, *Mass Entertainment: The Origins of a Modern Industry* (Adelaide, 1960).
[61] *ME*, 11 March 1911, 3 February 1910, 28 January 1911.

the Merthyr Electric Theatre that others were more than
willing to invest the £3,000–4,000 needed to set up such a business. In 1911 local money financed the Merthyr Picture Palace,
an impressive building which could accommodate 780 film-
goers.[62] The outlying districts were also well served with the
establishment of the Troedyrhiw Cinema Company and the
opening of the Victoria Cinema in Dowlais.[63] Local money
mixed with capital from national cinema companies to ensure
that the picture palaces quickly became permanent features.
By 1912 cinemas could be found in the Taff, Cynon, Rhymney
and Sirhowy Valleys. With their cheap prices, warm bright
surroundings, exciting entertainment and programmes which
fitted well with the working hours of men, women and even
schoolchildren, they were admirably placed to succeed. Little
wonder that one observer could remark that 'it will be a long
time before the cinema loses its popularity'.[64]

Predictably enough, such developments were not well
received by many Free Church members. Nonconformists, of
course, had a long history of opposition to all manner of theatrical ventures that stretched back to the late sixteenth century.
Old habits died hard. There were certainly a number of vocal
late Victorian chapelgoers who found the presence of a permanent theatre in the town difficult to accept, seeing it as a place
of sin and worldly temptation. Hence, a decision made by
a meeting of Wesleyan Sunday school teachers in 1904 to hold
a special religious service in the theatre was overturned when
several 'expressed great repugnance' at the idea; the sacred
space of Shiloh Chapel was decided upon as a more appropriate
venue.[65] The proprietors of the Merthyr Theatre were made
well aware of such hostility on a regular basis. For example,
every time the annual drinks licence of the theatre came
up for renewal, the anti-theatre lobby (with Nonconformist

[62] Amongst the directors were to be found a local provision merchant, a dentist, an
auctioneer and valuer, a solicitor and a music dealer (ibid., 11 November 1911).
[63] Ibid., 22 June 1912, 18 May 1912.
[64] Ibid., 13 July 1911.
[65] GRO, D/D Wes/MT 119, Wesley Sunday School Minute Book: Sunday School
Teachers' Meeting Minutes, 1891–1906, 3 October 1904. See also a letter from one
Merthyrian objecting to the Free Churches holding their mission meetings at the
theatre: 'I have very strong objections myself to familiarising our young men with the
interior of a place which is so much spoken against in our religious gatherings' (ME,
4 May 1901).

teetotallers in the van) was sure to object.[66] On other occasions throughout the year, objections were raised regarding the nature of the entertainment on offer at the theatre.

One of the most spectacular demonstrations of Nonconformist hatred of the theatre in Merthyr was occasioned by the staging of Wilson Barrett's *The Sign of the Cross* at the Theatre Royal in March 1897. Judged by the standards of many contemporaries, the play was a 'religious' one.[67] Set in ancient Rome at a time when Christians were being persecuted, the storyline involved a young, beautiful Christian woman winning over a noble Roman pagan from the paths of worldly vice and thoughtlessness. Notwithstanding such an ennobling and uplifting theme, news of its imminent arrival in Merthyr led to a major debate in Nonconformist circles, with much soul-searching as to the advisability of allowing chapel members to attend performances. One chapel resolved only to allow its deacons to enter the theatre, prompting a disbelieving *Merthyr Express* to note sarcastically, 'So you see the "Nonconformist Conscience" is not always as narrow as some people wish to make out'.[68] Meanwhile, a minister from Dowlais, after deciding that *The Sign of the Cross* was not suitable material for his congregation, was enraged to discover that some of his flock had disobeyed him. As a punishment he refused to administer the sacrament the following Sunday.[69] No such debate attended the arrival of the next production to be staged in the theatre: *Men of War*.[70]

The complexity of the situation needs, as always, to be acknowledged. Just as some Nonconformists felt able to hold mission meetings in the theatre, so others appear to have staged religious plays in their own chapels, 'to further the work of God'. Nevertheless, the point remains that every such venture was likely to produce a storm of protest from the more

[66] In 1908, for example, the Merthyr and District Free Church Council forwarded resolutions to Merthyr Council supporting any moves that restricted the sale of intoxicating drinks in the theatre (County Borough of Merthyr Tydfil, Minutes of Council Meeting, 21 September 1908, p. 795).

[67] See the comments of Michael R. Booth, who notes that the production 'met with immense clerical favour, and its reception was a striking episode in the history of ecclesiastical attitudes to the theatre . . . [It] even won over Nonconformists' (Michael R. Booth, *Theatre in the Victorian Age* (Cambridge, 1991), pp. 23–5).

[68] *ME*, 13 March 1897.

[69] Ibid., 10 April 1910.

[70] Ibid., 3 April 1910.

puritanically minded. Take, for example, a letter sent to the
Merthyr Express complaining of such plays in 1907. According to
the correspondent, John Brain of Abercannaid, all theatrical
performances 'belong[ed] to the devil and his friends and not to
Jesus Christ, who said that to be friendly with the world was to
be at enmity with God'. He accused the Nonconformists who
organized these plays of setting up 'the idol of pleasure' and
fostering 'an inordinate love of pleasure' among the people
which 'will have to be accounted for in the Judgement Day'.[71]
There was little room for compromise in such a position.

The arrival of the picture palaces produced similar responses
from hardliners. Conceived of by many as a close relative of the
theatre (many theatres included cinematographic entertainments on their bill during these years), they were thought of as
legitimate targets of Nonconformist denunciation. In October
1911, for instance, Alderman D. W. Jones urged his fellow
councillors not to renew the Merthyr Electric Theatre's seven-
day licence. He argued strongly that 'the seventh day should
be kept holy' and that everyone should have a day of rest.[72]
Although unsuccessful in his attempt to win over his colleagues,
and despite Jones's own removal from office at the local elections two weeks later, the debate on the place of the cinemas in
Merthyr rolled on.[73] All manner of 'experts' offered contributions, including the Merthyr Branch of the National Union of
Teachers which reported in May 1912 on the impact that the
picture palaces were having upon the children of the district.[74]
Nevertheless, it was the Nonconformists who were the standard-
bearers in the battle to rid the town of this new moral threat.
In August 1912 the Free Church Council successfully stopped
the showing of films in Treharris on Sunday evenings, notwithstanding the numerous petitions that had been signed in favour
of the Sunday theatre.[75] Similarly, in 1913, the Free Church
Council lobbied the Merthyr Borough Council and pressured
councillors into refusing a seven-day licence for the local
theatre. The effect of this decision was to make it impossible for

---

[71] Ibid., 20 April 1907. Note the similarity of the language used by Brain and the
Wesleyan Sunday School rule book considered above, p. 183.
[72] Ibid., 21 October 1911.
[73] Ibid., 4 November 1911.
[74] Ibid., 18 May 1912.
[75] Ibid., 17 August 1912.

the management to show films on a Sunday – an entertainment which it had been offering to an appreciative public for over two years.[76] Two months later, a 'strong deputation' of the Free Church Council in Treharris mounted another offensive on the town's cinema proprietors when they reapplied for a seven-day licence. Once again, there were spirited attempts by supporters of the picture palace to thwart their efforts.[77]

The degree to which the Free Churches were out of touch with popular opinion is well illustrated by the outcry that followed every move to shut the cinemas on Sundays. When the Merthyr Electric Theatre was threatened, a petition was raised and within ten days of the Borough Council's decision, 6,500 Merthyrians – including five justices of the peace and 'a large number of leading citizens' – signed their names to it. A deputation was led by Captain Southey and included, according to one source, 'whole streets of inhabitants and men representing thousands of workers'. They persuasively argued that hitherto there had been no complaints from the local authorities and that admirable order was maintained by the management. 'The Voice of Labour' was represented in the corporeal form of Mr John Griffiths. Speaking for a number of workers from Troedyrhiw, he harangued councillors for bending to the will of the Nonconformists. As he put it:

> He objected to the ministerial friends coming to the Council trying to influence the members in a 'left-handed' way. There were people who did not attend churches or chapels, like in every town, as well as people who did, and he contended that the morals of the rising generation would be better cared for if they attended first-class cinemas than rushing up and down the streets.

He then proceeded to scotch the Sabbatarians' objections against the employment of Sunday labour by asking whether they should tell their wives and domestic servants not to wash, cook or purchase Sunday newspapers and milk.[78]

Apart from providing a telling glimpse of the patriarchal assumptions which could effortlessly link the concept of a wife

[76] Ibid., 26 April 1913.
[77] Ibid., 21 June 1913.
[78] Ibid., 26 April 1913.

with that of a domestic servant, Griffiths's argument is illuminating in the fashion in which it revolved around a sense of outrage at the hypocrisy of the Free Churches' approach. Not only did he question their right to act as guardians of the morality of the whole community when many considered themselves outside the influence of the chapels, but he also objected to their expecting compliance from the working population, for whom Sunday was still an important day of recreation, without being prepared themselves to follow the logic of their position. Notwithstanding the forcefulness of his reasoning, the subsequent vote of the council was extremely close, with twelve votes cast each way. Only after the mayor used his casting vote in favour of the granting of the seven-day licence was the matter finally resolved.

Cinema-lovers in Treharris were similarly stung into action by the activities of the Free Churches. The proprietors' solicitor dismissed the Nonconformists as being 'obsessed by religious fanaticism' and urged the councillors not to be swayed by their exhortations. He continued by pointing out:

> during the last twelve months people's views had changed, and those who a year ago ran down Sunday shows were now of the opinion that the shows were doing a wholesome and sensible work in providing a rational entertainment and driving away the dreadful monotony of the Sabbath, especially in the small towns.

After a trenchant defence of films as an educational tool, he assured the councillors that there had never been a single complaint against the pictures shown at Treharris and that the company's 'only object was to improve, elevate, and instruct'.[79] As in Merthyr, a petition had been raised within a few days. The 1,346 signatures (out of the village's total population of just over 8,800), including 'the most influential names in Treharris', had not been canvassed for, had not been obtained by door-to-door enquiries and included no one under the age of sixteen. A deputation of inhabitants in favour of the licence, which 'represented various shades of thought', condemned the hypocrisy of the Nonconformists. As one member of the group put it, 'the people

[79] Ibid., 21 June 1913.

wanted the privilege of citizenship, a right to exercise their Sunday evenings as they desired'. He continued: 'I should not care to stand here to-day and ask you to compel Parliament to close the churches.' Another pointed to the events at a certain chapel in the village where a resolution was passed to oppose the application, but no vote to the contrary was held. The conclusion he drew from this episode was that 'the ministers were afraid of their own congregations'.[80]

Part of the problem facing the Nonconformists was that the commercialization of leisure seriously undercut their ability to condemn recreations on grounds of lack of 'respectability'. The Merthyr Theatre Royal is a case in point. It was a prime example of an entertainment run purely on commercial lines, and so it was in the interests of the proprietors, directors and shareholders to appeal to as many Merthyrians as possible.[81] As Peter Bailey has pointed out, the Victorian music-hall impresario was a figure who traded in notions of sociability and friendship.[82] The proprietors of Merthyr Theatre certainly projected an image of themselves as friends of the people. In March 1896 Mr Will Smithson, then manager of the theatre, made the point succinctly. He organized a 'benefit' night in aid of the Plymouth colliers which raised over £50, itself a means of declaring his largesse. In a speech delivered to a packed house, Smithson articulated his desire to be all things to all people; he declared himself to be a 'Liberal-Unionist Conservative-Radical'.[83] This concern not to alienate sections of the public also led to proprietors placing great store upon the salubrity of the facilities on offer. Throughout the period the management was keen to draw attention to any structural improvements that had been undertaken as a means of emphasizing the building's modernity.[84] In March 1902 it was announced that a brand

---

[80] Ibid., 21 June 1913.

[81] For a consideration of the various phases in the history of the music halls, see John Earl, 'Building the halls', in Peter Bailey (ed.), *Music Hall: The Business of Pleasure* (Milton Keynes, 1986).

[82] Peter Bailey, 'A community of friends: business and good fellowship in London music-hall management, c. 1860–1885', in Bailey (ed.), *Music Hall*.

[83] *ME*, 7 March 1896.

[84] For a discussion of the importance of the 'discourse of modernity' in the presentation of commercialized entertainment, see T. Bennett, 'Hegemony, ideology, pleasure: Blackpool', in T. Bennett, C. Mercer and J. Woollacott (eds), *Popular Culture and Social Relations* (Milton Keynes, 1986), especially pp. 141–2.

new set of electric lights had been installed.[85] By November of that year, some £7,000 had been spent on renovation work.[86] In part, such improvements were effected as a means of attracting ever larger audiences into the theatre. However, the management was also required by the local council to keep its house in order. Thus, before the council granted a licence for the performance of stage plays, a number of criteria had to be met including various safety regulations and adequate sanitary arrangements.[87]

The success of Smithson and his successor, Albert Jackson, in appealing to large sections of Merthyr's population was impressive. Figures for the first two weeks in September 1908 showed an average attendance of 935 paying customers a night. In all, some 11,220 took their seats to watch the various theatrical entertainments on offer during that fortnight.[88] Importantly, women were not excluded from the theatre, and there is evidence that, at least during the 1890s, mothers attended evening performances with their young children.[89] By 1912 one commentator could sing the praises of the theatre by highlighting the 'heterogeneous crowd ... that ... filled the theatre nightly' to watch a performance by the famous Moody Manners Opera Company:

> Even chapel deacons, church dignitaries, and lay preachers forgot for the moment to assume the metaphysical aspect of vinegar vessels on the road to their Heaven. Parvenus and old roués forgot their pomp and circumstance, and allowed a little of their innate good fellowship to come to the surface. Rack-renting landlords, county-court haunting accountants, and money-lending tradesmen believed for a short space of time that there is a Divinity which shapes our ends.[90]

That chapel deacons and church dignitaries were included in his list of attenders is interesting, given the homiletic pronouncements on the evils of such entertainment that continued to emanate from the pulpits during these years. Even more telling is the manner in which it was now possible to describe the theatre as a civilizing, even a religious, force.

[85] *ME*, 22 March 1902.
[86] Ibid., 29 November 1902.
[87] See, for example, County Borough of Merthyr Tydfil Minutes of Council Meeting, 17 August 1908, p. 341.
[88] *ME*, 31 October 1908.
[89] Ibid., 5 May 1894.
[90] *MP*, 24 February 1912.

If the modern, permanent theatre was a far cry from the travelling companies that periodically arrived in the town during the 1870s and 1880s, the same was true of the cinema. Once again, the language of Welsh Nonconformity, shot through with a highly developed sense of righteousness and sin, found it difficult to condemn convincingly the picture palaces that were thrown up with such rapidity in the early years of the century. These elegant expressions of modernity were advertised in such a way as to emphasize the respectable nature of the entertainment they offered.[91] Spacious, air-conditioned, well-regulated by the local authorities, with comfortable seating arrangements and a self-conscious desire to become centres of family entertainment, the cinemas were worlds away from the cramped, dark, portable theatres of the nineteenth century.[92] That some of the films on show were of a high moral character seems clear; in 1911, for instance, it was possible to watch a picture which took as its subject the Oberammergau Passion Play.[93] Moreover, just like the proprietors of the Merthyr theatre, the managers of these cinemas were masters of the munificent gesture. In December 1912 the *Merthyr Express* noted that every afternoon Frank French, manager of the Merthyr Electric Theatre, treated his patrons to 'a nice cup of tea and biscuits'. The same report carried details of a special Saturday morning children's session in which the harmless nature of the proceedings was underlined. 'It was a treat to witness the joy of the youngsters. They cheered lustily at the stirring episodes in the cowboy pictures, and when the comics came on they screamed with delight.'[94] Three weeks later, French's generosity was again being celebrated in the pages of the paper, this time as a result of his decision to let over 600 children in free of charge on Christmas Eve.[95]

[91] As symbols of progress, the picture palace was often welcomed by civic leaders. Thus, in 1912, the Palace Electric Theatre was formally opened by the mayor, Alderman J. M. Berry (*ME*, 29 June 1912).
[92] For the background to Nonconformist hostility to the theatre in the nineteenth century, see Booth, *Theatre in the Victorian Age*, pp. 21–6. For evidence of women attending cinemas in Salford, see Robert Roberts, *The Classic Slum: Salford Life in the First Quarter of the Century* (London, 1990 edn), p. 175; Davies, *Leisure, Gender and Poverty*, pp. 73–9.
[93] *ME*, 8 April 1911. In February and March 1912, the cinema was 'besieged with crowds' keen to see high-brow films including *Dante's Inferno* and *The Merchant of Venice* (ibid., 22 February 1912, 1 March 1912).
[94] Ibid., 7 December 1912.

Such competitors were extremely difficult to dismiss by using language better suited to the vilification of the lowly beer house. Indeed, the continued employment of a puritanical discourse that condemned all but the holiest of recreations can be seen to have played a part in the marginalization of organizations such as the Free Church Council. We have already noted how the debates that raged over the opening of cinemas on Sundays provoked some to question publicly the ability of Nonconformists to represent the views of the town. Even Harry Southey's *Merthyr Express* came out on the side of the cinema-goers. 'Polonius', while noting the dangers of promoting anything that might lead to the 'continental Sunday', and lamenting the way in which 'the vast majority of the present generation view things in a very different light from their parents', nonetheless urged Nonconformists to move with the times. In order to make his point, he directed readers' attention to the condition of Merthyr's streets; people left the chapels after Sunday service and paraded the streets without 'a scrap of sanctity about them or their conduct'. He continued:

> Is it best that they should walk the streets, indulging in conduct which
> smacks more of gaiety and pleasure than sobriety of thought, or gather
> at the picture palace, and have their minds occupied in the seeing and
> contemplating of living moving pictures of life?[96]

Here was a measure of just how much 'civic Merthyr' had altered; a commercialized place of entertainment was now being justified as an effective means of ridding the district's public urban spaces of uncivilized crowds of chapelgoers.

III. NONCONFORMISTS, THE 'WHIT WALK' AND THE SYMBOLISM OF AN URBAN RITUAL

It has been suggested thus far that a number of prominent Nonconformists found it difficult to accommodate commercial

---

[95] Ibid., 28 December 1912. For an indication of the way in which other entrepreneurs of leisure explicitly acknowledged the values of respectable society, see the announcement that accompanied the news that the South Wales Rinks Company was to open a rink in Merthyr in 1909: 'The rules and regulations for the proper conduct of the place will be very strict and no rowdyism of any kind will be permitted. Every effort will be made to help the patrons enjoy themselves in a rational way' (ibid., 21 August 1909).
[96] Ibid., 26 April 1913.

entertainment within their particular vision of Merthyr. Theirs was a spiritual Merthyr that appeared to be constantly threatened by an apparently unremitting pursuit of worldly pleasures on the part of some urbanites. The use of an older, condemnatory discourse to describe new, respectable sites of leisure, such as the permanent theatre and the cinemas, seems to have alienated many Merthyrians. This alienation did not necessarily entail a total rejection of the chapel. As the observations of 'Polonius' suggest, it was possible for individuals to combine attendance at religious service with a trip to the cinema on a Sunday evening. However, the aggressive and unbending stance adopted by organizations such as the Free Church Council did much to encourage public debate about the role of Nonconformity in the town. And at a time when fears were being expressed generally about the vitality of organized religion, the appearance of leading Nonconformists as puritanical kill-joys out of sympathy with their fellow townsfolk did little to strengthen their cause. The final section of this chapter returns us to the streets and public spaces of urban south Wales. For it is contended here that Nonconformity's rivalry with commercialized entertainments, and its increasing inability to dominate the public sphere, can be illustrated by a consideration of a Nonconformist cultural practice that was inherently spatial, namely the 'Whit Walk'.

The Whitsuntide celebrations were observed in almost every town and settlement in south Wales throughout the second half of the nineteenth century, and had long been an occasion in which the secular competed with the sacred.[97] In 1873, a year notable for its typicality rather than for any extraordinary happenings, the *Western Mail* remarked on the general observance of the holiday in south Wales, and provided detailed reports of the various events that were held in each of the main towns. If nothing else, the description alerts us to the dangers of underestimating the amount of commercialized entertainments on offer to south Walians in the pre-1890 period.

In Cardiff, thousands embarked upon excursions, both on land and sea. Many were organized by Sunday schools.

---

[97] For background on the Whit holidays, see J. M. Golby and A. W. Purdue, *The Civilization of the Crowd: Popular Culture in England, 1750–1900* (London, 1984), pp. 98–100.

No fewer than 6,000 'scholars, teachers and friends' visited rural destinations courtesy of the Rhymney Railway Company alone. Likewise, the Brecon and Merthyr Railway Company transported large numbers of Dowlaisians to a monster fête and gala held on the banks of the lake at Dolygaer in the Brecon Beacons, whilst the picturesque seaside village of Mumbles, near Swansea, was 'besieged' by holidaymakers, much to the satisfaction of one publican who was heard to remark that he 'shouldn't care if Whit Monday came every day in the year'. The inhabitants of Newport enjoyed nothing less than a 'high festival'. Here the Order of the Foresters held a procession in full regalia from the centre of the town to the nearby Marshes, where an *al fresco* entertainment had been organized to raise money for their Widows and Orphans Fund. They were followed on their perambulations by a large crowd willing to part with an entrance fee of 1*s*. After seven o'clock in the evening a larger crowd was even more willing to pay the reduced sum of 6*d*. What awaited them amounted to an almost total assault on the senses:

> The general aspect of the field was more like that of a fair of the olden times . . . There were several drinking booths on the ground; a number of shooting galleries, merry-go-rounds, and swings; and a large waxworks and other exhibitions . . . 'Mr C. Roberts's talented company of London artistes' gave a variety of performances, including singing, dancing, floating in the air &c. Athletic sports were also provided, including flat and hurdle races, long jump, bicycle races, jumping in the sacks, climbing a greasy pole, &c. for each of which prizes were offered.

The day ended on a fittingly spectacular note with a fireworks display staged by Mr Edwin Tucker of London.[98]

Apart from the widespread desire to pack cheap-day excursion trains and attend fêtes and fairs, the other constant in the celebrations was the Whitsuntide parade. Usually organized by Sunday schools, this event involved large numbers of local children, their teachers and other assorted helpers. By the late Victorian period, its history was already a long one. In Manchester the first recorded walk by Anglicans took place in 1801. During the 1840s, and after the arrival of Irish immigrants fleeing the hardship of the famine, the Catholic Walk

[98] *WM*, 3 June 1873.

became a regular feature of the holiday.[99] Peter Bailey has noted that in Bolton Nonconformists began Whit walking in the early 1840s.[100] Certainly by the 1850s, the practice had been established in south Wales.[101] By the 1870s the Whit Walk had come to occupy an important position in the Nonconformist calendar; it had also taken on all the characteristics of an urban ritual. For what is most striking about the event is the similarity of the celebrations, regardless of location. From the old iron towns of Merthyr and Ebbw Vale down to the ports of Cardiff and Newport, the Whit Walk maintained its basic shape as a cultural practice.

Attempts to deconstruct rituals and understand them in terms of the 'rules' which govern their performance are fraught with difficulties.[102] Nonetheless, it is both possible and useful to abstract from the actual practice a general model of description. Usually, Sunday schools in the region celebrated the holiday on Whit Monday by joining forces, often at a central point in their local town, in the morning. For the purposes of the parade, denominational differences within the Nonconformist fold were overlooked. Once the young scholars had assembled, all dressed in their finest 'Sunday best' outfits, they proceeded to parade around the main thoroughfares of the town accompanied by their adult teachers and helpers, singing hymns and carrying banners inscribed with assorted religious motifs and the names of their chapels. Their destination was usually a large chapel in which the children were treated to a sermon often delivered by a special guest. After this, the congregation divided itself into individual schools and spent the afternoon playing games and picnicking at a venue either in the environs of the town or at a beauty spot situated at the end of a short train ride or boat journey.

Deviations from this pattern could, and did, occur. Occasionally, the celebrations were held on a day other than Whit Monday. In some towns it was common for the schools to attend the same service after the parade, while in others they

---

[99] Steve Fielding, 'The Catholic Whit Walk in Manchester and Salford, 1890–1939', *Manchester Region History Review*, 1, no. 1 (1987), 3–9, 3.
[100] Peter Bailey, *Leisure and Class* (London, 1987, paperback edn), p. 57.
[101] *CMG*, 2 June 1855.
[102] Clifford Geertz highlights the impossibility of simply 'describing' rituals in his *The Interpretation of Cultures* (London, 1973, 1993 edn), ch. 1.

returned to their respective chapels. Moreover, the order in which the constituent elements of the celebration took place could vary somewhat. In some instances the service followed the afternoon's frolics rather than preceded it. Nevertheless, despite these minor differences in execution, it is the over-all uniformity of practice that impresses most. Above all, the walks provided Nonconformists with an annual opportunity to colonize the main public spaces of their town.

When examining rituals, anthropologists have suggested that we are dealing with 'communicative events', events that communicate messages to those participating in the ritual.[103] To cite the oft-quoted musical metaphor used by Edmund Leach, 'the performers and the listeners are the same people. We engage in rituals in order to transmit collective messages to ourselves.'[104] Historians have not been altogether unaware of the importance of such events.[105] Peter Burke, for example, has provided us with a compelling study of the early modern carnival, arguing that it is useful to see it as both a ritual of reversal and a potential rite of protest.[106] Similarly, the British variants of the *charivari* have been analysed most powerfully by E. P. Thompson, as a means of gaining insights into eighteenth-century popular culture.[107] A Welsh ritual that can also be placed within this wider tradition of 'rough music' – the *ceffyl pren* (or 'wooden horse') – has also found its historian.[108] Nevertheless, despite these vital contributions, there is still much work to be done on these and similar rituals, especially the more 'respectable' ones such as the Whit Walk.

The need for such work is all the more pronounced given the variety of parades and processions that confronted the late

[103] The phrase is used by D. Hymes in his 'Toward ethnographies of communication', reprinted in P. P. Giglioli (ed.), *Language and Social Context* (Harmondsworth, 1972).
[104] Edmund Leach, *Culture and Communication: The Logic by which Symbols are Connected* (Cambridge, 1976), p. 45.
[105] For example, David Cannadine, 'The transformation of civic ritual in modern Britain: the Colchester Oyster feast', *Past and Present*, 94 (1982), 107–30. Early modern historians have lavished much attention on urban rituals; particularly noteworthy is Richard Trexler, *Public Life in Renaissance Florence* (New York, 1991 edn).
[106] Peter Burke, *Popular Culture in Early Modern Europe* (Aldershot, 1994, revised edn), ch. 7.
[107] E. P. Thompson, *Customs in Common* (London, 1993, paperback edn), ch. 8.
[108] Rosemary A. N. Jones, 'Women, community and collective action: the *ceffyl pren* tradition', in Angela V. John (ed.), *Our Mothers' Land: Chapters in Welsh Women's History, 1830–1939* (Cardiff, 1991).

Victorian urbanite on a regular basis. These could range from the informal, loosely organized event through to the highly choreographed piece of street theatre. The celebration of the wakes at Christmas, and the weekly march of the faithful to their various places of worship on a Sunday, are examples of the former; the parades organized by local friendly societies, and the Whit Walks themselves, examples of the latter. Many were already well established, although it is worth noting that there were some innovations during the period. In Merthyr, for example, 1891 witnessed the inauguration of the annual May Day celebrations. These were held under the auspices of the local tradesmen and included an impressive parade around the main thoroughfares.[109] Other ritualized events were occasional, yet none the less organized. Thus, in December 1898 the long-awaited visit of Lord and Lady Wimborne to the Merthyr district was the occasion for a 'public welcome' that involved a meticulously planned procession through the town. A leaflet was published informing inhabitants of the itinerary. On arriving at Merthyr station at 2.24 p.m., the Wimbornes were to be received by E. P. Martin and a reception committee. Once in their carriage, a procession was to form made up of police, Dowlais agents and workmen, the Dowlais National League Band and the Dowlais Volunteer Band, the reception committee, the Dowlais Chamber of Trade, and the 'General Public' who were 'invited to join the Procession'. The 'Tradespeople and Inhabitants of Dowlais and Penydarren' were asked to decorate their shops and homes to brighten up the route which included the High Streets of Merthyr, Penydarren, and Dowlais. Upon arriving at Dowlais School's playground, a welcome address was to be read out.[110]

This civic ritual, marking as it did the return to Dowlais of the prodigal son and daughter-in-law, was clearly thought of as an important part of their visit.[111] The procession, if it was to be effective, required the active involvement of the inhabitants of Merthyr, Penydarren and Dowlais, as both spectators and

[109] John G. E. Astle, *The Progress of Merthyr* (Merthyr Tydfil, 1897), p. 48; *ME*, 14 May 1892.
[110] GRO, D/DG C8/18, Official Programme of the Visit of Lord and Lady Wimborne, 1898.
[111] The deteriorating relationship between the Wimbornes and Dowlais is discussed in ch. 2.

participants. The resulting parade was nothing less than Dowlais society on the move, from the most prominent of local notables, down through the ranks of agents, managers, tradespeople and workers. Onlookers were presented with a living, breathing, music-playing representation of the social order itself.[112]

The Whit Walks can be similarly interpreted, although here, for the most part, we are dealing with members of a single social group (the Nonconformists) attempting to define their relationship with the rest of urban society. Throughout, recognition of the multi-vocality of such symbolic performances is important. Different messages could be received by different sections of the population. For example, for those participating in the Walk itself, the unity of the Nonconformist churches and the sense of belonging that such unity brought with it may have been an important feature of the day. Denominational differences within Nonconformity, as has been mentioned, were overlooked, although the division between the Free Churches on the one hand, and the Established Church and the Roman Catholics on the other, was strictly maintained.[113] Thus, the Walk was an affirmation of the values of Nonconformity, and a ritualized celebration – in their 'Sunday best' – of the triumph of respectability. The sense of pride felt by organizers of the events, which the *Cardiff Times* observed were '[a]lmost the only red-letter days in the history of the Sunday-school life in Wales', reflected the importance attached to order and a respectable appearance.

> For weeks beforehand, preparations are made for this event, and pastors of churches, Sunday school teachers, and members of congregations feel some reward for their labours in witnessing the long procession of nicely-dressed children marching slowly through the principal streets of the town . . .[114]

But if the Walk could celebrate the values that brought individuals together under the banner (literally) of Nonconformity,

[112] For a discussion of a similar civic ritual, albeit in a different time and place, see Robert Darnton, *The Great Cat Massacre and Other Episodes in French Cultural History* (London, 1991, paperback edn), ch. 3, especially pp. 113–21.

[113] See Stewart Williams (ed.), *Cardiff Yesterday*, Vol. 26 (Barry, 1992), photographs 147–50 for pictures of the 1911 Corpus Christi procession – the Catholic equivalent of the Whit Walk – held in Cardiff in 1911.

[114] *Cardiff Times* (*CT*), 22 May 1875.

the ritual also marked a boundary dividing insiders from out-siders.[115] For when considering the power of rituals to com-municate messages it is essential to concentrate not only on those who are participating, but also on those who take on – sometimes unwillingly – the role of spectators.[116] Certainly for those who were not Nonconformists, the activities of the Sunday schools were difficult to ignore. Take, for example, the scenes in the valley community of Ebbw Vale in 1875. As elsewhere in the region, the Free Churches organized a monster procession for the morning of Whit Monday, involving fifteen of the town's Sabbath schools. The children, walking anything between two and eight abreast, formed a line that was some three-quarters of a mile in length and which slowly wound its way along two miles of the main thoroughfares of the town. In case onlookers were left in any doubt as to the nature of the proceedings, the scholars announced their presence with the help of fifteen 'powerful' choirs and twenty banners. After playing 'moral' sports in the afternoon, they returned in the evening to remind Ebbw Valians of the vitality of Nonconformity. Public meetings were held at 'nearly every chapel' and the strains of hymn singing filled the night air.[117]

The effect that Nonconformist domination of the public spaces of a town had upon 'outsiders', and particularly those less respectable urbanites, is difficult to gauge. An indication of one possible response is contained in *Black Parade*, Jack Jones's imaginative re-creation of *fin-de-siècle* Merthyr. As Glyn, one of the central characters of the novel, is out walking after a Saturday night spent in some of the numerous drinking-places in the town, he encounters a procession of chapelgoers making their way to their respective places of worship.

> Yes, there they were, marching, those Nonconformist Christian soldiers, to their chapels, 'marching on to war', as Glyn was returning home. If the boozers, bouncers, bullies, wife-beaters and children starvers had had it all their own way the day previous, they certainly did not on the Sabbath, when the Nonconformist battalions marched proudly to Nebo,

---

[115] For more on this, see A. P. Cohen, *The Symbolic Construction of Community* (London, 1985), pp. 50–63.
[116] See Gerd Baumann, 'Ritual implicates "Others": rereading Durkheim in a plural society', in Daniel de Coppet (ed.), *Understanding Rituals* (London, 1992).
[117] *CT*, 22 May 1875.

Caersalem, Shiloh, Noddfa, Tabernacle, Beulah, Moriah and scores of other citadels. Even Glyn, son of a stalwart Nonconformist though he was, was made to feel unworthy and he wilted as he walked with downcast eyes past his more righteous brethren; so what must 'them old Irish' and 'those old church people' have felt like as they slunk by on their way to sit at the feet of priests and clergymen who knew not how to preach.[118]

Hence, Jones was alert to the powerful symbolism of the chapel parade, a symbolism from which an individual could learn one's place. The potential of the Whit Walk – an organized, combined display of Nonconformist unity – to generate such feelings was doubtless even greater.[119]

The manner in which the Walk dominated the public spaces of the town not only 'encouraged multiple readings of [its] symbolic messages', it actually demanded that such multiple readings be made.[120] The very staging of the parade – with its use of the main streets and the inescapable strains of the choirs – forced observers into a relationship with the Nonconformist cause. Individuals were obliged to fix their position *vis-à-vis* the Chapel, either as a sympathetic onlooker or as a disgruntled outsider. Moreover, the power of the Whit Walk to transmit its symbolic messages was enhanced by the local newspapers. Particularly during the late Victorian period, the widespread coverage of the Whitsuntide activities of the Sabbath schools in the pages of local and regional newspapers was impressive indeed. As we have seen, editors were keen to include often detailed reports from across south Wales relating the various forms that the holiday celebrations took, and the Nonconformist events were generally guaranteed extensive treatment. Even if townsfolk managed to miss the youthful walkers as they made their way excitedly through the main thoroughfares of Merthyr, they were still likely to confront them in the local papers a few days later. Certainly, it was a flattened, more muted procession, but at least a hint of its symbolism remained.

---

[118] Jack Jones, *Black Parade* (London, 1935), pp. 71–2.
[119] For evidence of the rivalry felt between Catholics and Protestants in Manchester and Salford at the time of the Walks during the first half of the twentieth century, see Davies, *Leisure, Gender and Poverty*, pp. 124–5. Also see Fielding, 'The Catholic Whit Walk', pp. 3–9.
[120] Baumann, 'Ritual implicates "Others"', p. 100.

IV. THE WHIT WALK IN A CHANGING CONTEXT

On one level, the extent to which the Whitsuntide holidays retained their basic shape down to (and beyond) the Edwardian period is remarkable.[121] The blend of the pursuit of pleasure, on the one hand – most notably in the form of the day excursion – and the activities of the chapels, on the other, had been well established by the beginning of the late Victorian era and was still largely in place during the interwar years.

Nevertheless, the ability of the Whit Walkers to make themselves heard appears to have been weakened somewhat. Nonconformists increasingly found themselves having to compete with other groups intent on laying claim to the main public spaces of the towns of south Wales. Perhaps one of the most startling examples of this direct competition in Merthyr occurred in 1912, the year in which the town played host to the annual conference of the Independent Labour Party.[122] As usual, the Nonconformists were highly active throughout the Whitsuntide period, twenty-one Sunday schools staging their customary walk around the main thoroughfares. However, their efforts were overshadowed by the visiting politicians who not only redirected public attention away from the chapels, but actually stole the Nonconformists' ritual in the process. For an integral part of the ILP conference proceedings was a 'church parade', a procession that employed the same 'rules' of performance as those that governed the Whit Walk itself. Thus, after delegates had been given a civic welcome by the mayor of the borough on the Saturday, the Sunday saw Merthyr's main streets colonized by the labour movement.

> Over 1,000 members of the ILP and trade unionists, wearing red ties, red rosettes, or badges, assembled with a picturesque array of banners and bannerettes outside the ILP institute, and headed by a band marched to the Tabernacle Church, Brecon Rd. where a sermon was preached by the Revd Rowland Jones on the 'Message of Jesus'.[123]

[121] In contrast, see T. Kelly's 'Suburbanization and the decline of a Catholic public ritual in Pittsburgh', *Journal of Social History*, 28, no. 2 (1994), 311–30, for an account of a religious ritual that declined significantly.

[122] Independent Labour Party, *Twentieth Annual Conference of the Independent Labour Party, Merthyr Tydfil, Easter 1912* (Cardiff, 1912). Notwithstanding the misleading (and erroneous) title of this pamphlet, the conference was held during the Whitsun, not the Easter, holidays.

[123] *ME*, 1 June 1912.

The delegates – 'miners, iron-workers, railway men, shop assistants, and suffragettes' – proceeded along Glebeland Street, down Castle Street, along Victoria Street, then up the High Street to Pontmorlais and then on to the church itself. At the head of the procession was a banner with the words 'God Save the People'. Meanwhile, 'large crowds', taking advantage of the beautiful weather, turned out to see the spectacle, and partake of the carnival atmosphere.

The event alerts us to the complexity of the situation facing the Nonconformists in Merthyr in that decade. The parade of the ILP can be seen as supportive of organized religion. The religious dimension was very much to the fore; it was formally defined as a 'church parade' after all, and ended in the traditional way with a sermon given by a Nonconformist minister. Nevertheless, in other respects the procession served to undermine the efforts of the Free Churches that year. This was perhaps most obvious with regard to the publicity that was accorded the political visitors at the expense of the local schoolchildren. The parading ILP, with such high-profile figures as Keir Hardie (one of the local members of Parliament) and Sylvia Pankhurst, enjoyed extensive coverage in the local newspapers. Whilst by no means absent from the pages of the papers, the Whit Walkers proper were clearly not such newsworthy items in 1912.

Significantly, the explosion of commercialized entertainment was also beginning to have an unfortunate impact upon the Whit Walk. Yet again the complexity of the situation needs to be fully acknowledged. We have already noted how the commercial entertainment – the fair, the sports event and the like – was a feature of the Whitsuntide holidays in the 1870s. As such, Nonconformists had always found themselves competing against various impresarios and promoters for the attention of the public. However, the point remains that by the 1900s and 1910s, the scale of the problem facing the Free Churches had altered considerably. The 'pursuit of pleasure', cited by so many observers as a corrosive influence on the religiosity of the people, began to dominate the Whitsuntide proceedings. In the year of the ILP conference, for example, the Whit Walkers found themselves in competition with a number of commercial entertainments. The Merthyr Electric Theatre was showing *War on the*

Plains, a film detailing the travails of white settlers attacked by 'Red Indians'. A short film of King George engaged in ceremonial duties was also included on a bill that attracted 'crowded houses'. Meanwhile, 'thousands' of Merthyrians took part in their own procession around the streets of the town with the intention of visiting Cyfarthfa Park and the Thomastown Recreation Grounds. The 'Three Musketeers' put in an appearance at the Theatre Royal, while there was a grand opening ceremony of the Victoria Electric Hall in Dowlais. For those desirous of leaving Merthyr, and thus avoiding the Whit Walkers altogether, trains were laid on to take pleasure-seekers to a sports and horse-racing competition in Pontypool.[124] Other inhabitants could head north to the Brecon Beacons, where an increasing number of resorts had developed during the later years of the nineteenth century. Thus, destinations such as Dolygaer Lake, Llangorse Lake, Pontsarn and Brecon itself, all connected to the 'old metropolis of Wales' by the Brecon and Merthyr railway, became increasingly popular with daytrippers.[125]

An indication of the extent to which the Whit Walk had become just one more event in a packed diary of entertainments and excursions is provided by a glimpse of Whitsuntide 1930. In many respects, the holiday celebrations in the interwar period would have been recognizable to Merthyrians of the 1850s and 1860s. Certainly, according to the *Western Mail,* the holiday had lost none of its popularity. Chapel-sponsored events jostled with commercial entertainments for the patronage of the people. By late May the paper was warming to the prospect of the forthcoming festivities: 'Whitsun is the great national holiday carnival. It is the gateway to summer, the jumping-off ground for the thousands who make their annual bid for freedom.'[126] Two weeks later, readers were treated to detailed reports of the celebrations as they had unfolded around south Wales. The sheer range of entertainments on offer in this age of mass leisure quickly reveals itself. Just as had been the case in the late Victorian period, excursions of all sorts were well

[124] Ibid., 25 May 1912.
[125] For an indication of the extent to which the Beacons had begun to take advantage of the excursion trade, see Charles Wilkins, *Merthyr and Aberdare Illustrated* (Merthyr Tydfil, 1902), pp. 74–81.
[126] *WM*, 27 May 1930.

patronized. Cardiff was 'crowded in the morning', but by the afternoon 'presented the appearance of a deserted city except for the steady stream of traffic passing through'. The coastal resorts of Barry, Penarth, Southerndown and Porthcawl were especially popular with holidaymakers, with bathing and 'open-air sports . . . in full swing all day'. And for those unwilling, or unable, to make the journey out of the city, the public parks of Cardiff served as suitable alternative destinations. Amidst all this activity, the Nonconformists continued to observe the holiday in a traditional fashion, and the paper informed its readers that the Sunday school treats 'were the most popular events in South Wales'. Yet for all that popularity, the Whit Walk only managed the briefest of appearances – a single reference to the walk staged in Newport, where the 'main streets were thronged with people on the occasion of the annual procession of the Newport Sunday School Union Whitsuntide festival'.[127] Meanwhile, a 'photopage' detailing the various events around the region – including pictures of the 'destroyer flotilla' at Barry, the Ely races and a general shot of the crowded beach at Barry Island – had only one dealing with Nonconformist celebrations. In keeping with the general tone, this was of a group of girls drinking bottles of 'pop' at Dinas Powys as part of a Baptist chapel treat. The Nonconformist invasion of the public spaces of urban south Wales, whilst still profound enough, was no longer guaranteed the sort of publicity that mid- and late Victorian walkers could hope to attract.

The contrast with the situation as it obtained in south Wales sixty years earlier is as instructive as it is subtle. According to the *Cardiff and Merthyr Guardian*, Whitsuntide in 1870 was as much a holiday as a holy day. It referred to the 'immense number of pleasure seekers' who packed the numerous pleasure steamers leaving Cardiff in the morning. Similarly, readers' attention was drawn to the 'streets of Cardiff [which] became crowded with pitmen and artizans, their wives and their children'. Nevertheless, whilst giving ample room to the pursuit of pleasure, the activities of the Sunday school children were accorded full consideration. Detailed descriptions of the various walks, including information on the participating schools, the

[127] Ibid., 10 June 1930.

routes taken, the sports indulged in afterwards, and the local dignitaries who had deigned to help, were presented to the readership.[128] Put simply, the Whit Walks made news in 1870 in a way that they did not in 1930.

V. CONCLUSION

The shifting position of the Whit Walk in the urban culture of late Victorian and Edwardian south Wales serves as a metaphor for the changing fortunes of organized religion itself during these years, and in particular draws our attention to the complicated relationship that obtained between religion and leisure. That the commercialization of leisure had an impact upon Nonconformists is clear. Contemporary observers were quick to point to the damage that the pursuit of pleasure was inflicting upon the churches and chapels, especially in the aftermath of the religious revival. In part this damage revealed itself in falling attendances. The picture of the half-empty chapel was a powerful one, and was frequently invoked by commentators keen to bemoan the apparent decline in the influence of Nonconformity. Nevertheless, we should be wary of arguing that commercialized leisure necessarily turned congregations into audiences. As suggested by the religious revival itself, it was clearly possible to be members of both at the same time.

Apart from simply highlighting the diversionary nature of leisure, it is important to acknowledge the manner in which new patterns of popular culture had the effect of marginalizing Nonconformity. The commercialization of various leisure pursuits and entertainments – itself not a straightforward or novel experience – is important here. Whilst there had for long been a commercialized aspect of Merthyr's popular culture, the 1890s witnessed something qualitatively and quantitatively different. The establishment of the Merthyr Theatre Company can be seen as a significant development in this respect. Never before had local tradesmen and professionals been willing to commit such large sums of money to an entertainment venture. Run strictly along business lines, the theatre was well-regulated and policed. The proprietors made much of its modernity and

[128] *CMG*, 11 June 1870, 3 June 1871.

traded on the idea that it was a centre of good taste, decorum and respectability. As such it was difficult to condemn by using the well-established puritanical discourse so beloved of some Nonconformists. The same was true of the cinemas and skating rinks that were thrown up during these years. By repeatedly trying to shut such institutions on Sundays, it seems as if organizations like the Free Church Council did much to alienate large sections of Merthyr's population. This alienation did not necessarily entail a complete rejection of the Chapel and its set of values. Rather it seems to have encouraged a feeling that Nonconformist leaders were meddling in affairs that were outside their rightful sphere of influence; they were seen as constituting a vested interest that, on this occasion at least, was unrepresentative of the wider community.

Interlaced with this increasing dissatisfaction with Nonconformists' general approach to recreational matters was a willingness to recognize and even celebrate the pursuit of pleasure. In an earlier chapter, attention was drawn to the process whereby organized sport had become part of the cultural mainstream. Civic leaders in Merthyr felt happy enough publicly celebrating the promotion of Merthyr Town to the first division of the Southern League. Such individuals could also take pride in the arrival of the permanent theatre and the electric cinemas in the town. Importantly, Harry Southey was one such figure. Far from being antipathetic to the development of Merthyr as an entertainment centre, the *Merthyr Express* relished such a prospect. Space was always found for the promotion of such ventures in the town, and through 'Polonius' and the correspondents who wrote to complain about the unbending attitudes of the Nonconformists, the idea that theatrical entertainments and their like were both respectable and acceptable was given a welcome fillip.

This picture should not be overdrawn. Nonconformists, despite their increasing marginality, were still significant players in the social life of south Wales. Indeed, the willingness of impresarios to celebrate the virtues of respectability and morality can be seen as a triumph of Nonconformist values. Furthermore, as demonstrated by the continued vitality of the Whit Walk, marginalization was not the same as ossification. Yet, for all that, there can be no denying the altered situation in which the Free Churches found themselves operating during the early years of the twentieth century. Whit walkers could now be upstaged by socialists who had filched all the best features of their annual ritual. And in a world in which the pursuit of pleasure had apparently triumphed, the juvenile walkers found themselves treated as just one more spectacle to be consumed; they were youthful actors in another piece of street theatre. Perhaps the most telling indication of the degree to which matters had altered for the Nonconformists is provided by a letter published in the *Merthyr Express* in October 1910. The correspondent felt moved to contribute to a long-running debate on the thorny issue of amusements on the Sabbath. Obviously frustrated at the numerous homilies that had been offered up by various Nonconformist correspondents, the letter-writer set forth his views on the subject. He asked how chapelgoers would respond if protests were mounted against places of worship being open on Sundays on the following grounds:

(1) That the people attending such places caused obstructions in the street;
(2) that Sunday, being a day of rest, it was an inducement to deprive themselves of such rest, as the day was commonly intended for; and also that any Council member advocating the keeping open of these places on Sunday should be penalised by being deprived of their seats when they next contested them.[129]

The masters of the condemnatory discourse now found themselves duly condemned.

[129] *ME*, 1 October 1910.

CONCLUSION

When, in the 1860s, Charles Wilkins – post-office clerk, librar-
ian, antiquarian, historian, newspaper contributor, friend of
the south Walian literati and most avid booster of all things
Merthyrian – set to work on his sprawling *History of Merthyr
Tydfil*, he had to confront a prickly historical legacy. Only
thirty years previously, the place he was intent on celebrating
had marked itself out as a storm centre of industrial unrest,
social disorder and political radicalism. While he could not
ignore the events of June 1831, the spectacle of thousands
of working-class men, women and children – inspired by calls
for 'Reform', and desperate to unhinge a system that so easily
took their poverty, hunger and suffering for granted – seizing
control of the town, facing down the troops and sustaining
casualties in the process was not one that fitted neatly into his
argument. He resolved the problem by transforming, flattening
and diminishing the Merthyr 'Rising' into the Merthyr 'Riots'.
For if a lived history refused to conform to civilized sensitivities,
at least a written history could knock off the rough edges and
soften the focus. As he put it, 'the times were excessively bad.
The demand for iron was small, the price low, and great distress
prevailed... Politics had little to do with the matter... As it
was, Reform cries were occasionally heard ... misleading some
to think it a political riot.'[1] Thus, the good citizens of Merthyr
emerged from his analysis as just that, good citizens who had
been driven to riot by the desperate nature of their situation.
Yet, by the time that Wilkins turned his mind to extending and
revising his book, the turbulent 1830s seemed as remote as the
Dark Age days of Tydfil the Martyr. The frontier settlement
had been tamed; the urban dystopia had been brought back
from the brink. The town which had for so long suffered from a
lack of governance had, by 1905, been granted its charter of
incorporation, and by 1908 had achieved county borough
status. Certainly, the forty-one years that separated the first

[1] Charles Wilkins, *The History of Merthyr Tydfil* (Merthyr, 1867), p. 295.

edition from the second edition of Wilkins's *magnum opus* had been crucial ones in the history of Merthyr.

This book has traced elements of that fascinating journey from the 'urban' to the 'civic', dwelling in particular at the point where urban meaning, popular culture and the public spaces of the town intersected. It has often done so in the company of Wilkins and his fellow middle-class urbanites. They were such significant players in the civic project that it is inconceivable that they could have been left out. In the most unpropitious of circumstances, they continued to imagine a future for their town that was different from both its past and its present. Operating in a settlement in which the bourgeoisie had been noticeable only by their absence, these boosters embarked upon a civilizing campaign with remarkable single-mindedness. Their arguments in favour of civic initiatives, their pronouncements about popular culture and their worries about the condition of the streets reverberated through a public sphere which was growing ever more robust, thanks in no small measure to a burgeoning local newspaper culture. The resulting 'civic discourse' turned around identities such as 'the town', 'the public', 'the citizenry' and 'the people'. Such identities could – and often were intended to – transcend class understandings of the social order. The 'civilized' urbanite, after all, could hail from the working classes, the middle classes or the upper classes.

That said, it would be disingenuous to suggest that the discourse of the civic projectors was one emptied of all class content. No matter how inclusive identities such as 'the public' may have appeared, they could be assembled in ways which closely followed lines of class division. And, in any case, class could be present in the historical equation even when other terms were being deployed, a point that has been made by some critics of the 'linguistic turn'.[2] Moreover, many of the popular cultural pursuits which so upset civilized middle-class opinion, and which so problematized public space, were pastimes enjoyed exclusively by members of the working class. So frequently was this the case that to deny that the civic project was, in key respects, a class project would be curious indeed.

[2] See the discussion in Martin Hewitt, *The Emergence of Stability in the Industrial City: Manchester, 1832–1867* (Aldershot, 1996), ch. 1.

Such an argument has not been expounded in this study. Instead it has been maintained that, while class was an ever-important ingredient in the civilizing mission, it was by no means the only one. Although it is true that 'the public', for instance, could be put together in ways that made it synonymous with 'middle class', it was an identity which could possess its own dynamic. The public spaces of the town were never simply middle-class spaces. Likewise, while 'civility' could be interpreted as shorthand for bourgeois values, it could also be articulated in ways – and in contexts – that made it stand for something more. As Peter Bailey demonstrated in his analysis of 'respectability', such virtues could mean different things to different groups of people (or even the same person) at different times.[3] There certainly seems little reason to conclude that the middle class were guardians of the 'essence' of civility or respectability, any more than there is to suppose that the working class had a monopoly of 'truly' immoral or barbarous behaviour. It is perhaps at this point that advocates of the 'linguistic turn' have done so much to blow fresh air through older certainties. They at least have taken other identities seriously, and not simply assumed that everything is reducible, if boiled down long enough, to the master category of class. A consequence has been the production of histories which put illuminating spins on familiar themes. By breaking free from the assumption that discourses merely emanate from classes, historians have begun to explore the possibilities that classes (along with other social identities) could also emanate from discourses.

If class should be seen as just one – albeit vitally important – identity amongst others, then a more nuanced understanding of how power operated in the context of the civic project is also required. That class power was a dominant feature of the drive to clear the streets of the uncivilized hobbledehoys and loungers is clear. But the 'gaze of civilization' had the potential to work its disciplinary magic upon all urbanites. Indeed, shame was more likely to be effective when applied to those townspeople who had most completely internalized the civilizing messages. Publicity of one's misdemeanours could only serve as a deterrent

---

[3] Peter Bailey, 'Will the real Bill Banks please stand up? Towards a role analysis of mid-Victorian working-class respectability', *Journal of Social History*, 12, no. 3 (1978–9), 336–53.

to those who cared what a civilized citizenry thought about them. The Redmond Colemans and Nora Booths of Merthyr's streets, while susceptible to other forms of punishment, were not only beyond shame, they actually relished the notoriety that bad publicity brought in its wake. Contrariwise, respectable citizens (of all classes) who lost their reputation lost everything. The futile attempts at keeping one's name out of the paper on the part of those charged with public drunkenness, the indignation displayed by 'Alice' when she realized that her – perfectly innocent – public behaviour was being commented upon in a 'gossip' column, point to the seriousness with which the prospect of a public shaming was viewed by those schooled in the lessons of civility. As a consequence, it has been contended here that arguments which privilege class power above all else can conceal the complexities of the civic project. Although the pugilists who were chased out of the streets to their 'bloody spots', or the blacklisters who so frequently displayed their contempt for civilized street etiquette, may have been justified in considering themselves the targets of both class prejudice and class power, they could also be resented by more 'refined' and sober members of their own class. And as the newspapers carried stories of 'civilization' registering its victories over such recalcitrant adversaries, working-class readers could share the same satisfaction as their bourgeois counterparts; their streets, too, would be a little quieter, a little safer.

CLOSURE POSTPONED

It is certain that on Charter Day 1905, these working-class, 'civilized' Merthyrians rubbed shoulders with their social superiors as they gathered together in the pouring rain to hear the town's civic leaders weave yet more 'narratives of progress'. As D. A. Thomas and others spoke about the long struggle that had finally been brought to a conclusion, as John Astle, Harry Southey and Colonel Lewis reflected upon the great strides that had been made within the course of their own lives, so inhabitants of the town could be forgiven for thinking that the journey to that place of the imagination, 'civic Merthyr', had been completed. Only a few years later, events in the trenches of the Western Front made such unshakeable faith in the idea of progress seem hopelessly naïve.

Citizens of the 'old metropolis of Wales' were required to learn the hard way just how fragile civic identities could be. After the trauma of war, they witnessed the final collapse of the iron industry. Although this decline had been predicted by commentators for almost as long as there had been an iron industry to feel gloomy about, it was nonetheless shocking when it actually happened. The agony was intensified as a consequence of the general economic depression which had caught the rest of south Wales firmly in its grip in the 1920s and 1930s. Even the youthful, vibrant pit villages situated to the south of the parish could not shield Merthyr from the withering and icy blasts that accompanied economic dislocation. Thus, when the rest of the coalfield entered the 'locust years', Merthyrians once again found themselves, albeit unwillingly, in the van. The experience, however one gauges it, was devastating. Of the 24,000 men employed in Merthyr's pits in 1913, only 16,000 were working in them in 1924. By 1935 this figure had plummeted to a mere 8,000.[4] In the years after 1921, there was an annual exodus from the town of some 900 persons. The population of Merthyr in the mid-1930s was 14.2 per cent down on the 1921 total.[5] A consequence of this haemorrhaging of human resources was a Royal Commission appointed in 1935 to inquire into Merthyr's status as a county borough. The resulting document reads like an urban obituary. The commissioners saw little hope of a rebirth in fortunes and bluntly recommended that it be downgraded to a municipal borough.[6] Four years later, Political and Economic Planning (PEP) went a step further and recommended that the town be abandoned, and its population moved elsewhere.[7] In effect, 'civic Merthyr' was pronounced dead a mere thirty years after its birth.

Many of the historical processes set in motion during those interwar years are still being worked through. There is little doubt that the town image of Merthyr still bears the imprint of the harrowing 1920s and 1930s, as do (rather more pressingly)

[4] *Report of the Royal Commission on Merthyr Tydfil*, 1935, Cmd. 5039, p. 15.
[5] Ibid., p. 16.
[6] Ibid., pp. 53–60.
[7] J. W. England, 'The Merthyr of the twentieth century', in Glanmor Williams (ed.), *Merthyr Politics: The Making of a Working-Class Tradition* (Cardiff, 1966), p. 82.

its inhabitants who are forced to confront high levels of unemployment and social deprivation. This phase of the town's urban history is largely uncharted territory, and would doubtless repay detailed examination. Yet there is still much that is unknown about the nineteenth-century experience. This study has focused on aspects of the civic project in Merthyr in order to explore the relationship between popular culture, space and urban meaning. Other approaches would raise different questions and provide different insights. It seems appropriate in a book which has maintained that the construction of a town image was a process that denied closure, to conclude by pointing to areas which require further investigation. Given the particularities of Merthyr's urban history, two such areas demand especial attention. The first is rooted in the district's status as the paradigmatic industrial community and is concerned with the means by which Merthyr's social élite began to organize itself economically, socially and politically in the mid-Victorian years. We know next to nothing about the formation of the district's middle class during this critical period. Such were the horrors that Rammell and other mid-Victorians described that a raft of questions surrounds the impulses that brought the bourgeoisie into the town, and eventually decided them to stay. The relationships that those middle-class citizens entered into with the ironmasters, with organized religion, with the social élites in neighbouring towns (as well as in urban centres located further afield), the patterns of their cultural life, the development of an associational life, all are significant themes worthy of investigation. That the making of Merthyr's middle class would be a narrative as compelling and revealing as those which detail the making of the bourgeoisie in other towns and cities is clear.[8] It would simultaneously cast light on a vital aspect of the civic project's prehistory.

Secondly, Merthyr, along with other towns in urban south Wales, provides an opportunity to consider identities deployed

[8] There is now a burgeoning historiography of the middle class in nineteenth-century urban Britain. See, for example, Richard H. Trainor, 'The élite', in W. Hamish Fraser and Irene Maver (eds), *Glasgow: Volume II, 1830–1912* (Manchester, 1996); Stana Nenadic, 'The Victorian middle classes', ibid.; R. J. Morris, *Class, Sect and Party: The Making of the British Middle Class: Leeds, 1820–1850* (Manchester, 1990); Hewitt, *Emergence of Stability*; Simon Gunn, 'The ministry, the middle class and the "civilizing mission" in Manchester, 1850–1880', *Social History*, 21, no. 1 (1996), 22–36.

by civic projectors through the medium of Welsh. This book has concentrated upon evidence generated through the English-language public sphere. The overwhelming majority of the district's local papers, a major source for any history of this type, were English-language papers. Moreover, bilingualism had for long been a feature of Merthyr's social life. By the first year of the twentieth century some 43 per cent of those residing in the district had no knowledge of Welsh; by 1911 one in every two Merthyrians was without Welsh, while only 3.5 per cent were monoglot Welsh speakers.[9] Nevertheless, for much of the nineteenth century Welsh had been the language of choice for most inhabitants.[10] And there were certain social settings in which the Welsh language enjoyed an especially privileged status. The chapel was one such, and it is highly probable that Nonconformity's own distinctive version of the civic discourse contained key identities mediated through the Welsh language which had no direct equivalent in English. The concept of the *gwerin*, for instance, was one well suited to the discourses so beloved of the boosters, turning, as it did, around appeals to social inclusivity and harmony.[11] It would be interesting to see how the recovery of these Welsh-language identities might modify the argument developed here. That it would support the contention that 'class' was only one amongst many identities mobilized in the name of the civic project seems highly likely.

These are just two possible avenues of future research. For the moment it is enough to hope that this book has made a contribution to the interlocking historiographies of the civic project, popular culture and the urban, and to our understanding of Merthyr itself, the most written-about town in Welsh history. The need for histories of that town is as great today as it ever was in the era of Charles Wilkins. For an urban experience continues to unfold in the upper reaches of the Taff Valley, over 200 years after the ironmasters gave the settlement its *raison d'être*. Notwithstanding the recommendations made by

[9] For more on the changing position of the Welsh language in Merthyr, see Andrew J. Croll, 'Civilizing the urban: popular culture, public space and urban meaning, Merthyr c. 1870–1914', Ph.D. thesis, University of Wales (Cardiff), 1997, pp. 29–31.
[10] In 1891 the total number of Welsh speakers amounted to 68 per cent of the 110,000 who resided in the district. John Williams, *The Digest of Welsh Historical Statistics*, 2 vols. (Cardiff, 1985), Vol. 1, p. 83.
[11] Prys Morgan, 'The *gwerin* of Wales: myth and reality', in I. Hume and W. T. R. Pryce (eds), *The Welsh and their Country* (Llandysul, 1986).

the authors of the PEP report, subsequent developments were to
show that their hostile pronouncements were misplaced. The
Second World War gave Merthyr's economy something of a
kick-start, with an ordnance works opening at nearby Hirwaun.
A few companies, including Unilever and Rotax, were relocated
to the district during the war itself, while the development of the
Treforest Trading Estate, just outside Pontypridd, provided
employment opportunities for those Merthyrians willing to
travel outside the borough. Although the declaration of peace
brought with it the prospect of further economic decline, the
development of light industry during the postwar period at least
gave the district a future as an urban settlement.[12] Yet while it
remains an important centre of population, Merthyr is still
suffering from the painful effects of high unemployment, governmental neglect and chronic under-investment. And if it
retains features of a civic landscape fashioned in the late nineteenth and early twentieth centuries, it is a landscape that has
been significantly reworked. The transformation of Merthyr's
town hall into a nightclub, if nothing else, suggests that popular
culture still has the ability to shape urban meaning and undercut the civic project. Moreover, it is in the nature of things that
new understandings of 'civility' and 'civilization' constantly
emerge. Quite what the late Victorian boosters would have
made of it all can only be guessed. But today only the vapour
trails remain of the civic settlement that they and their non-élite
townsfolk continually strove for, created and problematized
as they wandered through the streets of Merthyr, the 'old
metropolis of Wales'.

[12] For a general survey of these themes, see G. Hopkins, 'The economic development
since 1939', in Merthyr Teachers' Centre Group, *Merthyr Tydfil: A Valley Community*
(Cowbridge, 1981).

BIBLIOGRAPHY

1. Manuscript Collections
2. Newspapers and Journals
3. Official Publications
4. Works of Reference
5. Published Works
   a) Pre-1914
   b) Post-1914
6. Theses

1. Manuscript Collections

Cardiff University Library
J. Hathren Davies, The tramways of Merthyr Tydfil (n.d.).

Glamorgan Record Office
D/D Wes/MT 129, Register of Class Members and Instructions to Leaders (1886).
D/D Wes/MT 119, Wesley Sunday School Minute Book: Sunday School Teachers' Meeting Minutes (1891–1906).
D/DG C8/18, Official Programme of the Visit of Lord and Lady Wimborne (1898).

Merthyr Tydfil Public Library
County Borough of Merthyr Tydfil, Minute Books.
Henry Allgood, Notes on Dowlais (1910).

2. Newspapers and Journals

Aberdare Times
Brewers' Almanack and Wine and Spirit Trade Annual
British Bandsman
British Musician
Cambrian (Utica)
Cardiff and Merthyr Guardian
Cardiff Times
Evening Express
Merthyr and Dowlais Times
Merthyr Express
Merthyr Express Almanack
Merthyr Guardian
Merthyr Pioneer
Merthyr Star
Merthyr Telegraph
Merthyr Times
National Review
Nineteenth Century

Orchestral Times and Bandsman
Pontypridd Chronicle
Reformer and South Wales Times
South Wales Daily News
South Wales Worker
The Times
Western Mail
Yorkshire Evening Press

3. OFFICIAL PUBLICATIONS

Census Reports: 1801, 1811, 1821, 1831, 1841, 1851, 1871, 1911.
Parliamentary Papers:
  Town Clauses Act, 1847 (10 and 11 Vict., Cap. 34).
  Royal Commission of Inquiry into the State of Education in Wales, Report (London, 1847), XXVII (870).
  Report to the General Board of Health into the Sewerage, Drainage, and Supply of Water, and the Sanitary Condition of Merthyr Tydfil, by Thomas Webster Rammell (London, 1850).
  Intoxicating Liquor (Licensing) Act [35 & 36 Vict.] ch. 94, 1872.
  Returns for England and Wales of the total number of convictions in respect of drunkenness, 1885–89, 1889, LXI (363).
  Royal Commision of Inquiry on the Operation of the Sunday Closing (Wales) Act, 1881, 1890 (C. 5994), XL (I) Report.
  Royal Commission on the Church of England and Other Religious Bodies in Wales and Monmouthshire, 1911, Cd. 5432–9.
  Public Health Acts Amendment Act, 7 Edw. VII c.53.

4. WORKS OF REFERENCE

Kelly's Directory of Monmouthshire and the Principal Towns and Places in South Wales.
The Dictionary of Welsh Biography (London, 1959).

5. PUBLISHED WORKS

a) PRE-1914
Almond, Hely Hutchinson, 'Football as a moral agent', *Nineteenth Century*, 34, no. 202 (December 1893), 899–911.
Anon., 'The eisteddfod and popular music in Wales', *Y Cymmrodor*, 5, pt. 2 (October 1882), 285–95.
Anon., *Aberdare: A Descriptive and Historical Sketch* (Aberdare, 1885), reprinted in Cynon Valley History Society, *Old Aberdare*, Vol. 1 (Newport, 1976).
Astle, John G. E., *The Progress of Merthyr* (Merthyr Tydfil, 1894).
——, *Illustrated Report of the Merthyr Tydfil Incorporation Inquiries, 1897 and 1903* (Merthyr, 1903).
Black, Adam and Black, Charles, *Black's Picturesque Guide Through Wales* (Chester, 1868).
Clarke, T. E., *A Guide to Merthyr Tydfil* (Merthyr Tydfil, 1848, reprinted 1894).
De Tocqueville, Alexis, *Journeys to England and Ireland*, tr. G. Lawrence and K. P. Mayer, ed. J. P. Mayer (New Jersey, 1988 edn).

Ensor, Ernest, 'The football madness', *The Contemporary Review*, 74 (November 1898), 753–60.

Evans, Harry, 'Welsh choral singing', in T. E. Stephens (ed.), *Wales: Today and Tomorrow* (Cardiff, 1907).

Fowler, John Coke, 'The Sunday Closing Act for Wales', *The Red Dragon*, I (1882), 49–56.

Griffith, Frederic (ed.), *Notable Welsh Musicians* (London, 1896).

Haweis, H. R., *Music and Morals* (5th edn, London, 1874).

Hume, J. O., 'A chat on amateur bands', *British Bandsman*, 12, no. 1421 (July 1899), 185.

Independent Labour Party, *Twentieth Annual Conference of the Independent Labour Party, Merthyr Tydfil, Easter 1912* (Cardiff, 1912).

J.H., 'Reminiscences of Merthyr Tydvil', *The Red Dragon*, 2 (August–December 1882), 337–43.

James, C. H., *Lectures* (Merthyr Tydfil, 1892).

Lyttleton, Edward, 'Athletics in public schools', *Nineteenth Century*, 7, no. 35 (January 1880), 43–58.

Malkin, B. H., *The Scenery, Antiquities, and Biography of South Wales* (Wakefield, 1970 edn).

Morgan, J. Vyrnwy, *The Welsh Religious Revival 1904–5: A Retrospect and Criticism* (London, 1909).

Nicholson, George, *The Cambrian Traveller's Guide* (2nd edn, London, 1813).

Rees, J. T., 'Music in the land of song', in T. E. Stephens (ed.), *Wales: Today and Tomorrow* (Cardiff, 1907).

Special Sanitary Commissioner, 'The housing problem in south Wales', *The Lancet* (21 January, 28 January, 4 February 1911), 193–4, 265–7, 333–4.

Sully, Eugene, 'Physical training and character', in T. E. Stephens (ed.), *Wales: Today and Tomorrow* (Cardiff, 1907).

Thomas, W. Beach, 'The failure of games', *The National Review* (February 1907), 1003–9.

Turner, Godfrey, 'Amusements of the English people', *Nineteenth Century*, 2, no. 6 (December 1877), 820–30.

Wilkins, Charles, *The History of Merthyr Tydfil* (Merthyr, 1867).

——, *Merthyr and Aberdare Illustrated* (Merthyr Tydfil, 1902).

——, *The History of the Iron, Steel, Tinplate and Other Trades of Wales* (Merthyr Tydfil, 1903).

——, *The History of Merthyr Tydfil* (2nd edn, Merthyr Tydfil, 1908).

Williams, Nestor R. et al., 'Where ought the Welsh university to be located?', *The Red Dragon*, 1 (February–July 1882), 186–90.

b) Post-1914

Allsobrook, David Ian, *Music for Wales* (Cardiff, 1992).

Ambrose, G. P., 'The Aberdare background to the South Wales Choral Union: Y Côr Mawr 1853–1872', in S. Williams (ed.), *Glamorgan Historian*, Vol. 9 (Barry, n.d.).

Anderson, Patricia, *The Printed Image and the Transformation of Popular Culture, 1790–1860* (Oxford, 1991).

Appleby, Joyce, Hunt, Lynn and Jacob, Margaret, *Telling the Truth about History* (London, 1994).

Bailey, Peter, *Leisure and Class in Victorian England: Rational Recreation and the Contest for Control, 1830–1885* (London, 1978).

——, 'Will the real Bill Banks please stand up? Towards a role analysis of mid-Victorian working-class respectability', *Journal of Social History* , 12, no. 3 (1979), 336–53.

——, 'A community of friends: business and good fellowship in London music-hall management, *c*. 1860–1885', in Peter Bailey (ed.), *Music Hall: The Business of Pleasure* (Milton Keynes, 1986).

——, 'The politics and poetics of modern British leisure: a late twentieth-century review', *Rethinking History*, 3, no. 2 (1999), 131–75.

——, *Leisure and Class* (London, 1987, paperback edn).

Barry, Andrew, Osborne, Thomas and Rose, Nikolas, 'Introduction', in Andrew Barry, Thomas Osborne and Nikolas Rose, *Foucault and Political Reason: Liberalism, Neo-Liberalism and the Rationalities of Government* (London, 1996).

Baumann, Gerd, 'Ritual implicates "Others": rereading Durkheim in a plural society', in Daniel de Coppet (ed.), *Understanding Rituals* (London, 1992).

Bennett, T., 'Hegemony, ideology, pleasure: Blackpool', in T. Bennett, C. Mercer and J. Woollacott (eds), *Popular Culture and Social Relations* (Milton Keynes, 1986).

Booth, Michael R., *Theatre in the Victorian Age* (Cambridge, 1991).

Brailsford, Dennis, *Bareknuckles: A Social History of Prizefighting* (Cambridge, 1988).

Bramwell, Bill, 'Public space and local communities: the example of Birmingham, 1840–1880', in Gerry Kearns and Charles W. J. Withers (eds), *Urbanising Britain: Essays on Class and Community in the Nineteenth Century* (Cambridge, 1991).

Briggs, Asa, *Mass Entertainment: The Origins of a Modern Industry* (Adelaide, 1960).

——, *Victorian Cities* (Harmondsworth, 1990, paperback edn).

Burke, Peter, *Popular Culture in Early Modern Europe* (Aldershot, 1994, revised edn).

Cannadine, David, 'The transformation of civic ritual in modern Britain: the Colchester Oyster feast', *Past and Present*, 94 (1982), 107–30.

Carter, Harold and Wheatley, Sandra, *Merthyr Tydfil in 1851: A Study of the Spatial Structure of a Welsh Industrial Town* (Cardiff, 1982).

——, 'The structure of Glamorgan towns in the nineteenth century', in Prys Morgan (ed.), *Glamorgan County History, Vol. VI: Glamorgan Society, 1780–1980* (Cardiff, 1988).

Cohen, A. P., *The Symbolic Construction of Community* (London, 1985).

Cosgrove, Denis, 'The myth and the stones of Venice: an historical geography of a symbolic landscape', *Journal of Historical Geography*, 8, no. 2 (1982), 145–69.

Croll, Andy, 'From bar-stool to choir-stall: music and morality in late Victorian Merthyr', *Llafur*, 6, no. 1 (1992), 17–27.

——, '"Naming and shaming" in late Victorian and Edwardian Britain', *History Today*, 47, no. 5 (May 1997), 3–6.

——, 'Writing the insanitary town: G. T. Clark, slums and sanitary reform', in Brian Ll. James (ed.), *G. T. Clark: Scholar Ironmaster in the Victorian Age* (Cardiff, 1998).

——, 'Street disorder, surveillance and shame: regulating behaviour in the public spaces of the late Victorian British town', *Social History*, 24, no. 3 (1999), 250–68.

Cunningham, Hugh, *Leisure in the Industrial Revolution, c. 1780–1880* (London, 1980).

——, 'Leisure and culture', in F. M. L. Thompson (ed.), *The Cambridge Social History of Britain, 1750–1950*, 3 vols. (Cambridge, 1990), Vol. 2, 'People and their Environment'.

Darnton, Robert, *The Great Cat Massacre and Other Episodes in French Cultural History* (London, 1991, paperback edn).

Daunton, M. J., *Coal Metropolis: Cardiff, 1870-1914* (Leicester, 1977).

——, 'Public place and private space: the Victorian city and the working-class household', in D. Fraser and A. Sutcliffe (eds), *The Pursuit of Urban History* (London, 1983).

——, 'Coal to capital: Cardiff since 1839', in Prys Morgan (ed.), *Glamorgan County History, Vol. VI: Glamorgan Society, 1780–1980* (Cardiff, 1988).

Davies, Andrew, *Leisure, Gender and Poverty: Working-Class Culture in Salford and Manchester, 1900–1939* (Buckingham, 1992).

——, 'Street gangs, crime and policing in Glasgow during the 1930s: the case of the Beehive Boys', *Social History*, 23, no. 3 (1998), 251–67.

Davies, E. T., *Religion in the Industrial Revolution in South Wales* (Cardiff, 1965).

Davies, John H., 'Rhondda choral music in Victorian times', in K. S. Hopkins (ed.), *Rhondda: Past and Future* (Rhondda, 1975).

Dingle, A. E., 'Drink and working-class living standards in Britain, 1870–1914', *Economic History Review*, 2nd series, 25, no. 4 (1972), 608–22.

Earl, John, 'Building the halls', in Peter Bailey (ed.), *Music Hall: The Business of Pleasure* (Milton Keynes, 1986).

Edwards, W. J., *From the Valley I Came* (London, 1956).

Eley, Geoff and Nield, Keith, 'Starting over: the present, the post-modern and the moment of social history', *Social History*, 20, no. 3 (1995), 355–64.

England, J. W., 'The Merthyr of the twentieth century', in Glanmor Williams (ed.), *Merthyr Politics: The Making of a Working-Class Tradition* (Cardiff, 1966).

Epstein, James, 'Spatial practices/democratic vistas', *Social History*, 24, no. 3 (1999), 294–310.

Evans, Chris, *'The Labyrinth of Flames': Work and Social Conflict in Early Industrial Merthyr Tydfil* (Cardiff, 1993).

Evans, Neil, 'The Welsh Victorian city: the middle class and civic and national consciousness in Cardiff, 1850–1914', *Welsh History Review*, 12, no. 3 (1985), 350–87.

Evans, R. S., 'The development of local government', in Merthyr Teachers' Centre Group, *Merthyr Tydfil: A Valley Community* (Cowbridge, 1981).

Fielding, Steve, 'The Catholic Whit Walk in Manchester and Salford, 1890–1939', *Manchester Region History Review*, 1, no. 1 (1987), 3–9.

Finlayson, Geoffrey, *Citizen, State, and Social Welfare in Britain, 1830–1990* (Oxford, 1994).

Fishwick, Nicholas, *English Football and Society, 1910–1950* (Manchester, 1989).

Foucault, Michel, *Madness and Civilization: A History of Insanity in the Age of Reason* (London, 1967).

——, *Discipline and Punish: The Birth of the Prison* (London, 1977).

——, 'Space, knowledge and power', in Sylvère Lotringer (ed.), *Foucault Live* (New York, 1989).

Fraser, David, *The Evolution of the British Welfare State* (2nd edn, Basingstoke, 1984).

Garrard, John, *Leadership and Power in Victorian Industrial Towns, 1830–80* (Manchester, 1983).

Gattrell, V. A. C., *The Hanging Tree: Execution and the English People, 1770–1868* (Oxford, 1994).

Geertz, Clifford, *The Interpretation of Cultures* (London, 1973, 1993 edn).

Gill, R., *The Myth of the Empty Church* (London, 1993).

Ginswick, J. (ed.), *Labour and the Poor in England and Wales, 1849–51*, Vol. 3 (London, 1983).

Girouard, Mark, *The English Town* (London, 1990).

Goheen, P. G., 'The ritual of the streets in mid-nineteenth-century Toronto', *Environment and Planning D: Society and Space*, 11 (1993), 127–45.

——, 'Negotiating access to public space in mid-nineteenth-century Toronto', *Journal of Historical Geography*, 20, no. 4 (1994), 430–49.

Golby, J. M. and Purdue, A. W., *The Civilization of the Crowd: Popular Culture in England, 1750–1900* (London, 1984).

Gordon, Colin (ed.), *Power/Knowledge: Selected Interviews and Other Writings, 1972–1977, by Michel Foucault* (Brighton, 1980).

Grant, Raymond K. J., 'Merthyr Tydfil in the mid-nineteenth century: the struggle for public health', *Welsh History Review*, 14, no. 4 (1989), 574–94.

Griffiths, Rhidian, 'Musical life in the nineteenth century', in Prys Morgan (ed.), *Glamorgan County History, Vol. VI: Glamorgan Society, 1780–1980* (Cardiff, 1988).

——, 'Welsh chapel music: the making of a tradition', *Journal of Welsh Ecclesiastical History*, 6 (1989), 35–43.

Guest, Revel and John, Angela V., *Lady Charlotte: A Biography of the Nineteenth Century* (London, 1989).

Gunn, Simon, 'The "failure" of the Victorian middle class: a critique', in J. Wolff and J. Seed (eds), *The Culture of Capital: Art, Power and the Nineteenth-Century Middle Class* (Manchester, 1988).

——, 'The ministry, the middle class and the "civilizing mission" in Manchester, 1850–1880', *Social History*, 21, no. 1 (1996), 22–36.

Habermas, Jürgen, *The Structural Transformation of the Public Sphere: An Inquiry into a Category of Bourgeois Society*, tr. Thomas Burger with Frederick Lawrence (Cambridge, 1989).

Hamlin, Christopher, 'Muddling in Bumbledom: on the enormity of large sanitary improvements in four British towns', *Victorian Studies*, 32, no. 1 (1988), 55–83.

Harrison, Brian, 'Pubs', in H. J. Dyos and M. Wolff (eds), *The Victorian City: Images and Realities*, 2 vols. (1973), vol. 1.

——, *Drink and the Victorians: The Temperance Question in England, 1815–1872* (2nd edn, Keele, 1994).

Harrison, Mark, *Crowds and History: Mass Phenomena in English Towns, 1790–1835* (Cambridge, 1988).

Harvey, David, *Consciousness and the Urban Experience: Studies in the History and Theory of Capitalist Urbanization* (Oxford, 1985).

Harvey, J., 'The visions of the 1904–5 Revival', *Llafur*, 6, no. 2 (1993), 75–93.

Herbert, Trevor, 'The virtuosi of Merthyr', *Llafur*, 5, no. 1 (1988), 60–9.

——, 'Introduction' and 'Nineteenth-century bands: the making of a movement', in Trevor Herbert (ed.), *Bands: The Brass Band Movement in the Nineteenth and Twentieth Centuries* (Buckingham, 1991).

——, ' "A softening influence": R. T. Crawshay and the Cyfarthfa Band', in T. F. Holley (ed.), *The Merthyr Historian*, Vol. 5 (Merthyr Tydfil, 1992).

Hewitt, Martin, *The Emergence of Stability in the Industrial City: Manchester, 1832–67* (Aldershot, 1996).

Hignell, Andrew, *A 'Favourit' Game: Cricket in South Wales before 1914* (Cardiff, 1992).

Hobsbawm, E. J., *Worlds of Labour: Further Studies in the History of Labour* (London, 1984).

—— and Rudé, G., *Captain Swing* (London, 1970).

Holt, Richard, 'Working-class football and the city: the problem of continuity', British *Journal of Sports History*, 3, no. 1 (1986), 5–17.

——, *Sport and the British: A Modern History* (Oxford, 1989).

Hopkin, Deian, 'The *Merthyr Pioneer*, 1911–1922', *Llafur*, 2, no. 3 (1978), 54–64.

Hopkins, G., 'The economic development since 1939', in Merthyr Teachers' Centre Group, *Merthyr Tydfil: A Valley Community* (Cowbridge, 1981).

Horn, Pamela, *The Victorian Town Child* (Stroud, 1997).

Humphries, Stephen, *Hooligans or Rebels? An Oral History of Working-Class Childhood and Youth, 1889–1939* (Oxford, 1983, paperback edn).

Hymes, D., 'Toward ethnographies of communication', reprinted in P. P. Giglioli (ed.), *Language and Social Context* (Harmondsworth, 1972).

Israel, Jonathan I., *The Dutch Republic: Its Rise, Greatness and Fall, 1477–1806* (Oxford, 1995).

Jackson, Peter, 'The politics of the streets; a geography of Caribana', *Political Geography*, 11, no. 2 (1992), 130–51.

Jacobs, Jane, *The Death and Life of Great American Cities* (New York, 1961).

Jones, Aled, *Press, Politics and Society: A History of Journalism in Wales* (Cardiff, 1993).

Jones, Anthony, *A Thesis and Survey of the Nonconformist Chapel Architecture in Merthyr Tydfil* (Merthyr, 1962).

Jones, Brynmor P., *Voices from the Welsh Revival, 1904–5* (Brigend, 1995).

Jones, D. J. V., *Crime in Nineteenth-Century Wales* (Cardiff, 1992).

Jones, David and Bainbridge, Alan, 'The "Conquering of China": crime in an industrial community 1842–64', *Llafur*, 2, no. 3 (1978), 7–37.

Jones, Ieuan Gwynedd, 'The Merthyr of Henry Richard', in Glanmor Williams (ed.), *Merthyr Politics: The Making of a Working-Class Tradition* (Cardiff, 1966).

——, 'Politics of Merthyr Tydfil', in Stewart Williams (ed.), *Glamorgan Historian*, Vol. 10 (Barry, 1974).

——, 'Merthyr Tydfil: the politics of survival', *Llafur*, 2, no. 1 (1976), 18–31.

——, 'The election of 1868 in Merthyr Tydfil: a study in the politics of an industrial borough', in Ieaun Gwynedd Jones, *Explorations and Explanations: Essays in the Social History of Victorian Wales* (Llandysul, 1981).

——, *Communities: Essays in the Social History of Victorian Wales* (Llandysul, 1987).

Jones, Jack, *Black Parade* (London, 1935).

Jones, P. N., 'Population migration into Glamorgan, 1861–1911: a reassessment', in P. Morgan (ed.), *Glamorgan County History, Vol. VI: Glamorgan Society, 1780–1980* (Cardiff, 1988).

Jones, Rosemary A. N., 'Women, community and collective action: the *ceffyl pren* tradition', in Angela V. John (ed.), *Our Mothers' Land: Chapters in Welsh Women's History, 1830–1939* (Cardiff, 1991).

Jones, W. D., *Wales in America: Scranton and the Welsh, 1860–1920* (Cardiff, 1993).

Joyce, Patrick, *Work, Society and Politics: The Culture of the Factory in Later Victorian England* (London, 1980).

——, *Visions of the People: Industrial England and the Question of Class, 1848–1914* (Cambridge, 1991).

——, *Democratic Subjects: The Self and the Social in Nineteenth-Century England* (Cambridge, 1994).

——, 'The end of social history?', *Social History*, 20, no. 1 (1995), 73–91.

——, 'The return of history: postmodernism and the politics of academic history in Britain', *Past and Present*, 158 (1998), 207–35.

Keating, Peter, 'Fact and fiction in the East End', in H. J. Dyos and M. Wolff (eds), *The Victorian City*, 2 vols. (London, 1973), Vol. 2.

——, *Into Darkest England, 1866–1913: Selections from the Social Explorers* (Glasgow, 1976).

Kelly, T., 'Suburbanisation and the decline of a Catholic public ritual in Pittsburgh', *Journal of Social History*, 28, no. 2 (1994), 311–30.

Kidd, A. J., 'Introduction: the middle class in nineteenth-century Manchester', in A. J. Kidd and K. W. Roberts (eds), *City, Class and Culture: Studies of Cultural Production and Social Policy in Victorian Manchester* (Manchester, 1985).

Lambert, W. R., 'The Welsh Sunday Closing Act, 1881', *Welsh History Review*, 6, no. 2 (1972), 161–89.

——, 'Drink and work-discipline in industrial South Wales, c. 1800–1870', *Welsh History Review*, 7, no. 3 (1975), 289–306.

——, 'Thomas Williams, J.P., Gwaelod-y-Garth (1823–1903): a study in nonconformist attitudes and action', in Stewart Williams (ed.), *Glamorgan Historian*, Vol. 11 (Cowbridge, 1975).

——, 'Some working-class attitudes towards organised religion in nineteenth-century Wales', *Llafur*, 2, no. 1 (1976), 4–17.

——, *Drink and Sobriety in Victorian Wales, c. 1820–c. 1895* (Cardiff, 1983).

Leach, Edmund, *Culture and Communication: The Logic by which Symbols are Connected* (Cambridge, 1976).

Lile, B. and Farmer, D., 'The early development of association football in south Wales, 1890–1906', *Transactions of the Cymmrodorion Society* (1984), 193–215.

Linebaugh, Peter, *The London Hanged: Crime and Civil Society in the Eighteenth Century* (London, 1993).

Lord, Peter, *The Visual Culture of Wales: Industrial Society* (Cardiff, 1998).

Lotringer, Sylvère (ed.), *Foucault Live* (New York, 1989).

Lowerson, John, *Sport and the English Middle Classes, 1870–1914* (Manchester, 1995, paperback edn).

Mason, Tony, *Association Football and English Society, 1863–1915* (Brighton, 1980).

——, *Sport in Britain* (London, 1988).

Mayne, Alan, 'Representing the slum', *Urban History Yearbook*, 17 (1990), 66–84.

——, *The Imagined Slum* (Leicester, 1993).

Meller, Helen, *Leisure and the Changing City, 1870–1914* (London, 1976).

Morgan, Dennis, *The Cardiff Story* (Cowbridge, 1991).

Morgan, Kenneth O., 'D. A. Thomas: the industrialist as politician', in Stewart Williams (ed.), *Glamorgan Historian*, Vol. 3 (Cowbridge, 1966).

——, 'The Merthyr of Keir Hardie', in Glanmor Williams (ed.), *Merthyr Politics: The Making of a Working-Class Tradition* (Cardiff, 1966).

Morgan, Prys, 'The *gwerin* of Wales: myth and reality', in I. Hume and W. T. R. Pryce (eds), *The Welsh and their Country* (Llandysul, 1986).

Morgans, David, *Music and Musicians of Merthyr and District* (Merthyr, 1922).

Morris, J. H. and Williams, L. J., *The South Wales Coal Industry, 1841–1875* (Cardiff, 1958).

Morris, R. J., 'The middle class and British towns and cities of the industrial revolution, 1780–1870', in D. Fraser and A. Sutcliffe (eds), *The Pursuit of Urban History* (London, 1983).

——, *Class, Sect and Party: The Making of the British Middle Class: Leeds, 1820–1850* (Manchester, 1990).

Mumford, Lewis, *The City in History* (London, 1961).

Nead, Lynda, 'Mapping the self: gender, space and modernity in mid-Victorian London', in Roy Porter (ed.), *Rewriting the Self: Histories from the Renaissance to the Present* (London, 1997).

Nenadic, Stana, 'The Victorian middle classes', in W. Hamish Fraser and Irene Maver (eds), *Glasgow: Volume II, 1830–1912* (Manchester, 1996).

Obelkevich, James, *Religion and Rural Society: South Lindsey, 1825–1875* (Oxford, 1976).

——, 'Religion', in F. M. L. Thompson (ed.), *The Cambridge Social History of Britain, 1750–1950*, 3 vols. (Cambridge, 1990), Vol. 3, 'Social Agencies and Institutions'.

Ploszajska, Teresa, 'Moral landscapes and manipulated spaces: gender, class and space in Victorian reformatory schools', *Journal of Historical Geography*, 20, no. 4 (1994), 413–29.

Pollock, Griselda, 'Vicarious excitements: *London: A Pilgrimage* by Gustave Doré and Blanchard Jerrold, 1872', *New Formations*, 4 (1988), 25–50.

Pope, Robert, *Building Jerusalem: Nonconformity, Labour and the Social Question in Wales, 1906–1939* (Cardiff, 1998).

Pretty, David, 'John Owen Jones ('Ap Ffarmwr') and the labour movement in Merthyr Tydfil, 1894–96', *Morgannwg*, 38 (1994), 101–14.

Raban, Jonathan, *Soft City* (London, 1988 edn).

Richter, Donald, 'The role of the mob-riot in Victorian elections, 1865–85', *Victorian Studies*, 15, no. 1 (1971), 19–28.

Roberts, David, *Paternalism in Early Victorian England* (London, 1979).

Roberts, Robert, *The Classic Slum: Salford Life in the First Quarter of the Century* (London, 1971, 1990 edn).

Rose, Nikolas, *Towards a Critical Sociology of Freedom* (Inaugural Lecture, Goldsmith's College, Univ. of London, 3 May 1992), reprinted in Patrick Joyce (ed.), *Class* (Oxford, 1995).

——, 'Governing "advanced" liberal democracies', in Andrew Barry, Thomas Osborne and Nikolas Rose, *Foucault and Political Reason: Liberalism, Neo-Liberalism and the Rationalities of Government* (London, 1996).

——, 'Assembling the modern self', in Roy Porter (ed.), *Rewriting the Self: Histories from the Renaissance to the Present* (London, 1997).

Rouse, Joseph, 'Power/knowledge', in Garry Gutting (ed.), *The Cambridge Companion to Foucault* (Cambridge, 1994).

Rubinstein, David, 'Cycling in the 1890s', *Victorian Studies*, 21, no. 1 (1977), 47–72.

Rudé, George, *The Crowd in History: A Study of Popular Disturbances in France and England, 1730–1848* (New York, 1964).

Russell, Dave, 'Popular musical culture and popular politics in the Yorkshire textile districts, 1880–1914', in John K. Walton and James Walvin (eds), *Leisure in Britain, 1780–1939* (Manchester, 1983).

——, *Popular Music in England, 1840–1914: A Social History* (Manchester, 1987).

Savage, Mike, 'Urban history and social class: two paradigms', *Urban History*, 20, pt. 1 (1993), 61–77.

Savage, Mike and Warde, Alan, *Urban Sociology, Capitalism and Modernity* (Basingstoke, 1993).

Schivelbusch, Wolfgang, *Disenchanted Night: The Industrialisation of Light in the Nineteenth Century* (Oxford, 1988).

Sennett, Richard, *The Fall of Public Man* (London, 1993, paperback edn).

——, *Flesh and Stone: The Body and the City in Western Civilization* (London, 1994).

Shurmer-Smith, P. and Hannam, K., *Worlds of Desire, Realms of Power* (London, 1994).

Silver, Allan, 'The demand for order in civil society: a review of some themes in the history of urban crime, police, and riot', in D. J. Bordua (ed.), *The Police: Six Sociological Essays* (New York, 1967).

Smith, Dai, *Aneurin Bevan and the World of South Wales* (Cardiff, 1993).

Smith, David, 'Tonypandy 1910: definitions of community', *Past and Present*, 87 (1980), 158–84.

——, 'Wales through the looking glass', in David Smith (ed.), *A People and a Proletariat: Essays in the History of Wales, 1780–1880* (London, 1980).

—— and Williams, Gareth, *Fields of Praise: The Official History of the Welsh Rugby Union, 1881–1981* (Cardiff, 1980).

Springhall, J., ' "A life story for the people?" Edwin J. Brett and the London "low-life" penny dreadfuls of the 1860s', *Victorian Studies*, 33, no. 2 (1990), 223–46.

Stead, Peter, 'Amateurs and professionals in the cultures of Wales', in J. Beverley Smith and Geraint H. Jenkins (eds), *Politics and Society in Wales, 1840–1922: Essays in Honour of Ieuan Gwynedd Jones* (Cardiff, 1988).

Stedman Jones, Gareth, 'Working-class culture and working-class politics in London, 1870–1900: notes on the remaking of a working class', *Journal of Social History*, 7, no. 4 (1983), 460–508.

——, *Languages of Class: Studies in English Working Class History, 1832–1982* (Cambridge, 1983).

Storch, Robert D., 'The plague of the blue locusts: police reform and popular resistance in Northern England, 1840–57', *International Review of Social History*, 20, no. 1 (1975), 61–90.

——, 'The policeman as domestic missionary: urban discipline and popular culture in Northern England, 1850–80', *Journal of Social History*, 9, no. 4 (1976), 481–509.

Strange, Keith, 'In search of the Celestial Empire: crime in Merthyr, 1830–1860', *Llafur*, 3, no. 1 (1980), 44–86.

Sullivan, Kate, ' "The biggest room in Merthyr": working-class housing in Dowlais, 1850–1914', *Welsh History Review*, 17, no. 2 (1994), 155–85.

Suttles, Gerald D., 'The cumulative texture of local urban culture', *American Journal of Sociology*, 90, no. 2 (1984), 283-304.

Taylor, Margaret S., *The County Borough of Merthyr Tydfil: Fifty Years a Borough, 1905–1955* (Merthyr Tydfil, 1955).

Tebbutt, Melanie, 'Women's talk? Gossip and "women's words" in working-class communities, 1880–1939', in Andrew Davies and Steven Fielding (eds), *Workers' Worlds: Cultures and Communities in Manchester and Salford, 1880–1939* (Manchester, 1992).
——, *Women's Talk? A Social History of 'Gossip' in Working-Class Neighbourhoods, 1880–1960* (Aldershot, 1995).
Thane, Pat, 'Government and society in England and Wales, 1750–1914', in F. M. L. Thompson (ed.), *The Cambridge Social History of Britain, 1750–1950*, 3 vols. (Cambridge, 1990), Vol. 3, 'Social Agencies and Institutions'.
Thompson, E. P., 'The moral economy of the English crowd in the eighteenth century', *Past and Present*, 50 (1971), 76–136.
——, *Customs in Common* (London, 1993, paperback edn).
Thompson, F. M. L., 'Town and city', in F. M. L. Thompson (ed.), *The Cambridge Social History of Britain, 1750–1950*, 3 vols. (Cambridge, 1990), Vol. 1, 'Regions and Communities'.
Trainor, Richard H., 'The élite', in W. Hamish Fraser and Irene Maver (eds), *Glasgow: Volume II, 1830–1912* (Manchester, 1996).
Trexler, Richard, *Public Life in Renaissance Florence* (New York, 1991 edn).
Turner, Christopher B., 'Conflicts of faith? Religion and Labour in Wales, 1890–1914', in Deian R. Hopkin and Gregory S. Kealey (eds), *Class, Community and the Labour Movement in Wales and Canada, 1850–1930* (Aberystwyth, 1989).
Vamplew, Wray, 'The economics of a sports industry: Scottish gate-money football, 1890–1914', *Economic History Review*, 2nd series, 35, no. 4 (1982), 549–67.
Vernon, James, *Politics and the People: A Study in English Political Culture, c. 1815–1867* (Cambridge, 1993).
Vincent, David, *Literacy and Popular Culture: England, 1750–1914* (Cambridge, 1989).
Walkowitz, Judith R., *City of Dreadful Delight: Narratives of Sexual Danger in Late-Victorian London* (London, 1992).
Walters, R. H., *The Economic and Business History of the South Wales Steam Coal Industry, 1840–1914* (New York, 1977).
Ward, David, 'Victorian cities: how modern?', *Journal of Historical Geography*, 1, no. 2 (1975), 135–51.
——, 'Environs and neighbours in the "Two Nations": residential differentiation in mid-nineteenth century Leeds', *Journal of Historical Geography*, 6, no. 2 (1980), 133–62.
Warnes, A. M., 'Early separation of home from workplace and the urban structure of Chorley, 1780 to 1850', *Transactions of the Historic Society of Lancashire and Cheshire*, 72 (1970), 105–35.
Waters, Chris, *British Socialists and the Politics of Popular Culture, 1884–1914* (Manchester, 1990).
Williams, C. R., 'The Welsh religious revival of 1904–5', *British Journal of Sociology*, 3, no. 3 (1952), 242–59.
Williams, Gareth, 'How amateur was my valley: professional sport and national identity in Wales, 1890–1914', *British Journal of Sports History*, 2, no. 3 (December 1985), 248–69.
——, 'Rugby Union', in Tony Mason (ed.), *Sport in Britain: A Social History* (Cambridge, 1989).
——, *Valleys of Song: Music and Society in Wales, 1840–1914* (Cardiff, 1998).
Williams, Gwyn A., *The Merthyr Rising* (Cardiff, 1988).
Williams, John, *Digest of Welsh Historical Statistics*, 2 vols. (Cardiff, 1985).
Williams, Raymond, *The Long Revolution* (Harmondsworth, 1965).
Williams, Stewart (ed.), *Cardiff Yesterday*, Vol. 26 (Barry, 1992).
Winter, James, *London's Teeming Streets, 1830–1914* (London, 1993).

Wohl, Anthony S., *Endangered Lives: Public Health in Victorian Britain* (London, 1984, paperback edn).
Yeo, Stephen, *Religion and Voluntary Organisations in Crisis* (London, 1976).

6. THESES

Barclay, Martin, 'Aberdare, 1880–1914: class and community', MA thesis, University of Wales (Cardiff), 1985.
Croll, Andrew J., 'Civilizing the urban: popular culture, public space and urban meaning, Merthyr *c.*   1870–1914,' Ph.D. thesis, University of Wales (Cardiff), 1997.
Johnes, Martin O., 'Association football in South Wales, 1906–40', Ph.D. thesis, University of Wales (Cardiff), 1998.
Strange, Keith, 'The condition of the working classes in Merthyr Tydfil, *c.* 1840–1850', Ph.D. thesis, University of Wales (Swansea), 1982.

INDEX